Jakarta Pitfalls

Time-Saving Solutions for Struts, Ant, JUnit, and Cactus

Bill Dudney
Jonathan Lehr

Wiley Publishing, Inc.

Executive Publisher: Robert Ipsen
Vice President and Publisher: Joe Wikert
Executive Editor: Robert Elliott
Assistant Development Editor: Eileen Bien Calabro
Editorial Manager: Kathryn A. Malm
Senior Production Editor: Angela Smith
Text Design & Composition: Wiley Composition Services

This book is printed on acid-free paper. ∞

Copyright © 2003 by Bill Dudney and Jonathan Lehr. All rights reserved.

Published by Wiley Publishing, Inc., Indianapolis, Indiana

Published simultaneously in Canada

No part of this publication may be reproduced, stored in a retrieval system, or transmitted in any form or by any means, electronic, mechanical, photocopying, recording, scanning, or otherwise, except as permitted under Section 107 or 108 of the 1976 United States Copyright Act, without either the prior written permission of the Publisher, or authorization through payment of the appropriate per-copy fee to the Copyright Clearance Center, Inc., 222 Rosewood Drive, Danvers, MA 01923, (978) 750-8400, fax (978) 646-8700. Requests to the Publisher for permission should be addressed to the Legal Department, Wiley Publishing, Inc., 10475 Crosspoint Blvd., Indianapolis, IN 46256, (317) 572-3447, fax (317) 572-4447, E-mail: permcoordinator@wiley.com.

Limit of Liability/Disclaimer of Warranty: While the publisher and author have used their best efforts in preparing this book, they make no representations or warranties with respect to the accuracy or completeness of the contents of this book and specifically disclaim any implied warranties of merchantability or fitness for a particular purpose. No warranty may be created or extended by sales representatives or written sales materials. The advice and strategies contained herein may not be suitable for your situation. You should consult with a professional where appropriate. Neither the publisher nor author shall be liable for any loss of profit or any other commercial damages, including but not limited to special, incidental, consequential, or other damages.

For general information on our other products and services please contact our Customer Care Department within the United States at (800) 762-2974, outside the United States at (317) 572-3993 or fax (317) 572-4002.

Trademarks: Wiley, the Wiley Publishing logo and related trade dress are trademarks or registered trademarks of Wiley Publishing, Inc., in the United States and other countries, and may not be used without written permission. All other trademarks are the property of their respective owners. Wiley Publishing, Inc., is not associated with any product or vendor mentioned in this book.

Wiley also publishes its books in a variety of electronic formats. Some content that appears in print may not be available in electronic books.

Library of Congress Cataloging-in-Publication Data:

ISBN: 0-471-44915-6

Printed in the United States of America

10 9 8 7 6 5 4 3 2 1

For Sarah
—BD

For my wife, Kathryn
—JL

Contents

Acknowledgments		ix
About the Authors		xi
Introduction		xiii
Chapter 1	**Testing: Cactus and JUnit**	1
	Pitfall 1.1: No Assert	4
	Example	6
	Solving Pitfall 1.1: Assert the Intent	9
	Step-by-Step	9
	Example	10
	Example 2: Cactus	15
	Pitfall 1.2: Unreasonable Assert	20
	Example	21
	Solving Pitfall 1.2: Assert the Intent	23
	Pitfall 1.3: Console-Based Testing	24
	Example	25
	Solving Pitfall 1.3: System.out Becomes Assert	28
	Step-by-Step	29
	Example	29
	Example 2: Cactus	31
	Pitfall 1.4 Unfocused Test Method	34
	Example	35
	Solving Pitfall 1.4: Keep It Simple	38
	Step-by-Step	38
	Example	39

	Pitfall 1.5: Failure to Isolate Each Test	45
	Example	46
	Solving Pitfall 1.5: Use setUp and tearDown and	
	Introduce Test Decorators	50
	Step-by-Step	51
	Example	52
	Example 2: Introduce Test Decorators	55
	Pitfall 1.6: Failure to Isolate Subject	58
	Example	59
	Solving Pitfall 1.6: Introduce Mock Objects	62
	Step-by-Step	62
	Example	62
Chapter 2	**Struts ActionForms**	**67**
	Pitfall 2.1: Copy/Paste Formatting	70
	Example	72
	Solving Pitfall 2.1: Consolidate and Generalize	
	Formatting Code	74
	Step-by-Step	75
	Example	76
	Pitfall 2.2: Copy/Paste Conversion	96
	Example	98
	Solving Pitfall 2.2: Consolidate and Generalize Bean	
	Population Code	101
	Step-by-Step	101
	Example	102
	Pitfall 2.3: Copy/Paste Validation	119
	Example	121
	Solving Pitfall 2.3: Consolidate and	
	Generalize Validation Code	123
	Step-by-Step	126
	Example	127
Chapter 3	**Struts Actions**	**147**
	Pitfall 3.1: Business-Tier Code in Actions	149
	Example	151
	Solving Pitfall 3.1: Move Business-Tier	
	Code to BusinessDelegate	157
	Step-by-Step	158
	Example	159
	Pitfall 3.2: Copy/Paste Code in Actions	172
	Example	172
	Solving Pitfall 3.2: Move Common Code to Base Class	173
	Step-by-Step	174
	Example	174

	Pitfall 3.3: Accessing ActionForms in the Session	182
	Example	183
	Solving Pitfall 3.3: Add ActionForm	
	Locator Method to Base Class	187
	Step-by-Step	188
	Example	188
	Pitfall 3.4: Overloaded ActionMappings	192
	Example	192
	Solving Pitfall 3.4: Create Separate ActionMappings	
	for Navigation and Form Submission	195
	Step-by-Step	195
	Example	195
Chapter 4	**Struts TagLibs and JSPs**	**197**
	Pitfall 4.1: Hard-Coded Strings in JSPs	199
	Example	200
	Solving Pitfall 4.1: Move Common Strings to	
	Resource Bundles	201
	Step-by-Step	201
	Example	201
	Pitfall 4.2 Hard-Coded Keys in JSPs	203
	Example	203
	Solving Pitfall 4.2:Replace Hard-Coded Keys with Constants	204
	Step-by-Step	205
	Example	205
	Pitfall 4.3: Not Using Struts Tags for Error Messaging	209
	Example	210
	Solving Pitfall 4.3: Replace Custom Messaging with	
	Struts Messaging	210
	Step-by-Step	211
	Example	211
	Pitfall 4.4: Calculating Derived Values in JSPs	214
	Example	214
	Solving Pitfall 4.4: Move Calculations to Value Object	215
	Step-by-Step	216
	Example	216
	Pitfall 4.5: Performing Business Logic in JSPs	218
	Example	219
	Solving Pitfall 4.5: Move Business Logic to a Helper Class	220
	Step-by-Step	221
	Example	221
	Pitfall 4.6: Hard-Coded Options in HTML Select Lists	224
	Example	224
	Solving Pitfall 4.6: Move Options Values to a Helper Class	225
	Step-by-Step	225
	Example	226

Contents

	Pitfall 4.7: Not Checking for Duplicate Form Submissions	229
	Example	229
	Solving Pitfall 4.7: Add Tokens to Generated JSP	230
	Step-by-Step	230
	Example	230
Chapter 5	**Ant**	**233**
	Pitfall 5.1: Copy-and-Paste Reuse	235
	Example	235
	Solving Pitfall 5.1: Introduce Antcall	237
	Step-by-Step	237
	Example	238
	Pitfall 5.2: No Distinction between Different Types of Builds	243
	Example	244
	Solving Pitfall 5.2: Introduce Properties File	245
	Step-by-Step	245
	Example	246
	Pitfall 5.3: Building Subprojects	249
	Example	249
	Solving Pitfall 5.3: Centralize the Build	251
	Step-by-Step	252
	Example	253
	Pitfall 5.4: No Logging from Custom Tasks	257
	Example	257
	Solving Pitfall 5.4: Add Logging	259
	Step-by-Step	259
	Example	260
Appendix A	**Pitfall Catalog**	**263**
Appendix B	**References**	**273**
Appendix C	**What's on the Web Site**	**277**
Index		**279**

Acknowledgments

I would like to thank first and foremost Christ, for all He has done in my life to teach me to be more than I was and to inspire me to be more than I am. I would also like to thank my wonderful wife Sarah, without her support and love I'd be lost. And I'd also like to thank my great kids that keep life interesting. Andrew, Isaac, Anna and Sophia you are the definition of joy. I'd also like to thank my mom for always making me look the word up in the dictionary even though I complained enough to deserve to be sent to my room. I'd also like to thank Jon Crater and Bill Willis for all their great feedback on the content of this book. It's a better book because of them. I would also like to thank my co-workers Chris Noe and Sridhar Valavala for teaching me so much, and for listening to my endless Monty Python quotes. My hovercraft is indeed full of eels. And finally I'd like to thank Eileen Bien Calabro for all her hard work on turning my gibberish into English and helping me to deliver a better book. I hope you learn as much from reading this book as I did in writing it.

—**Bill Dudney**

Writing this book has truly been an adventure for me, and I am grateful to my co-author, Bill Dudney, for inviting me to participate. As is the case I suppose with most technical books, this one is the work of many hands, and I am indebted to Bill Willis, Jon Crater, and Eileen Calabro for their invaluable assistance.

For the past year and a half, I have had the very good fortune of working with a wonderful team of developers who have shared many insights that helped deepen my understanding of the Struts framework and the possibilities of web applications in general. In particular, I owe much to Carl

Acknowledgments

Lindberg and Harshal Chaudhari, as well as Shailesh Patel, Shoekai Yeh, Jason Jobe, Michael Cymerman, Nikolai Teleguine, Diana Schmidt, and Sergey Muzyka. I would also like to thank Chris Cordrey of Gale Force Software for his help in assembling the team, with a special note of thanks to Bob Leonard.

Above all, I am grateful to my beloved wife, Kathryn, for her patience, support, and sacrifice while I juggled the full-time responsibilities of leading a framework development team with the demands of co-authoring this book.

—Jonathan Lehr

About the Authors

Bill Dudney is a Java Architect with Object Systems Group. He has been building J2EE applications and software for 5 years and has been doing distributed computing for almost 14 years. Bill has been using Jakarta tools since there was a Tomcat and has been a major advocate of using open source tools and building unit tests on all his projects. After struggling for years to keep *make* off his resume he discovered Ant and was glad to be known as the 'build guy' again. He is the co-author of both *J2EE AntiPatterns* and *Mastering JavaServer Faces* (Wiley).

Jonathan Lehr is an independent consultant in the Washington, D.C., area with over twenty years experience in software development and developer training. He is the author of over a dozen courses on Object-Oriented Programming and other development topics, and for the past eight years has designed and architected e-commerce applications in Objective C and Java for Fortune 100 financial and telecommunications companies. He currently leads a user-interface framework team that provides reusable Struts-based components and infrastructure enhancements for use by development teams at a major financial institution. He is also the co-author of *Mastering JavaServer Faces* (Wiley).

Introduction

What Is a Pitfall?

A pitfall is a common, overlooked, unsound way of developing and designing software. The consequences of pitfalls vary: Some are as mild as slightly decreased performance, but some have more severe consequences, like slipping schedules, difficult maintenance, and lack of changeability. Pitfall-strewn code can also be a major problem for new developers. The time it takes for a new developer to become effective is directly related to the cohesiveness of the code. Cohesive code is easy to follow and understand because it flows logically. Code filled with pitfalls is hard to follow because it does not flow logically.

The need to avoid pitfalls is paramount. Over time, any application that is being used will have bugs that need to be fixed and new features that need to be added, and thus it will require maintenance. The fewer pitfalls that are in the design and code, the easier this maintenance will be to perform. To illustrate this principal, imagine a shopping cart application. The application has browse, add products, checkout, and ship functionality. Over time, customers might request more functionality, such as the ability to search the product catalog. If some of the code to implement the search functionality is in the StrutsAction classes and some of the code is in a business tier object such as a JavaBean or an EJB, adding the new search functionality will be more difficult than if the original code is contained solely in the business tier.

Oddly, pitfalls rarely keep systems from working. An application can be riddled with pitfalls and still not have a problem functioning early on, but the consequences of the pitfalls will eventually surface. For example, a project can be proceeding according to plan for months. Then, the second iteration begins, and mass chaos ensues. Many projects have failed during later iterations because the early code was too hard to maintain.

Also, unlike other development problems, the consequences of pitfalls don't make themselves obvious. If we do something like cast an object to the wrong type, the Java runtime is kind enough to inform us of that fact with an exception the first time the code is executed. But if our code is stuck in a pitfall, there is no runtime to tell us; we simply have to wait for the consequences to manifest themselves. This is why it is important to study the pitfalls that others have fallen into and to recognize them before we fall into them ourselves.

As a result of the delayed nature of the consequences, it is sometimes hard to justify fixing code stuck in a pitfall. After all, management is rarely keen on rewriting the whole system just to remove a couple of pitfalls (and rightly so because there would almost certainly be other pitfalls introduced as a result). So how do you get buy-in to fix the code? The most important thing to keep in mind when trying to justify fixing code is the longer-term payoff of code that is easier to understand and maintain. For example, copying and pasting the formatting code in one of your Struts forms (Pitfall 4.1) is particularly bad for the long-term maintainability of the form.

It is also important to remind management of the long-term consequences of pitfalls if you hope to ask for the time and resources to address them. The most important aspect to communicate to management is that fixing pitfalls does not have to mean rewriting. Instead, inform management that the code is changed in a disciplined way to achieve better design and implementation without starting over. Also emphasize that when fixing pitfalls, the internal structure of the code might change a lot, but the interface changes only slightly.

Of course, studying pitfalls before any of these issues occurs will save both you and management time, energy, and money down the road. But remember that studying pitfalls is not enough. You also need to find a way to work out of them when necessary or, better yet, to avoid them altogether. The good news is that every pitfall has at least one solution, and all of the Jakarta pitfalls discussed in this book come with both solutions and tips for avoidance.

Pitfalls in Jakarta

Jakarta is part of the Apache open source project, and its emphasis is on server-side Java solutions. There are many great projects hosted by the

Jakarta folks, but we focused on these three subprojects because they are widely used: Ant, Cactus, and Struts.

Ant

Ant has almost entirely replaced *make* as the build tool for Java developers. Ant allows developers to declare how their applications should be built and packaged. The declaration is written in a straightforward XML-based configuration file that is used to direct Ant from step to step. Ant is also customizable to allow developers to build their own tasks and use them in their configuration files.

Pitfalls in Ant arise typically from a lack of experience. Another area that gives rise to pitfalls is the perceived similarity between make files and build files. Many developers making the switch from make to Ant end up writing make files instead of build files. Chapter 5, "Ant," deals with these issues.

Cactus

Cactus is a derivative of JUnit that provides server-side unit testing for J2EE components. With Cactus, unit tests can be written to perform on the server side fully integrated with the application server. This setup provides a great way to ensure that your components will perform as expected in an actual J2EE runtime environment. Because Cactus runs in the application server environment, the tests can use the actual server objects instead of having to try to build mock objects.

Although unit testing server-side objects with Cactus is far easier than it would be without Cactus, developers still make mistakes and end up with code that is hard to understand or maintain. The most common cause for these mistakes is lack of understanding of how to do unit testing in the first place. Chapter 1, "Testing: Cactus and JUnit," explains in depth what goes wrong and how to fix it.

Struts

Struts is the Web-based UI framework that has become a de facto standard in the J2EE community. Struts provides an implementation of the Model-View-Controller (MVC) framework for building Web applications. The view is built from a large array of custom tags and JSPs. There are two controllers in Struts: a central servlet that listens to requests and delegates to application-specific controllers to perform the task specified in the request, and the Action that you write. The model is left to the developer to build. The application controller classes (that is, Actions) are responsible for converting the model-level data into data that Struts is able to understand (that is, Action-Forms) as well as converting from the ActionForms back to the application-specific model.

Struts makes building Web-based applications easier than it has ever been before, but there is a common set of things that developers, especially new Struts developers, do wrong. Several pitfalls come from not having a good understanding of the architecture of Struts. Other pitfalls arise from not building the Struts components (Actions and ActionForms) in a way that will work well in a three-tier environment. Chapters 2, 3, and 4 capture these pitfalls as well as their solutions.

These three tools from Jakarta have proven to be a major force in the J2EE community. Many projects have been greatly enhanced by using Struts for their Web-based UI, Ant to build, and Cactus to test the project.

Why This Book?

The kinds of mistakes that are chronicled in this book are real-world experiences we have faced as developers working with these tools—the kinds of experiences that cause actual delays in schedule, or allow major bugs to get into the users' hands, or led to lots of rewrites in maintenance because the code was so hard to change or understand.

The Jakarta open source community has exploded over the last couple of years with insanely popular—and useful—projects, including the ones covered here: Ant, Cactus, and Struts. Given the relative newness of the technology, many developers are inexperienced with these tools and are getting trapped by the same pitfalls over and over. This book is an attempt to capture some of the most common pitfalls and the means to arrive at solutions. It is our hope that you will be saved the frustration of being trapped by the same pitfalls that have trapped us.

Even if you are an experienced developer, that doesn't mean that you can't get something out of this book. After all, just because everyone uses a technology does not always mean that they use it correctly. It takes time for common mindshare to develop around a concept and for common problems and solutions to become well known. For example, early adoptors of Ant, Cactus, and Struts suffered from poor documentation. Over time, the documentation has become very good for all three of these Jakarta projects, but some developers are still building bad code out of habit. What we provide here, therefore, is not an introductory Ants, Cactus, or Struts book; it's a way to improve code incrementally and to find out about the nooks and crannies that could make your code hard to maintain or perform poorly. In the end, the pitfalls and solutions in this book will help you build better applications that are easier to maintain and that will perform better.

Organization of the Book

In each chapter, we first give a brief introduction to the chapter topic and offer lists of pitfalls and their related solutions. Sometimes, a single solution applies to one or more pitfalls in a chapter. When that happens, we cover the solution in detail under the first pitfall to which it applies and refer you to the original solution the next time it is applicable.

Pitfalls

Every pitfall in this book is numbered and named. We describe each pitfall in detail, and we explain how developers typically become trapped in it. We also provide information on how a developer can avoid being trapped and what the common symptoms and consequences of each pitfall are. For example, Pitfall 5.1: Business Tier Code in Chapter 5 documents the typical bad practice of putting code that belongs in the model into the StrutsAction classes and describes how to clean up the code so that it is better partitioned.

Where applicable, the pitfall descriptions also document the pitfall from different perspectives. Often a pitfall will manifest in different ways, depending on a number of factors. The pitfall descriptions in this book address each of these different manifestations in a way that will help developers identify the pitfall in their code or design.

To make the discussion more concrete, we also provide an example for each pitfall. Sometimes, the example is abbreviated in an effort to make it more clear. It is better to have an example that clearly illustrates the pitfall than to explain all the details.

Solutions

After each pitfall's example, we offer a solution, called Solving Pitfall X.X. Each solution contains general information, ways the solution can be applied to all the variations of the pitfall, step-by-step guidance, and a detailed example. The solutions essentially walk you through taking your pitfall-riddled code and converting to better, pitfall-free code.

Some solutions will affect the design of the application, but others will affect only the code. During the discussion of the solutions, however, we will focus mostly on the code because as the code is changed the design will be changed as well.

A Note about JUnit Testing

Testing often gets a bad reputation. It is often pushed to the end of a project, then dropped because of schedule issues. Then the project goes into the hands of testers without any developer-based testing, leading to a landslide of bugs. A unit test makes sure that small units of functionality on a particular class are working correctly, so this cycle doesn't repeat itself. With enough unit tests in place, the official testers on your project will be bored, and your application will sail through testing.

Why Unit Test?

First and foremost, it is necessary to have unit tests in place in order to refactor code—or, for our purposes, dig yourself out of pitfalls. Unit tests help you to make sure that what is documented in the API of your classes is actually what you have implemented—which is, of course, valuable if you want to change the implementation. When the change is complete (your pitfall is resolved), you can just rerun your unit tests. If the tests are complete, then you know the clients of your class will not be affected by your solution. Another benefit of unit tests is that as long as the tests are run before and after any change, problems will be found right away. Without unit tests, it can be quite a while before a bug related to the change surfaces, making the bug harder to track down.

Unit testing is also an efficient way to validate design and implementation assumptions. For example, with a unit test, you can validate your expectations about the way hashCode and equals work in a Hash Map or Set. If you have a set of unit tests that assert the contract as it is spelled out in the documentation, you can be fairly sure that when you put the object into the set it will act as expected. More tests to make sure that it is acting the correct way will expose missed requirements, assumptions, and bugs.

Unit testing is especially important in reusable components or frameworks. If you want your reusable code to be used by others, then you need to write tests for it. If that code is poorly tested, your teammates will lack confidence in your code; if it is well tested (and well documented), the code can be used with confidence. The tests not only will help to make sure that the code works but will give your users some valuable hints on how to use the framework. Further, code changes in one part of a system often show up as bugs in other parts of the system. Unit tests that are run often help prevent this from happening by isolating change and finding bugs right away.

Testing with JUnit

JUnit and its derivatives make unit testing easy. In fact, for some developers, testing with JUnit is addictive. It's a great feeling to have your code go into the hands of testers knowing that they won't find any major show-stopper bugs. And with any test, it's as simple as overriding setUp, tearDown, and the suite method; then you are ready to add test methods.

To prove how easy it is to perform a test with JUnit, here is an example test that examines the substring method on the String class.

```java
public StringTest extends TestCase {
  private String subject = "Monty Python";

  public static void main(String args[]) {
    String classes[] = {StringTest.class.getName()};
    junit.swingui.TestRunner.main(classes);
  }

  public static TestSuite suite() {
    return new TestSuite(StringTest.class);
  }

  public void testSimpleSubstring() throws Exception {
    assertEquals("Python", subject.substring(6));
  }

  public void testBeginEndSubstring() throws Exception {
    assertEquals("Monty", subject.substring(0, 4));
  }

  public void setUp() throws Exception {
    // no need to Initialize anything because the subject
    // Is already Initialized as 'Monty Python'
  }
}
```

That is it. In just these few lines, we have all that we need to build and run a JUnit test. You can visit www.junit.org for more information and motivation.

Note to the Reader

This book assumes that you are a Java/J2EE developer familiar with the technologies discussed. This is not a book on how to build Ant files or

Struts applications. Instead, this book is about how not to build Cactus tests, how not to do Struts, and how not to use Ant.

We hope both inexperienced and experienced developers enjoy reading this book as much as we enjoyed writing it. With the experience captured here, we hope that you will be able to avoid the countless hours we spent frustrated, trying to work our way out of the pitfalls we had created.

CHAPTER 1

Testing: Cactus and JUnit

With the advent of Extreme Programming (XP) and its emphasis on refactoring, unit testing has gained in popularity and exposure. In order to refactor anything, a good set of unit tests must be in place to make sure that current clients of the implementation will not be affected by the changes that are made. Many developers, as they embrace the XP approach, are suddenly "test infected" and writing all kinds of JUnit tests. Many developers who were doing unit testing with code in the main method of their Java classes are finding JUnit and Cactus to be a more thorough means to test their classes. This chapter is about what goes wrong when building a real-world test set for real-world applications with these tools.

Many pitfalls in unit tests come from the complexity of the components being tested or the complexity of the tests themselves. Also, the lack of assertions in the test code can cause problems. Without an assertion, a test just confirms that no exceptions were thrown. Although it is useful to know when exceptions are thrown, it is rarely enough. For example, not all unexpected state changes in a test subject will throw an exception. Developers shouldn't simply rely on printouts so that they can visually inspect the result of calling the tested code. While visual inspection is better than nothing, it's not nearly as useful as unit testing can be. This chapter shows several ways in which a lack of assertions shows up and provides strategies

> **MOCK OBJECT VERSUS "IN CONTAINER" TESTING**
>
> There are two ways to approach testing your server-side objects. They can be isolated from the containers in which they are intended to run and tested separately to ensure that the objects do what is expected of them. The other way is to build a framework that works with the container to allow your objects to be tested inside the container.
>
> The first approach, called Mock Object testing (or the Mock Objects Pattern), is very effective at isolating the test subject. There is significant burden, though, in building and maintaining the Mock Objects that simulate the configuration and container objects for the test subject. They have to be built and maintained in order for the testing to be effective. Even though there is virtually no complexity to the actual Mock Objects, there is a lot of complexity in maintaining the large number of Mock Objects required to simulate the container.
>
> Cactus takes the other approach and facilitates testing inside the container. Cactus gets between the test cases and the container and builds an environment for the test subject to be run in that uses the container-provided objects instead of Mock Objects. Both approaches are helpful in stamping out bugs.

to migrate existing tests (visual or not) to solid unit tests that assert the contract implied in the API being tested.

A quick word about the differences between JUnit and Cactus: JUnit tests run in the same JVM as the test subject whereas Cactus tests start in one JVM and are sent to the app server's JVM to be run. Cactus has a very clever means to do the sending to the remote machine. Just enough information is packaged so that the server side can find and execute the test. The package is sent via HTTP to one of the redirectors (ServletTestRedirector, FilterTestRedirector, or the JSPTestRedirector). The redirector then unpacks the info, finds the test class and method, and performs the test. Figure 1.1 represents this process.

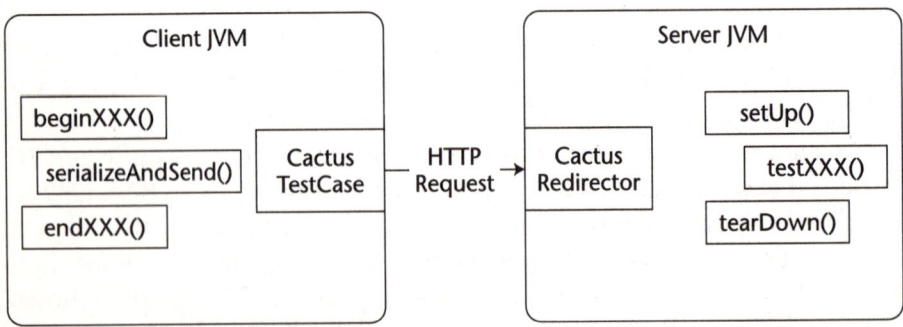

Figure 1.1 Cactus and test methods.

Misunderstanding the distributed nature of Cactus can lead to frustration if you are an old hand at building JUnit tests. Keep this in mind as you start to build Cactus tests.

Another thing to keep in mind as you build Cactus tests is that the redirector provides access to the container objects only on the server. Because the container objects are not available until the test is running on the server side, you cannot use container objects in the methods that are executed on the client side. For example, the config object in a ServletTest is not available in the beginXXX and endXXX methods, but you can use it in your setUp, textXXX, and tearDown methods.

JUnit has become the de facto standard unit testing framework. It is very simple to get started with it, and it has amazing flexibility. There are probably dozens, if not a couple of hundred, of extensions to JUnit available on the Web. This chapter focuses on JUnit (www.junit.org) and Cactus (www.jakarta.apache.org/cactus). Cactus allows "in container" testing of J2EE components. As stated earlier, this book assumes some experience with these tools.

> **Pitfall 1.1: No assert** is the result of developers that do not realize that calling a method is not the same as testing it.
>
> **Pitfall 1.2: Unreasonable assert** examines the tendency of developers new to unit testing to start asserting everything, even things that won't happen unless the JVM is not working properly.
>
> **Pitfall 1.3: Console-Based Testing** addresses the problem of developers who get into the habit of using "System.out" to validate their applications. This method of testing is very haphazard and error-prone.
>
> **Pitfall 1.4: Unfocused Test Method** is common to more experienced developers who get a little lazy about writing good tests and let the test become overly complex and hard to maintain.
>
> **Pitfall 1.5: Failure to Isolate Each Test** is fixed using the setUp and tearDown methods defined in the JUnit framework. These methods allow each test to be run in an isolation that contains only the test subject and the required structure to support it.
>
> **Pitfall 1.6: Failure to Isolate Subject** is related to the discussion of Mock Objects in the previous sidebar.

Pitfall 1.1: No Assert

This pitfall describes the tendency of developers new to unit testing to forget about asserts completely. New developers often assume that invoking the method is a sufficient test. They assume that if no exceptions are thrown when the method is called, then everything must be OK. Many bugs escape this kind of testing.

Here is some code for a simple addStrings method that returns the result of concatenating the value returned from the toString method of its two arguments. The current implementation should not be putting a space into the returned value, but it is. The initial test will not expose this bug because it is stuck in this pitfall; we will apply the solution to the test, though, and it will expose the bug.

```
public String appendTwoStrings(Object one, Object two) {
    StringBuffer buf = new StringBuffer(one.toString());
    buf.append(" ");
    buf.append(two.toString());
    return buf.toString();
}
```

Here is a sample test that simply invokes the method without really testing anything.

```
public void testAppendTwoStrings() throws Exception {
    myAppender.appendTwoStrings("one", "two");
}
```

This situation is typical of tests stuck in this pitfall. Even though it looks as if the appendTwoStrings method is tested, it is not. Users of the appendTwoStrings method have expectations of what the return value will be as a result of calling the method. And, in this case, the expectations will not be met. The API for a class is an implied contract for the users of the code. Whenever that contract is not met, the users of the code will see that failure as a bug. Unit tests should make sure that every unit of code performs as expected, that it fulfills the implied contract in the API. Unit tests that are stuck in this pitfall do not make sure that code is performing as expected, and they need to be fixed.

> **INTENT OF THE API**
>
> The "intent of the API" is what is documented or expected that the API will do with the inputs provided. It is also what the API will do to the internal state of the object on which the method is being called. For example, the *append* method on the StringBuffer class is documented to append the argument to its internal buffer such that the StringBuffer is longer by the length of the argument that is passed into the method. The internal state of the StringBuffer has changed, and nothing has happened to the argument. The test suite for StringBuffer should assert both "intents" of the StringBuffer API.
>
> A test should make sure that the stated intentions of the API are met by asserting that what is expected to be true actually is. Another way to think of the intent of the API is that the API is like a contract between the clients that use the API and the provider of the API. The provider of the API is guaranteeing that the class will perform certain tasks, and the consumer is expecting those tasks to be performed. Formal ideas surrounding Design by Contract (DBC) are helpful in building tests for classes.

No assert is usually exposed at the point at which the application is passed over to the testing team, which tests the application by looking at the state changes that are occurring. As the testing team looks into the database to confirm that what was supposed to change did change, they will notice that the data is not changing as expected. As a result, many bug reports will be filed, and the bug fixes will more often than not be made in code that was tested with few asserts. Bug reports are no fun, especially when some effort was made to do unit testing. This situation will make it appear that unit testing added little value.

One of two things, laziness or lack of knowledge and experience, usually causes this pitfall. Everyone gets lazy from time to time. Developers are no exception, but it is important that we build good unit tests so that we can afford to be a little lazy. A good set of unit tests will expose bugs right when they are introduced, which is when they are easiest to fix. And because the bugs are easier to fix, we have less work.

Lack of knowledge and experience is fixed only through mentorship and experience. Over time, developers will begin to see how valuable unit tests are, especially if they have found, fixed, and prevented anyone else from seeing bugs in their code. You can encourage and teach good unit testing by doing periodic peer reviews with junior members. Peer reviews provide a great mechanism to mentor people, and if the senior people allow junior people to review their code, junior people will be able to see good examples on a regular basis.

> **TESTING FIRST**
>
> Many people in the JUnit community suggest that tests be written before the code that they are intended to test. The tests become almost a coded set of requirements for the test subject. This is a great habit to get into. The next time you are transitioning from design to development, try writing a few tests for the new code before implementing. When it comes time to use the code, you will thank yourself. The great benefit of testing first is that it forces the developer to focus on providing good APIs to future clients. The tests will expose nuances of what was expected to be true at design time versus what is really true on the ground in the code. And besides, if you write the tests first you will have a concrete gauge of when the class is done (that is, when it passes all the tests, it is done).

To stay out of this pitfall, you have to assert the intent stated in the API being tested. The intent of the API is what is expected to happen when the API is called. The intent is usually captured in the form of JavaDoc and the exception list that a method throws (sometimes referred to as the contract for the class). Unit tests should make sure that each piece of the API is doing what it should. As an example, if a method claims to throw an IllegalArgumentException when a null is passed, at least one test should assert that that exception is thrown when a null is passed.

Example

This example of No assert relies on a test for the contrived class called StringPair. Instances of StringPair will be used as keys in a map. An object that will be used as a key in a map must implement two methods: "equals" and hashCode. The two methods must be consistent, which means that if true is returned from the two objects involved in an equals comparison (that is, the receiver of the method call and the argument to the method), then hashCode must return the same value for both objects.

The StringPair class has two string properties, *right* and *left*. These two values are used in the equals and hashCode methods. To further complicate the subject, let's say that the StringPair class is used in a performance-sensitive environment and that it caches the hashCode so that it does not have to be recomputed each time. The hashCode should be reset to –1 when either the right or left value changes. This resetting behavior is crucial to the functioning of the StringPair class as a signal that the hashCode should be recomputed. The unit test here makes sure that the important methods on the StringPair class are called.

A good test for the StringPair class would assert that every intent described earlier is true (that hashCode and equals are consistent). The

JUnit test, however, is not good, as the test in Listing 1.1 does not assert anything in particular; in other words, this test case is trapped in this pitfall.

```java
public class StringPairTest extends TestCase {
    private StringPair one = new StringPair("One", "Two");
    private StringPair oneA = new StringPair("One", "Two");
    private StringPair two = new StringPair("Three", "Four");
    private StringPair twoA = new StringPair("Three", "Four");

    public static Test suite() {
        return new TestSuite(StringPairTest.class);
    }

    public StringPairTest(String name) {
        super(name);
    }

    /**
     * Test equals.
     */
    public void testEquals() throws Exception {
        one.equals(oneA);
        oneA.equals(one);
    }

    /**
     * Test not equals.
     */
    public void testNotEquals() throws Exception {
        one.equals(two);
        two.equals(one);
    }

    /**
     * Test hashCode.
     */
    public void testHashCode() throws Exception {
        one.hashCode();
        two.hashCode();
    }

    /**
     * Test setting the values.
     */
    public void testSetValues() throws Exception {
        one.setRight("ROne");
        one.setLeft("LOne");
```

Listing 1.1 StringPairTest. *(continues)*

```
            two.setRight("RTwo");
            two.setLeft("LTwo");
    }

    /**
     * Should throw an exception.
     */
    public void testNullPointerProtection() throws Exception {
        // since this will throw an exception the test will fail
        StringPair busted = new StringPair(null, "Four");
    }
}
```

Listing 1.1 *(continued)*

There are no asserts in the code for StringPairTest, so it is actually not testing very much. For example, take a look at the testSetValues method. All that happens is that the right and left property set methods are called. No check is made to make sure that the expected state changes happened on the StringPair instances. All this test is making sure of is that if valid strings are passed into the set methods (that is, not null) no exceptions are thrown. A lot of code is written in this way and then called test code. The StringPairTest test case is a classic example of this pitfall.

In this example, because the StringPair class is so simple, it might seem like overkill to put tests in place to make sure that equals and hashCode are performing as they should. Others, however, will be using this class and will expect it to function as advertised in its API. Which kind of class would you rather depend on in your code, one that is well tested (even when the code seems simple) or code that is not tested? A well-tested StringPair class can be used confidently. A poorly tested StringPair class that is tested only in integrated tests with the larger process will likely lead to much harder-to-find bugs. If StringPair is tested only through the Big Process test cases, then bugs in StringPair will be much harder to find because it cannot be stated with certainty that the bug is not in StringPair. The test needs to assert that the intent of the class as laid out in its API is actually being met, meaning that the hashCode is being reset when a value changes. If tests are in place that assert the intent of the StringPair API, then when bugs arise in the Big Process, they can be attributed confidently to something in the Big Process code.

> **INCREMENTAL TEST IMPROVEMENT**
>
> **If a bug exposed in a higher-level test turns out to be in a lower-level component (as in the earlier StringPair, Big Process example), then use that occasion to improve the test of the lower-level component. Instead of just fixing the bug and moving on, write a test first that fails because of the bug. Then fix the bug so that the test passes. In the future, if someone attempts maintenance on the lower-level component, the test will help him or her avoid reintroducing the bug.**

Solving Pitfall 1.1: Assert the Intent

The way to get your tests out of Pitfall 1.1: No Assert is to introduce asserts. The intent of the API needs to be asserted to make sure that the documented behavior is actually happening. Building tests that assert the intent is making sure that the contract that is implied by the API and its documentation is being met.

This solution is the primary solution to Pitfalls 1.1 and 1.2: Unreasonable assert. Note that sometimes there are no asserts because the test is stuck in Pitfall 1.3: Console-Based Testing. Review that pitfall for a more in-depth discussion of the issues surrounding using System.out as a test tool and a description of the solution to Pitfall 1.3, "System.out becomes assert."

Step-by-Step

1. Start the process with the simplest-to-test subject method.
    a. If there is an existing test method that calls the method, the solution will start there; otherwise, a new test method should be created.
2. Review the documentation for the method to identify the intent (or contract) of the method.
    a. Some methods have no documentation so you will have to review the implementation of the method looking for intent.
    b. Sometimes bugs in the documentation will be exposed in implementing this process.
    c. Statements about what state changes will happen or what actions will be taken are good candidates for tests.
3. For each intent stated in the documentation, assert that what is documented to happen really has happened.

4. Repeat this process for the more complex methods.
    a. Be careful not to do a bunch of pointless tests. Too many tests that are testing simple accessory methods can be another pitfall. Test the important API of the class first.
5. Run the tests, and debug any failures.

Example

To illustrate, the JUnit test for StringPair (discussed earlier) will be put through this solution so that the test is cleaned up and accurately tests the StringPair class so we can be confident in using the StringPair as it is documented. The code for StringPair with its JavaDoc comments that will be used to determine the intent of the API is found in Listing 1.2.

```
/**
 * A class to provide a key into a map.
 */
public class StringPair {
    /**
     * <code>hashCode</code> is used to cache the hash code for
     * this class
     */
    private int hashCode = -1;
    /**
     * The right-hand side string.
     */
    private String right;
    /**
     * The left-hand side string.
     */
    private String left;

    /**
     * A simple constructor taking the right and left side strings.
     * @param right
     * @param left
     * @throws IllegalArgumentException if either <code>right</code> or
     * <code>left</code> are null.
     */
    public StringPair(String right, String left) {
        if (null == right || null == left) {
            throw new IllegalArgumentException(
                "Should not pass null "
                    + "right = "
                    + right
```

Listing 1.2 StringPair.

```java
                    + " left = "
                    + left);
        }
        this.right = right;
        this.left = left;
    }
    /**
     * Get the right side string.
     * @return String
     */
    public String getRight() {
        return right;
    }

    /**
     * Sets the right-hand side string, reinitializes the
     * hashCode so that it is recalculated the next time
     * hashCode  is called.
     * @param right
     */
    public void setRight(String right) {
        hashCode = -1;
        this.right = right;
    }

    /**
     * Returns the left-hand side string.
     * @return String
     */
    public String getLeft() {
        return left;
    }

    /**
     * Sets the left-hand side string, reinitializes the hashCode
     * so that it is recalculated the next time hashCode is called.
     * @param left
     */
    public void setLeft(String left) {
        hashCode = -1;
        this.left = left;
    }

    /**
     * Calculates the hashCode in a way consistent with equals.
     * @see java.lang.Object#hashCode()
     * @see java.util.Map
     */
    public int hashCode() {
```

Listing 1.2 *(continues)*

```
            if (-1 == hashCode) {
                hashCode = right.hashCode() ^ left.hashCode();
            }
            return hashCode;
        }

        /**
         * Implements the equals method consistent with the hashCode method.
         * @see java.lang.Object#equals(Object)
         * @see java.util.Map
         */
        public boolean equals(Object o) {
            boolean flag = false;
            if (o instanceof StringPair) {
                StringPair other = (StringPair) o;
                if (other.hashCode() == hashCode()) {
                    if (right.equals(other.getRight())
                        && left.equals(other.getLeft())) {
                        flag = true;
                    }
                }
            }
            return flag;
        }
    }
```

Listing 1.2 *(continued)*

None of the tests in the original JUnit test class (Listing 1.2) specifically asserts anything. This kind of test code is deceiving because it looks as if there are tests in place, but there is no actual testing happening. With a test case like this one in place, StringPair looks as if it's fully tested when, in fact, the equals method (as tested in the testNotEquals method in the code listing) could be returning true when it should return false and vice versa. So how does the code get out of this pitfall? Let's apply the steps outlined previously to StringPairTest and solve this pitfall.

The first step is to start with the simplest-to-test method. The absolute simplest methods are the property accessors (the *get* methods). Although they are the easiest, they are not very important to test because there is no actual code, so let's move to the next method in complexity, the equals method. Because methods to test the equals method already exist, we can start there. Here is the original test code intended to test the equals method.

```
    /**
     * Test equals.
     */
```

```
    public void testEquals() throws Exception {
        one.equals(oneA);
        oneA.equals(one);
    }

    /**
     * Test not equals.
     */
    public void testNotEquals() throws Exception {
        one.equals(two);
        two.equals(one);
    }
```

The next step to solving this pitfall is to review the intent of the API. The equals method is supposed to provide the typical equals behavior—that is, return true if the receiver and the argument should be considered the same object. The equals method also claims to be consistent with the hashCode method, meaning that if two objects are equal to each other then their hash-Code will be the same. Both statements need to be tested. In order to test the two different aspects of the equals method we will introduce two methods: testEqualsReturn and testEqualsHashCodeConsistency (one is simply a rename from testEquals to testEqualsReturn). The third method, testNotEquals, simply uses asserts where there were none before. The code for the methods is shown here.

```
    /**
     * Test equals.
     */
    public void testEqualsReturn() throws Exception {
        assertTrue(one.equals(oneA));
        assertTrue(oneA.equals(one));
    }
```

Notice that the difference between testEquals and testEqualsReturn is very small; all we did was add two method calls. The two new method calls made all the difference. Now there is a test in place so that the computer can make sure that what is expected to happen is actually happening. In other words, the responsibility for making sure that the program is doing what it should has shifted from the programmer to the computer.

```
    /**
     * Test equals & hashCode consistency.
     * @throws Exception
     */
    public void testEqualsHashCodeConsistency() throws Exception {
        assertTrue(one.equals(oneA));
```

```
        assertEquals(one.hashCode(), oneA.hashCode());
    }
    /**
     *  Test not equals.
     */
    public void testNotEquals() throws Exception {
        assertTrue(!one.equals(two));
        assertTrue(!two.equals(one));
    }
```

These two methods have assertions to make sure that the hashCode and equals methods are indeed doing what they are documented to do. The first method checks that the two methods are consistent with each other, and the next method checks that the equals is returning false when it should.

The final step in the process is to apply what we did before (that is, assert the intent of the API in the tests) to each of the methods in StringPair that need to be tested. The next method that needs to be tested would be the hashCode method, and there are many statements in the documentation of the class that are important to look at. Specifically, each time a set method is called (for example, setRight), the hashCode must be recalculated. A test should be written that makes sure the hashCode is different after a set method is called with a different value. Another interesting test that should probably be done is to test that the hashCode is the same after a set method is called with the same value that was there before. The last statement about hashCode that needs to be verified is in its consistency with equals. That aspect of the two methods is already tested in the code we saw earlier. Here is a list of methods that test the intent stated for hashCode.

```
    /**
     *  Test hashCode.
     */
    public void testHashCode() throws Exception {
        assertTrue(one.hashCode() == oneA.hashCode());
    }

    public void testHashCodeChanges() throws Exception {
        int initialHashCode = one.hashCode();
        one.setRight("Wowzer");
        assertTrue(initialHashCode != one.hashCode());
    }

    public void testHashCodeNoChanges() throws Exception {
        int initialHashCode = one.hashCode();
        one.setRight(one.getRight());
        assertTrue(initialHashCode == one.hashCode());
    }
```

The final aspect of the StringPair API and its old JUnit test that needs to be addressed is the passing in of *null* to the constructor. The constructor is supposed to throw an exception if null is passed in. The old test code just called the method with null and documented that the runner of the test should expect a failure there. Although that approach kind of works on very small projects, it is troublesome on bigger projects because no one knows which tests should succeed and which are expected to fail without looking at the comments in the code. It is far better to catch the exception and fail the test if the exception is not thrown. Code that addresses this issue is shown here.

```
/**
 *  Test the constructor's protection against null
 */
public void testNullPointerProtection() throws Exception {
    try {
        StringPair busted = new StringPair(null, "Four");
        fail("The constructor should have thrown an exception");
    } catch(IllegalStateException e) {
        // just ignore the exception because we expect it
    }
}
```

We have completed our reworking of the StringPairTest JUnit test to cover all the stated intents of the StringPair class. Now we should run the test to make sure that everything passes. If you go back and review the differences between the two sets of code, you will notice that they are almost the same except for the addition of the asserts. The important thing to remember is that a test without an assert is not a very good test. Applying the steps outlined in this solution will help you fix any code you have that is stuck in this pitfall.

Example 2: Cactus

In this next example, we apply this solution to Cactus tests that are trapped in Pitfall 1.1: No assert. The steps to solve the pitfall do not change, but some of the details of Cactus tests need to be kept in mind while applying the steps. In particular, there is more API to review and assert, and each EJB has at least a home interface and a bean interface (local or remote and sometimes both). Also, because the code is running inside the application server, the test invocation will go through the container objects to get to your code. Because the container code is generated from your deployment descriptor, there are aspects of the descriptor that contribute to the contract of the API. For example, if it is important for one of your methods to participate in an existing transaction but not start one, then you might want to write a test that makes sure of that (that is, invoke the method without an existing transaction). Because there is so much detail (parts of the intent or contract) for each EJB method, the typical Cactus test will have a few asserts instead of one or two like the typical JUnit tests.

The Shopping Cart Session Bean (part of the Petstore demo application from the Sun Blueprints group) will be tested. The initial test is trapped in this pitfall and will be cleaned up so that it is not trapped anymore. The Shopping Cart Session Bean does all the things that a typical shopping cart does, and it uses methods to add and remove items. The quantity of a particular item can be updated, and a subtotal of the items currently in the cart can be calculated. The code in Listing 1.3 shows the interface for the cart that will be tested (all the comments have been removed for brevity; we will review the intent as we review the tests).

Listing 1.4 is the initial test class that is stuck in this pitfall. The only thing this test is really testing is that the methods can be called. While that might be a good test for the application server, the cart is deployed, and it is not what this test should be testing.

```
/**
 * This interface provides methods to add an item to the
 * shopping cart, delete an item from the shopping cart,
 * and update item quantities in the shopping cart.
 */
public interface ShoppingCartLocal extends EJBLocalObject {
    /*
     * Methods to update the state of shopping cart.
     */
    public void addItem(String itemID);
    public void setLocale(Locale locale);
    public Collection getItems();
    public void deleteItem(String itemID);
    public void updateItemQuantity(String itemID, int newQty);
    public Double getSubTotal();
    public Integer getCount();
    public void empty();
}
/**
 * The home interface for the shopping cart.
 */
public interface ShoppingCartLocalHome extends EJBLocalHome {
    public ShoppingCartLocal create() throws CreateException;
}
```

Listing 1.3 ShoppingCart interface.

Testing: Cactus and JUnit

```java
public class ShoppingCartCactusTest extends ServletTestCase {
... constructor and main
    public void testDeployed() throws Exception {
        InitialContext ic = new InitialContext();
        // if it's not deployed this will throw an exception
        // this is a pointless test because the rest of the tests
        // will expose any problem in deploying the bean.
        ShoppingCartLocalHome sHome = (ShoppingCartLocalHome)ic.
            lookup(JNDI_NAME);
    }

    public void testCreate() throws Exception {
        InitialContext ic = new InitialContext();
        ShoppingCartLocalHome sHome = (ShoppingCartLocalHome)ic.
            lookup(JNDI_NAME);
        // assume it is deployed and try a create
        // if something goes wrong this will throw an
        // exception
        ShoppingCartLocal cart = sHome.create();
    }

    public void testGetItems() throws Exception {
        InitialContext ic = new InitialContext();
        ShoppingCartLocalHome sHome = (ShoppingCartLocalHome)ic.
            lookup(JNDI_NAME);
        ShoppingCartLocal cart = sHome.create();
        // assume we can create and call the getItems method
        cart.getItems();
    }

    public void testUpdateItemQuantity() throws Exception {
        String itemId = "EST-3";
        InitialContext ic = new InitialContext();
        ShoppingCartLocalHome sHome = (ShoppingCartLocalHome)ic.
            lookup(JNDI_NAME);
        ShoppingCartLocal cart = sHome.create();
        cart.addItem(itemId);
        cart.updateItemQuantity(itemId, 2);
        Collection items = cart.getItems();
        CartItem item = (CartItem)items.iterator().next();
    }
... other tests here
}
```

Listing 1.4 ShoppingCartCactusTest.

The first indication that this test is stuck in this pitfall is that there are no asserts in any of the tests. The tests are counting on exceptions being thrown if something is not correct. But, as discussed earlier, a test that does not assert the intent of the API is not actually testing anything of value.

Chapter 1

As with a JUnit test, start the solution by tackling the simplest method to test first. The simplest method on this bean is the getCount method. The existing test does not have a test for this method so we will add one. The code for the new method is listed here.

```
public void testGetCount() throws Exception {
    // get the shopping cart home
    InitialContext ic = new InitialContext();
    ShoppingCartLocalHome sHome =
        (ShoppingCartLocalHome) ic.lookup(JNDI_NAME);
    // create the cart
    ShoppingCartLocal cart = sHome.create();
    // add an item
    cart.addItem("EST-3");
    // update the quantity of that item to 4
    cart.updateItemQuantity("EST-3", 4);
    // assert that what we put in is there
    assertEquals(cart.getCount().intValue(), 1);
}
```

Notice that the test asserts what is expected. The quantity of items that should be in the cart is one, and that is asserted through the assertEquals method call. This test covers the stated intent of the getCount method so the next step in the process is to improve the tests for the rest of the intent of the API.

The next method to test is the updateQuantity method. The testUpdateItemQuantity test method will be updated by applying the steps to the solution as before. The original test method code is listed here.

```
public void testUpdateItemQuantity() throws Exception {
    String itemId = "EST-1";
    InitialContext ic = new InitialContext();
    ShoppingCartLocalHome sHome = (ShoppingCartLocalHome)ic.
        lookup(JNDI_NAME);
    ShoppingCartLocal cart = sHome.create();
    cart.addItem(itemId);
    cart.updateItemQuantity(itemId, 2);
}
```

Notice that there are no asserts here; the test is not doing what it should in making sure the quantity has been updated as expected. The next step is to identify the intent of the API. The updateQuantity method is supposed to find the item, identified by the itemID argument, and update the quantity of that item in the cart to the amount specified by the second argument. In order to assert that the update has happened, the test must get the list of

CartItems from the cart and look at the quantities stored there. The new test code is listed here.

```java
public void testUpdateItemQuantity () throws Exception {
    String itemId = "EST-";
    InitialContext ic = new InitialContext();
    ShoppingCartLocalHome sHome = (ShoppingCartLocalHome)ic.
        lookup(JNDI_NAME);
    ShoppingCartLocal cart = sHome.create();
    cart.addItem(itemId);
    cart.updateItemQuantity(itemId, 2);
    Collection items = cart.getItems();
    assertNotNull("Items should not be null", items);
    assertEquals("There should be exactly one item", 1,
              items.size());
    // the direct call of next here is ok because we just checked
    // that the count is 1 in the previous line
    CartItem item = (CartItem)items.iterator().next();
    assertEquals("The item id is wrong", itemId, item.getItemId());
    assertEquals("The quantity of " + itemId + " is wrong",
              2, item.getQuantity());
}
```

This test method is much more complete in asserting the state changes that should have occurred because of the change to the quantity of the item.

If you are new to Cactus testing, note that the test is interacting with the local home interface for the shopping cart. Remember that the test begins in a client JVM but is routed into the server's JVM by the specialized test classes and the redirectors in the Cactus framework. As discussed previously, Cactus runs inside the container in the application server so that you do not have to have Mock Objects for JNDI and the other server-side services provided by the application server.

TESTING EXISTING CODE

This last test on updating the quantity of a particular item in the cart is illustrative of the difficulty of working with existing code and trying to write tests for that code. Because the cart has no way of getting the quantity for a particular item other than through the CartItem class, there is no way to get at the value from outside. A better unit test would be interacting only with the bean and not with any of the helper classes like CartItem. The only way to accomplish a strict unit test, though, would be to modify the ShoppingCart bean. So this test makes due with what is available and manages to test the intent of the API.

Pitfall 1.2: Unreasonable Assert

Unreasonable assert is the tendency of inexperienced developers to assert everything that can be imagined. Often developers new to unit testing will take one of two tracks: They will have read about asserts before and thus recognize the concept when they see it in JUnit, or they will not have heard of asserts before and skip over them. The first kind of developer typically gets trapped in this pitfall. Tests end up bloated with a lot of asserts that basically just make sure that the JVM is working. Most JUnit tests will have only one assert; some tests will have a couple of asserts. If a JUnit test has several asserts, then it is very probable that either the test needs to be pulled into many tests or the underlying class needs to be simplified so that a single method is not doing so much. In Cactus, the number of asserts is usually a few instead of one due to the nature of testing in a distributed environment.

> **CACTUS AND UNIT TESTING**
>
> The strictest definition of unit testing requires that each test subject and each test run in complete isolation from all the supporting classes on which the test subject relies. This definition is a guide but is hard to accomplish in a J2EE environment. For example, in order to strictly unit test an entity EJB, the test harness must have Mock Objects implemented for each of the container-generated classes that support that bean. The harness must also provide mock implementations of all the container services (transactions, security, and so on).
>
> Cactus takes a pragmatic approach to this debate and makes tests pseudo-units (according to the strict definition outlined earlier) that use the actual container-generated classes and the services provided by the container. In a typical test of an EJB there is usually more than one thing that can and should be asserted. In an earlier example, the Shopping Cart Session Bean that returns the list of items in the cart was tested. Instead of strictly applying the unit test definition, the test asserted several things that should be true about that collection of objects in one test. This approach, while not purely a unit test, provides a practical approach to testing EJBs.
>
> Each invocation of the getItems method takes considerable time to set up and execute; if only one small part of the intent of that method were executed with each test, the whole test suite would take too long to run. If the tests take too long to run, developers will often stop running them. The best tests in the world are useless if they are never run. The approach outlined here takes a pragmatic approach to testing.

Just like a lack of asserts, many pointless asserts do not provide enough unit testing. When the test team tests the application, many bugs will be exposed that should have or could have been caught by good unit testing. Other symptoms include a reluctance to maintain the tests because they do not appear to add much value. Ultimately, spending lots of time and energy building tests that make sure the JVM is working wastes effort.

Usually this pitfall takes the form of tests that assert things that are almost impossible. For example, here is some code that ensures that the JVM is functioning properly.

```
public void testRidiculous() throws Exception {
    StringPair subject = new StringPair("One", "Two");
    assertNotNull(subject);
}
```

This test is making sure that the constructor does not return null. If the JVM is working, it's not possible to get null back from a constructor. If the JVM is unable to allocate memory for the new object, it will throw an OutOfMemoryException. If something else goes wrong with constructing the object, an exception will be thrown. None of the things that should be tested in this method is being tested. For example, the two strings that are passed into the constructor are supposed to initialize the right and left properties on the StringPair object. The test should assert this intent of the StringPair API.

Example

This JUnit test case is intended to test the StringPair class, but it is not asserting anything about the API of the class. The actual testing needs of the StringPair class are being missed in all the noise of the useless asserts, as you can see in Listing 1.5. Notice that there are lots of asserts, but none of them is making sure that what the class should be doing is actually being done. The test subject is the same StringPair class that was tested in Pitfall 1.1: No assert.

```
public class StringPairTest extends TestCase {
    StringPair subject = new StringPair("One", "Two");

    public static Test suite() {
        return new TestSuite(StringPairTest.class);
```

Listing 1.5 StringPairTest. *(continues)*

```java
    }

    public StringPairTest(String name) {
        super(name);
    }

    public void testConstructor() throws Exception {
        StringPair localSubject = new StringPair("One", "Two");
        assertNotNull(localSubject);
        assertTrue(null != localSubject.getRight());
        assertTrue(null != localSubject.getLeft());
    }

    public void testRightValue() throws Exception {
        subject.setRight("Three");
        assertTrue(null != subject.getRight());
    }

    public void testLeftValue() throws Exception {
        subject.setLeft("aValue");
        assertTrue(null != subject.getLeft());
    }

    public void testHashCode() throws Exception {
        int hash = subject.hashCode();
        assertTrue(subject.hashCode() == hash);
    }

    public void testEquals() throws Exception {
        assertEquals(subject, subject);
    }

    public void setUp() throws Exception {
    }
    public void tearDown() throws Exception {
    }
}
```

Listing 1.5 *(continued)*

The most important thing for the test writer to know is the intent of the API; the writer then should make sure the tests are asserting that. In this test case, nothing much is being asserted. For unit tests to be useful, they need to ensure that the expected behavior is what is actually happening.

Solving Pitfall 1.2: Assert the Intent

Just as with Pitfall 1.1: No assert, the solution to this pitfall is asserting only the intent of the test subject. Developers of the tests should know the intent of the API being tested and write tests that make sure that intent is met. In addition to adding asserts that make sure the API is acting as it should, many asserts (as described earlier in the solution to Pitfall 1.1) will have to be removed to fix the code. While applying the steps ask the question, "What aspect of the API does this assert test?" for each assert that is in the test. If there is no clear answer, then remove the assert. The new asserts will be added just as they were to solve Pitfall 1.1.

Pitfall 1.3: Console-Based Testing

Pitfall 1.3: Console-Based Testing is the practice of using System.out.println in the test code and then visually inspecting the output to validate that the test subject is doing what it should. Developers new to unit testing typically don't know how to write good test code and will not have enough experience to write good assertions. Often in these cases, the developer knows something more needs to be done but does not know quite what to do, so he or she decides that the results should be printed to the console. The developer is then forced to inspect the output visually to determine if the test succeeded.

Most of the time, this common practice leads to a numb stare at the console as untold numbers of lines stream by. After some experience with this blank-stare syndrome, developers often resort to putting strange leading and trailing characters into the logs so that the output in question catches the eye. As we all know, there are just not enough special characters on a keyboard to make every interesting thing eye-catching. Besides, with enough strange characters streaming by, nothing will catch the eye. Usually when the code is transitioned to a test team, they will find many bugs that should and could have been discovered via the unit tests.

The typical way to get trapped in this pitfall is to put lots of logging messages (for example, System.out.println) into the code, manually stimulate the application either through clicking around on the UI or writing simple client programs that invoke the remote API, and then review the output for correct values. For some reason, this practice seems to give most of us a warm fuzzy feeling that we have done what we can to make sure everything is working as it should. It's strange that developers would think this way; we are writing software to automate some part of the user's task, but we are unwilling to use a computer to automate some of our task. This is like a bad habit that is very hard to break.

The form this pitfall usually takes is big test methods with little else but println in them. In these test methods, there are many lines of test code, but the value of that code is small. A typical test method trapped in this pitfall usually looks something like this.

```
public void testFindCustomerByName() throws Exception {
    CustomerPO customer = new CustomerPO();
    customer.setFirstName("Al");
    customer.setLastName("Capone");
    // print out the presentation object
    System.out.println("Al Capone = " + customer);
    InitialContext ic = new InitialContext();
```

```
        CustomerSearchHome csHome =
(CustomerSearchHome)ic.lookup(JNDINames.CUSTOMER_SEARCH_NAME);
        CustomerSearch search = csHome.create();
        // pass null as the address because the address is not
        // important for this search
        CustomerPO alCapone = search.findCustomer(customer, null);
        // print out the first and last name
        System.out.println("Found Al Capone = " + alCapone);
    }
```

This test would let the developer know that the values are what they should be, but imagine 200 tests running that look something like this. Now imagine that this is the simplest of the 200. Clearly, with all that output, any bugs or unexpected behavior will be hard to spot.

The best way to avoid being stuck in this pitfall is to develop the discipline of removing println code in test code as soon as possible. A basic rule of thumb is that wherever a call to System.out.println is tempting, put an assert statement instead.

Example

The test subject for this example is a cache. The cache keeps two lists of customer objects, one ordered for the presentation layer and another map that is keyed on the customer's social security number for quick lookup during processing. The CustomerCache is shown in Listing 1.6.

```
public class CachedCustomerList {
    private List customers = new ArrayList();
    private Map customerMap = new HashMap();

    /**
     * Add newCustomer to both collections.
     * @param newCustomer
     */
    public void addCustomer(CustomerPO newCustomer) {
        customers.add(newCustomer);
        customerMap.put(newCustomer.getSSN(), newCustomer);
    }

    /**
     * Return the list of customers. This list should be in the same
     * order that the customer objects were placed into the cache.
     * @return List
     */
```

Listing 1.6 CachedCustomerList. *(continues)*

```java
    public List getCustomers() {
        return customers;
    }

    /**
     * Return the customer identified by <code>ssn</code>.
     * This method uses the hash map for quick lookup.
     * @param ssn
     * @return CustomerPO
     */
    public CustomerPO getCustomer(String ssn) {
        return (CustomerPO)customerMap.get(ssn);
    }

    /**
     * Returns true if the customer is in this cache, false
     * otherwise.
     *
     * @param testCustomer
     * @return boolean
     */
    public boolean containsCustomer(CustomerPO testCustomer) {
        return customerMap.get(testCustomer.getSSN()) != null;
    }
}
```

Listing 1.6 *(continued)*

The intent of this API is captured in its comments. The JUnit test in Listing 1.7 is stuck in Console-Based Testing so there is very little assurance that the intent of the API is being met.

```java
public class CachedCustomerListTest extends TestCase {
    private CachedCustomerList cache = new CachedCustomerList();

    public CachedCustomerListTest(String name) {
        super(name);
    }

    public static Test suite() {
        return new TestSuite(CachedCustomerListTest.class);
    }

    /**
     * Test getting the customers from the cache.
     */
    public void testGetCustomers() throws Exception {
```

Listing 1.7 CachedCustomerListTest.

Testing: Cactus and JUnit 27

```java
        List customers = cache.getCustomers();
        // there is no check here (except visually by the developer)
        // of what the count is, and it's not altogether apparent
        System.out.println("Count = " + customers.size());
        System.out.println("Customers = " + customers);
    }

    /**
     * Test getting the customer map from the cache.
     */
    public void testCustomerMap() {
        CustomerPO one = cache.getCustomer(ONE_SSN);
        System.out.println("Customer = " + one);
        System.out.println("ssn should be " + ONE_SSN);
    }

    private final String ONE_SSN = "999-00-8888";
    private final String TWO_SSN = "888-00-9999";
    private final String THREE_SSN = "333-00-3456";

    public void setUp() throws Exception {
        // customer one
        CustomerPO cust = new CustomerPO();
        cust.setFirstName("Willy");
        cust.setLastName("Wonka");
        cust.setSSN(ONE_SSN);
        cache.addCustomer(cust);
        // customer two
        cust = new CustomerPO();
        cust.setFirstName("Mogilla");
        cust.setLastName("Gorrila");
        cust.setSSN(TWO_SSN);
        cache.addCustomer(cust);
        // customer three
        cust = new CustomerPO();
        cust.setFirstName("Speed");
        cust.setLastName("Racer");
        cust.setSSN(THREE_SSN);
        cache.addCustomer(cust);
    }
}
```

Listing 1.7 *(continued)*

Take a look at the testGetCustomers method, which prints out the customer collection. It is up to the test runner to parse the output and determine if the subject is performing as expected. Also notice that it is hard to tell exactly what is being tested in this method. Is the intent to test that the size of the returned collection is proper, or is the test intended to test the objects in the list?

Keep in mind that building tests with lots of output is OK as long as the intent of the API is being asserted. If you prefer reviewing logged output to stepping through the code in a debugger, then feel free to put in println, but make sure that you also assert the intent of the API. Each time a println is added, try to add an assert as well. If you are not sure what to assert, then think through what intent of the API the printout is supposed to help you confirm. As the println code is removed from the test code, the assert statements remain and continue to ensure silently that the test subject is behaving as expected. If the expected value is not known, then add the assert statement as soon as the expected value is known. A good approach to adding asserts when the values are not known is to run the test, then assert that the value is whatever shows up on the console. As the data varies, the test will expose misunderstandings about the API, leading to better assertions.

Solving Pitfall 1.3: System.out Becomes Assert

The solution System.out Becomes assert is the best means to solve this pitfall. (A related solution, assert the intent from Pitfall 1.1: No assert, can also be helpful.) Tests trapped in this pitfall usually have the same issues that code trapped in Pitfall 1.1 do, namely the intent of the API is not asserted. As you are working through this solution references will be made to the intent of the API being put into the asserts in places where the intent of the printout is not clear. In those cases it might be helpful to refer back to that solution for more context. The steps to that solution can be found earlier in this chapter as the solution to Pitfall 1.1.

Many developers become console blind because of having too many debugging statements in their code. As the program runs, debugging statements come spraying out of the console as fast as the console can write text. The same thing happens with test code that is stuck in this pitfall. As the printouts come streaming by on the console, the developer is forced to pay very close attention and then must be able to look through all the output to make sure that what was expected is what actually happened. There is no way that a developer will catch everything in a long stream of printouts, and a developer cannot possibly provide as much detail checking as a program can. With asserts in place, however, the test can actually make sure that whatever is being looked for in the output is found. And, as an added bonus, nothing will show up on the console unless there is a failure. This approach leads to more repeatable and reliable tests. Using asserts allows the computer to review the state of the test subject and make sure that the expected state of the subject (that is, what is documented in the API) is the actual state. When tests rely on the output to the console and a human to review that output, there are often a lot of missed bugs.

Step-by-Step

1. Start with the simplest existing test method.
2. For each System.out.println, try to discern what the intent of the output is.
   a. This is absolutely the hardest part of this solution. Sometimes it's just not apparent why some piece of data is printed out or what the value should be.
   b. There are usually two flavors of printouts—one is just to see what is there and to check if an object is null; the other is to print the expected value and the actual value so that they can be compared. The first case is harder to convert to an assert; the second is easier.
3. For each simple review discovered in the second step (an "I just want to see it" printout), place an assertNotNull.
4. For each println with a value to compare use an assertEquals.
   a. Typically, this shows up as a printout of the expected value, followed by the value derived in the test.
5. Review the intent of the API being tested with these changes, and look for unchecked aspects that should be tested.
6. Deploy and test.
7. Repeat these steps for each test that is trapped in the pitfall.
   a. Often when applying this solution you will notice many pieces of the API that are not being tested. Add tests to cover the missing pieces while applying this solution.

Example

In this example, the CachedCustomerList JUnit test will be fixed so that it is no longer trapped in the pitfall. The first step in applying this solution is to find the simplest existing test method to start the cleanup on. Going back to the CachedCustomerListTest listing earlier, the simplest test method is testCustomerMap. The code for that method is listed here.

```
/**
 * Test getting the customer map from the cache.
```

```
    */
    public void testCustomerMap() {
        CustomerPO one = cache.getCustomer(ONE_SSN);
        System.out.println("Customer = " + one);
        System.out.println("ssn should be " + ONE_SSN);
    }
```

The next step is to figure out what intent is supposed to be tested by examining the values that are being printed out. In the two printouts in testCustomerMap, it is fairly straightforward to see what is intended to be tested. Because the customer with ONE_SSN is being asked for, that is what should be returned.

The next step in the solution is to provide an assert for each intent that is being tested. In the current code for testCustomerMap there are two printouts. It is not clear what the first printout is for, but we will assume it is there just to make sure the value is not null (System.out.println ("Customer = " + one)). The other printout is giving a value to be compared. This method should have one assertNotNull call and one assertTrue, so that the code looks like this.

```
public void testCustomerMap() {
    CustomerPO one = cache.getCustomer(ONE_SSN);
    assertNotNull("The customer with ssn "
            + ONE_SSN + " should not be null", one);
    assertEquals("The ssn should be " + ONE_SSN,
            ONE_SSN, one.getSSN());
}
```

On the first pass at inserting the asserts, leave the printouts in place in case the asserts fail. If the asserts do fail, you just might have uncovered a long-standing bug that escaped the output review testing that was happening.

The next step is to check for other untested intent. For each intent discovered that is not being tested, insert a new test method to cover that intent. The intent of the getCustomer API is fully tested so we should move on to the next method. The method to test the list of customers is next. The existing test method is listed here.

```
    /**
     * Test getting the customers from the cache.
     */
    public void testGetCustomers() throws Exception {
        List customers = cache.getCustomers();
        // there is no check here (except visually by the developer)
        // of what the count is, and it's not altogether apparent
        System.out.println("Count = " + customers.size());
```

```
        System.out.println("Customers = " + customers);
    }
```

The next step is to identify the reason for the printout—that is, what intent of the API is being reviewed. The first printout is showing what the actual size is, but there is no reference to the expected size. For this part of the test, though, we can easily know the expected size by looking at the setUp method to see how many customers were put into the cache. The other printout is not obvious. Is the intent to look at the content of the collection or just another way to see the length of the list, or is the test runner supposed to be looking at the order of the customer objects to make sure it is correct? Because we cannot tell exactly what the intent of the printouts was, we just press on and assert the intent of the API.

```
public void testCustomerSize() throws Exception {
    List customers = cache.getCustomers();
    // Check the size of the list
    assertEquals(
        "There should be 3 customers",
        3,
        customers.size());
}

public void testCustomerOrder() throws Exception {
    List customers = cache.getCustomers();
    CustomerPO one = (CustomerPO)customers.get(0);
    CustomerPO two = (CustomerPO)customers.get(1);
    CustomerPO three = (CustomerPO)customers.get(2);
    assertEquals(ONE_SSN, one.getSSN());
    assertEquals(TWO_SSN, two.getSSN());
    assertEquals(THREE_SSN, three.getSSN());
}
```

The name of the method testGetCustomers was changed to testCustomerSize in keeping with its new focus. A new test method was also added to assert that the order of the customer objects is correct.

The final step is to repeat the process for the rest of the methods in the test and to continue to review the intent of the test subject to make sure everything that should be tested is being tested.

Example 2: Cactus

This example tests the Populate servlet from Petstore. The Populate servlet takes data from an XML file and puts it into the database so there is a reference set of data loaded. The servlet takes initialization parameters from

32   Chapter 1

the web.xml file and uses them to find the data and load the database. The servlet is invoked from the welcome page after the Petstore is first installed. Listing 1.8 illustrates the initial test code to invoke the loading.

The first step to make this code better is to find out what is the intent of the test. This can be very hard if there are no comments in the test. Often, the source code for the subject must be reviewed to be able to discover the actual expected behavior. The PopulateServlet reads an XML file and pipes the data into a database; then, on success, it redirects the user to the main page (or the page on which the user clicked the Sign On button).

In the endSimplePopulate test method, the entire response is being printed. It is impossible to discern intent from that printout; there is just too

```java
public class PopulateServletCactusTest extends ServletTestCase {
    private PopulateServlet subject = null;

... more tests and JUnit required methods here

    public void beginSimplePopulate(WebRequest theRequest)
        throws Exception {
        // set the parameters
        theRequest.addParameter("success", "//petstore/main.screen");
        theRequest.addParameter("forcefully", "false");
    }

    public void testSimplePopulate() throws Exception {
        try {
            subject.init(config);
            subject.doPost(request, response);
        } catch(ServletException se) {
            System.out.println("This should not happen, an " +
                               "exception should not be thrown " +
                               se.getMessage());
        }
    }

    public void endSimplePopulate(WebResponse theResponse)
        throws Exception {
        System.out.println("theResponse = " +
                           theResponse.getText());
    }
... more tests here
    public void setUp() throws Exception {
        subject = new PopulateServlet();
    }
}
```

Listing 1.8   PopulateServletCactusTest.

much there, so instead the method should assert that the intent of the post method has been achieved. A couple of things should be checked: The title of the response should be checked to make sure that the store-front is being returned, and the database should be checked to make sure that the data is loaded properly. To test the title of the response it's best to use the HttpUnit integration in Cactus. The HttpUnit framework provides many simple-to-use APIs that make finding titles, buttons, and so on simpler. The endSimplePopulate method would change to look like this.

```
public void endSimplePopulate(com.meterware.httpunit.WebResponse
                        theResponse) throws Exception {
    assertEquals("Welcome to the BluePrints Petstore",
            theResponse.getTitle());
}
```

Checking the database is a bit more involved. The test needs to fetch some data from the database and assert that what is expected is what is there. To do that, a bit of JDBC code should be added to the test; specifically, there needs to be code to get a connection, execute a select statement, retrieve the results, and clean up. In this test, one method is written to perform all that and return what was found in a HashMap keyed on the column name and strings as values.

```
public void testSimplePopulate() throws Exception {
    try {
        // init the subject
        subject.init(config);
        subject.doPost(request, response);
    } catch(ServletException se) {
        fail("A servlet exception should not be thrown: " +
            se.getMessage());
    }
    String query = "select * from item where itemid = 'EST-1'";
    // get the data from the item table
    HashMap data = fetchData(query);
    // assert that it's what is expected
    assertEquals("FI-SW-01", (String)data.get("productid"));
    query = "select * from item_detail where itemid = 'EST-1'";
    // get some of the details
    data = fetchData(query);
    // assert the values
    assertEquals("16.50", data.get("listprice"));
}
```

This test does not assert everything that could be asserted about the data that was imported, but it does at least check part of it. Exhaustive tests are often more trouble than they are worth. It is often better to focus on testing the breadth of the API first.

Pitfall 1.4: Unfocused Test Method

Pitfall 1.4: Unfocused Test Method describes test methods that are unfocused in nature and tend to become unwieldy as they grow to test more and more of the API. It usually comes from experienced developers who have become lazy about building the setUp code for the test, so they cram all the testing they can into one large, complex test method. While this sometimes results in a well-tested subject, the tests become unwieldy and are less likely to be maintained over time.

The symptoms of this pitfall usually involve reluctance to modify a test method because it is too big. If during a typical maintenance cycle on the subject of a test you are tempted to get rid of the test because it's too large or complex, rather than update it, then the test is probably stuck in this pitfall. Keep in mind that as the complexity of the test code grows, so does the time taken to maintain the tests, which can lead to the tests being abandoned. Another symptom is the time it takes to execute each test method. As a test method attempts to test more, the time it takes for that method to execute grows. As the execution time grows, developers will run the tests less often, eventually resulting in the tests not being run at all. Tests that are not run are not very useful.

This pitfall usually takes the form of a few test methods that grow to many lines of code over time. The tests grow to test the entire API of the subject in only a few test methods. Here is an example of a test method stuck in this pitfall.

```
public void testCustomerAPI() throws Exception {
    InitialContext ic = new InitialContext();
    UserTransaction ut = (UserTransaction)ic.
        lookup(USER_TRANS_REF);
    ut.begin();
    CustomerHome cHome = (CustomerHome)ic.lookup(CUSTOMER_REF);
    Customer customer = cHome.findByPrimaryKey(new Long(14));
    assertEquals(new Long(14), customer.getId());
    // this should be in an address test method
    assertEquals("14 Mulberry Lane", customer.getAddress().
            getStreet());
    Collection invoices = customer.getInvoices();
    assertEquals(3, invoices.size());
    Invoice inv = (Invoice)invoices.iterator().next();
    // this should be in an invoice test method
    assertTrue(!(new BigDecimal(0.0)).equals(inv.getOrderTotal()));
    assertEquals("Inigo", customer.getFirstName());
```

```
        assertEquals("Montoya", customer.getLastName());
        assertEquals("555-33-4455", customer.getSsn());
        customer.setFirstName("Binigo");
        assertEquals("Binigo", customer.getFirstName());
        ut.commit();
    }
```

This method is testing several aspects of the Customer API as well as some of the Invoice API. By contrast, a good test method typically tests one method or aspect of an API. Some methods are quite complex, and a test method would have to be very large to test the whole intent of a single piece of the API. In cases like that, there are two choices: Refactor the subject so that its API is easier to test, or build several tests to cover all the different aspects of the complex method. It is usually better to refactor the subject (or, for our purposes, find a solution to the pitfall), but sometimes the source is not easy to change and the test has to accommodate.

Example

The test subject in this example is a Customer Entity Bean. The bean maintains information about customers—their name, their address, and other personal data The bean has two container-managed relationships: a one-to-one relationship with the customer's billing address and a one-to-many relationship with the list of invoices describing the orders the customer has placed. The customer interface is demonstrated in Listing 1.9; we will discuss the intent of particular pieces of this API later in the solution.

```
public interface Customer extends EJBLocalObject {
    public Long getId();

    public String getFirstName();
    public void setFirstName(String param);

    public String getLastName();
    public void setLastName(String param);

    public String getFullName();

    public String getSsn();
    public void setSsn(String param);

    public Address getAddress();
```

Listing 1.9 Customer bean API. *(continues)*

```
    public void setAddress(Address param);

    public void addInvoice(Invoice invoice)
        throws InvoiceException;
    public void removeInvoice(Invoice invoice)
        throws InvoiceException;
    public Collection getInvoices();
    public void setInvoices(Collection invoices);
}
public interface CustomerHome extends EJBLocalHome {
    public Customer create() throws CreateException;

    public Customer lookupCustomer(CustomerPO customer,
                                   AddressPO address)
        throws FinderException;

    public Customer findByPrimaryKey(Long pk) throws FinderException;
}
```

Listing 1.9 (continued)

The Customer bean API is tested by the following test class (Listing 1.10). There is only one test method, and it is very unfocused.

```
public class CustomerCactusTest extends ServletTestCase {
    private final String USER_TRANS_REF =
        "java:comp/UserTransaction";
    private final String CUSTOMER_REF = "invoice.Customer";
    private final String ADDRESS_REF = "invoice.Address";

    private UserTransaction ut = null;
    private Customer subject = null;
    private Address address = null;

    public CustomerCactusTest(String name) {
        super(name);
    }

    public static Test suite() {
        return new TestSuite(CustomerCactusTest.class);
    }

    public void testCustomerAPI() throws Exception {
        InitialContext ic = new InitialContext();
        UserTransaction ut = (UserTransaction)ic.
            lookup(USER_TRANS_REF);
        // need a user transaction so that we can traverse the
```

Listing 1.10 Cactus test for the Customer bean.

```
            // container-managed relationships, usually the transaction
            // would be opened and managed by a session facade.
            ut.begin();
            CustomerHome cHome = (CustomerHome)ic.lookup(CUSTOMER_REF);
            Customer customer = cHome.findByPrimaryKey(new Long(14));
            assertEquals(new Long(14), customer.getId());
            // this should be in an address test method
            assertEquals("14 Mulberry Lane", customer.getAddress().
                      getStreet());
            Collection invoices = customer.getInvoices();
            assertEquals(3, invoices.size());
            Invoice inv = (Invoice)invoices.iterator().next();
            // this should be in an invoice test method
            assertTrue(!(new BigDecimal(0.0)).
                            equals(inv.getOrderTotal()));
            assertEquals("Inigo", customer.getFirstName());
            assertEquals("Montoya", customer.getLastName());
            assertEquals("555-33-4455", customer.getSsn());
            customer.setFirstName("Binigo");
            assertEquals("Binigo", customer.getFirstName());
            ut.commit();
      }

      public void setUp() throws Exception {
      }

      public void tearDown() throws Exception {
      }
}
```

Listing 1.10 *(continued)*

The first clue that this test is unfocused is the inclusion of the JNDI name for other beans in this test. While it is not unreasonable to need the JNDI name for other beans, it is an indicator that the test might be unfocused. The biggest problem in this test class is the testCustomerAPI method. This test method is all over the place, asserting things about most of the API of the Customer bean. It starts off testing things about the customer but then moves to the invoices. Each test method should be focused on one aspect or intent of the API and should assert that one thing instead of several different, seemingly random parts of the API. Another thing to note is that a test class should focus on one subject class. Any tests that are written for the Invoice bean should be in a different test class altogether.

In some cases, the code being tested is just too complex to test in just a few asserts. As argued earlier, if the subject code is doing too much, the subject code should probably be refactored into more methods that each do less work. In some cases it will not be possible for you to refactor the test subject code. Whether you are able to change the subject or not, you should strive to keep the test methods as focused as possible so that your test code will stay out of this pitfall. The best way to keep the test methods focused is to limit the number of asserts in the test to one or two. We will see more on how to do this in the solution to this pitfall.

Solving Pitfall 1.4: Keep It Simple

The solution to Pitfall 1.4: Unfocused Test Method is simple: Keep it simple. Long test methods are hard to maintain and keep in sync with the ever-changing API of the subject. Instead, test methods should be short and have clearly defined goals. For each test method, only one aspect or intent of the subject's API should be asserted, leaving other asserts to other test methods. Make sure in applying this solution that each new test method is named after the kind of test being performed or the intent that is being tested. Another issue to consider in applying this solution is that lots of simple tests are likely to be more thorough than a few big tests. When a test method has a clearly defined piece of the subject to test, that method can be more focused. If, however, the method is just testing the subject, then the asserts can be haphazard in nature and fail to check critical aspects of the state of the subject.

Another thing to think about when applying this solution is the construction of the subject(s) of the tests. As the large tests are broken into more, smaller tests, the overhead of calling setUp and tearDown grows. If this overhead becomes too much, then the "run quickly and often" goal of unit tests can be compromised. In these cases, consider using a test decorator to initialize a common subject that can be used by many different tests.

Keep in mind that each test should be focused on one part of the intent of the subject API. As you are applying this solution to your tests, you might find it useful to look at the solution to Pitfall 1.1: No assert for pointers on capturing the intent of the subject's API. When you are applying this solution to your Cactus tests, keep in mind that getting to your test in the first place is a distributed method call (it takes some time to get set up and executed) so make sure that you test everything that makes sense to test in each test method.

Step-by-Step

1. For each large and complex test method, extract groups of asserts that relate to common intent of the subject API.
    a. "Large" and "complex" are, of course, subjective; the question to keep in mind is "Will this test method be likely to be abandoned

as the subject's API is changed?" If the answer is yes, then the method is probably too complex.
2. Place each related group of asserts into a separate test method.
    a. Name these new methods after the intent that is being asserted.
3. Further decompose the remaining complex test methods.
    a. As a general rule, each test method should have one assert.
4. Deploy and test.
5. Repeat these steps for each test that is trapped in the pitfall.

Example

In this example, a Cactus test is cleaned up from two very complex test methods to many, much simpler methods that test focused pieces of the API. The Invoice bean listed here will be the subject of the example test to which we will apply the solution. The bean manages orders for customers. A single invoice has one customer and the list of line items for that invoice. The initial test is haphazard in its approach to checking the invoice API, as you can see in Listing 1.11, but the fixed test will make sure that the line items are managed properly and that the customer-related methods work as expected.

```
public interface Invoice extends EJBLocalObject {
    public Long getId() throws EJBException;
    // Customer relationship
    public Customer getCustomer() throws EJBException;
    public void setCustomer(Customer customer) throws EJBException;
    // LineItem relationship
    public void addLineItem(LineItem newItem)
        throws EJBException, InvoiceException;
    public void removeLineItem(LineItem newItem)
        throws EJBException, InvoiceException;
    public Collection getLineItems() throws EJBException;
    public void setLineItems(Collection items) throws EJBException;
    // totaling this invoice
    public BigDecimal getOrderTotal() throws EJBException;
}
public interface InvoiceHome extends EJBLocalHome {
    public Invoice create(Customer customer) throws CreateException;
    public BigDecimal totalForCustomer(Customer customer);
    public Invoice findByPrimaryKey(Long pk) throws FinderException;
}
```

Listing 1.11 The API for the Invoice bean.

Chapter 1

This entity is responsible for keeping track of the invoices for individual customers. The entity is also able to sum all orders that a customer has ever made. The original test code in Listing 1.12 tries to test everything in only two test methods. The test methods are too long, overly complex, and not all that thorough as a result.

```java
public class InvoiceCactusTest extends ServletTestCase {
    // for JBoss this must be "UserTransaction" instead
    private final String TRANS_REF =
        "java:comp/UserTransaction";
    private static final String INVOICE_REF = "invoice.Invoice";
    private static final String CUSTOMER_REF = "invoice.Customer";
    private static final String LINEITEM_REF = "invoice.LineItem";

    private InvoiceHome iHome = null;
    // the subject of the tests in this class
    private Invoice invoice = null;
    // an invoice primary key for use in one of the tests
    private Long invoicePrimaryKey = null;
    // auxiliary objects
    private CustomerHome cHome = null;
    private Customer customer = null;
    private UserTransaction ut = null;

    public InvoiceCactusTest(String name) {
        super(name);
    }

    public static void main(String[] args) {
        String name = InvoiceCactusTest.class.getName();
        junit.textui.TestRunner.main(new String[] {name});
    }

    public static Test suite() {
        return new TestSuite(InvoiceCactusTest.class);
    }

    public void testBean() throws Exception {
        assertNotNull(invoice.getCustomer());
        assertNotNull(invoice.getLineItems());
        Collection lineItems = invoice.getLineItems();
        List removedItems = new ArrayList();
        assertEquals(4, lineItems.size());
        Iterator itr = lineItems.iterator();
        int count = 0;
        while(itr.hasNext()) {
            // remove the even items to test removal
```

Listing 1.12 InvoiceCactusTest.

```
            LineItem lineItem = (LineItem)itr.next();
            if((count % 2) == 0) {
                invoice.removeLineItem(lineItem);
                removedItems.add(lineItem);
            }
        }
        assertEquals(2, invoice.getLineItems().size());
        BigDecimal total = invoice.getOrderTotal();
        assertTrue(total.doubleValue() > 57.00 &&
                total.doubleValue() < 59.00);
        itr = removedItems.iterator();
        while(itr.hasNext()) {
            LineItem lineItem = (LineItem)itr.next();
            invoice.getLineItems().add(lineItem);
        }
        assertEquals(4, invoice.getLineItems().size());
        total = invoice.getOrderTotal();
        assertTrue(total.doubleValue() > 231.00 &&
                total.doubleValue() < 233.00);
    }

    public void testHome() throws Exception {
        customer = cHome.create();
        customer.setFirstName("Buzz");
        customer.setLastName("Lightyear");
        invoice = iHome.create(customer);
        assertNotNull(invoice.getCustomer());
        Invoice anInvoice = iHome.findByPrimaryKey(invoicePrimaryKey);
        assertEquals(invoicePrimaryKey, anInvoice.getId());
        BigDecimal total = iHome.totalForCustomer(customer);
        assertTrue(total.doubleValue() > 231.00 &&
                total.doubleValue() < 233.00);
    }
. . . the setUp and tearDown methods go here . . .
}
```

Listing 1.12 *(continued)*

The testBean method is all over the place, testing many different pieces of the invoice API. A much more effective way to test the entity is to test each intent in a different method. The first step of this solution is to group the asserts according to the intent that is to be tested. The local interface for this bean has three basic functions: manage the relationship with the customer, manage the relationship with the line items this invoice contains, and sum the list of line items to get the total for this invoice. The tests should make sure that these three parts of the API are functioning as expected. The home interface for this bean is very simple: one finder, one create, and one business method. The test should make sure that these aspects of the API are tested as well.

The testBean method is more or less testing each aspect of the API for the entity, but the depth of testing is not consistent. The asserts should be grouped into the three basic areas. The next step, after grouping the asserts, is to move them into another test method named after the function or intent they are supposed to be testing. The asserts can be cut and pasted into the new methods. Here is the code after being put through these first two steps.

```java
public void testCustomerRelationship() throws Exception {
    // check the customer relationship
    assertNotNull(invoice.getCustomer());
}

public void testLineItemRelationship() throws Exception {
    // check the lineitem relationship
    assertNotNull(invoice.getLineItems());
    Collection lineItems = invoice.getLineItems();
    List removedItems = new ArrayList();
    assertEquals(5, lineItems.size());
    Iterator itr = lineItems.iterator();
    int count = 0;
    while(itr.hasNext()) {
        LineItem lineItem = (LineItem)itr.next();
        // remove the even items (0, 2, 4) to test removal
        if((count % 2) == 0) {
            invoice.removeLineItem(lineItem);
            removedItems.add(lineItem);
        }
    }
    assertEquals(2, invoice.getLineItems().size());
    // test adding items
    itr = removedItems.iterator();
    while(itr.hasNext()) {
        LineItem lineItem = (LineItem)itr.next();
        invoice.getLineItems().add(lineItem);
    }
    assertEquals(5, invoice.getLineItems().size());
}

public void testTotaling() throws Exception {
    BigDecimal total = invoice.getOrderTotal();
    assertTrue(total.doubleValue() > 231.00 &&
            total.doubleValue() < 233.00);
}
```

Notice that this is basically the same code from the testBean method; it's just been grouped according to the functional area of the API that it was testing.

The next step in the solution is to further decompose the complex test methods into simpler test methods (aim for one assert per test method). The next method to attack would be the testLineItemRelationship method because it has several asserts. One aspect of the bean that can be pulled into another test is the totaling of the invoice. Specifically, if a line item is removed, the total should change. Here is a test to make sure that the total does change when items are removed.

```
public void testTotalingDiffers() throws Exception {
    BigDecimal total = invoice.getOrderTotal();
    removeEvenItems(invoice);
    BigDecimal smallerTotal = invoice.getOrderTotal();
    // total should be larger than smallerTotal
    assertTrue(total.compareTo(smallerTotal) > 0);
}
```

The rest of the testLineItemRelationship method needs to be broken up into several test methods. Listing 1.13 shows the code resulting from breaking up the original testBean method.

```
public void testCustomerRelationship() throws Exception {
    // check the customer relationship
    // this test will let us know if anything has
    // gone wrong in the container-managed relationships
    assertNotNull(invoice.getCustomer());
}

public void testLineItems() throws Exception {
    // check the lineitem relationship
    // this test will let us know if anything has
    // gone wrong in the container-managed relationships
    assertNotNull(invoice.getLineItems());
}

public void testLineItemsCount() throws Exception {
    // 5 line items are put in during setUp
    Collection lineItems = invoice.getLineItems();
    // make sure they are there
    assertEquals(5, lineItems.size());
}

public void testLineItemRemoval() throws Exception {
    Collection lineItems = invoice.getLineItems();
```

Listing 1.13 Fixed code from the original testBean method. *(continues)*

```
        Iterator itr = lineItems.iterator();
        // remove the first element
        while(itr.hasNext()) {
            LineItem lineItem = (LineItem)itr.next();
            invoice.removeLineItem(lineItem);
            break;
        }
        // make sure there are four items left
        assertEquals(4, invoice.getLineItems().size());
    }

    public void testTotaling() throws Exception {
        BigDecimal total = invoice.getOrderTotal();
        assertTrue(total.doubleValue() > 231.00 &&
                   total.doubleValue() < 233.00);
    }

    public void testTotalingDiffers() throws Exception {
        BigDecimal total = invoice.getOrderTotal();
        removeEvenItems(invoice);
        BigDecimal smallerTotal = invoice.getOrderTotal();
        // total should be larger than smallerTotal
        assertTrue(total.compareTo(smallerTotal) > 0);
    }
```

Listing 1.13 *(continued)*

The single unfocused testBean method is now cleaned up to be six separate test methods. The test code is much easier to follow and is more focused on the particular aspect that is being tested. The names of the test methods are also more descriptive.

This is a good time to bring up TestDecorators in Cactus. Keep in mind that a typical implementation of a JUnit test decorator in your Cactus tests will be run on the client side, not on the server side. This means that any access to a local EJB interface will fail because the test starts in a different JVM. In order to use test decorators they must interact with remote interfaces. You can accomplish this in several different ways. Placing a session façade is a popular way to provide a remote interface to the underlying entities. The typical problem with this approach, however, is that the session then needs specific methods to support testing. An alternative approach is to deploy your entities twice, once under their local interfaces and once with remote interfaces when doing testing. Placing remote interfaces over your entities is a maintenance burden so it is not without cost. Using the session façade is the recommended approach.

Pitfall 1.5: Failure to Isolate Each Test

Pitfall 1.5: Failure to Isolate Each Test usually takes the form of some external script that must be run before the tests will succeed. Examples of external scripts include things like initialization data (or scripts that clean out the database) in an SQL script that must be run against the database. Another typical form is for the test methods to have order dependencies. For example, one test might create an object, the next method makes a couple of state changes, and the last method deletes the object. In either form, the tests will become unreliable if they remain stuck in this pitfall because, over time, the order of the methods will change and they will start to fail. Often, developers will forget to run the database script often enough that they get fed up with the tests. Tests that are not reliable will cease to be used because they show too many false bugs and catch too few actual bugs.

Loading data into the database via a script prior to running a test suite is a very typical practice. The problem with this approach, though, is that the test is no longer self-sufficient. The developer (and anyone else running the tests) could be required to run the script before running the tests. If the test fails because the database script has not been run, the results can be confusing and lead to questions about the validity of the test or even the code being tested.

> **CACTUS AND MOCK OBJECT APPLICATION SERVERS**
>
> Some in the unit testing community go so far as to say that the application server configuration is another example of configuration or setup that should be part of the test. This is another place where the discussion of Mock Objects is prevalent. In some cases, people have developed entire mock application servers so that the tests can run in isolation from the application server configuration. While that makes for very isolated tests, the amount of work required to maintain these Mock Objects is often as much or more than the work required to maintain the tests.
>
> Cactus takes the opposite approach to the application server. Instead of seeing it as a factor to be isolated and removed from the test, Cactus embraces the application server. Instead of trying to supply Mock Objects for all the server-side services, Cactus provides the actual server-side objects to the tests. This approach does introduce a dependency on the application server and might cause tests to fail as a result of bugs in the underlying application server. If there are bugs in the underlying application server, it is probably better to know that up front instead and thus be able to work around them than to wait until the application is deployed to the test team for the bug to be exposed.

This pitfall usually develops because a developer got lazy about building sufficient test subject objects in the setUp method. Building good test subjects often takes time and sometimes even digging around in the subject code to make sure that the correct set of initial conditions is met to perform the test. It is often argued that this time is not worth the trouble because writing an SQL script to load the database could be done in half the time. That might be true for the first set of tests, but over time the data file becomes a constant source of trouble.

Another driver behind this pitfall is a lack of knowledge or experience with Cactus or JUnit. Inexperienced developers often put a bunch of test data into the database and then run their tests. The test runs once and then is not touched again for a while. In the meantime, other testing has modified the data in the database enough that the tests fail. False failures are a constant headache and often lead to unit testing being dropped from a project because developers and managers do not see value in the tests because of the maintenance overhead.

This pitfall also shows up in tests that add or remove data from the database. If each test does not clean up after it runs, then the data that the test changed must be reset, or the test might not run the next time. In other cases, this issue shows up as one test that can inadvertently delete the data on which another test depends. If the first test does not clean up, the second test will fail because its data has been removed.

The important thing to keep in mind is that the tests need to be isolated enough to be run without manual intervention by the test runner. In other words, requiring that the application server be running for the tests to succeed is fine, but requiring that an SQL script be run after each test is not. The difference between the two is subtle. If the application server is not running the failure is obvious, and it is easy to see from the failure that Cactus could not contact the server-side piece of the test. If, on the other hand, the data has not been reinitialized in the database, the failure might show up as a NullPointerException. Testers never like to see NullPointerExceptions; if they do happen, the testers can and often do lose confidence in the application.

Example

In this example, we will test a Customer Entity EJB. This bean manages the typical information needed to manage a customer, the name, address, and so on, as well as the list of invoices for goods the customer has purchased. The API the example will test is found in Listing 1.14. The intent of the particular parts of the API will be discussed as they are tested in the example. Because this is an Entity Bean, we will use Cactus to test.

```java
public interface Customer extends EJBLocalObject {
    public Long getId() throws EJBException;
    public String getFirstName() throws EJBException;
    public void setFirstName(String param) throws EJBException;
    public String getLastName() throws EJBException;
    public void setLastName(String param) throws EJBException;
    public String getSsn() throws EJBException;
    public void setSsn(String param) throws EJBException;
    public Address getAddress() throws EJBException;
    public void setAddress(Address param) throws EJBException;
    public Collection getInvoices() throws EJBException;
    public void setInvoices(Collection invoices) throws EJBException;
}
public interface CustomerHome extends EJBLocalHome {
    public Customer create() throws CreateException;
    public Customer lookupCustomer(CustomerPO customer,
                                   AddressPO address)
        throws FinderException;
    public Customer findByPrimaryKey(Long pk) throws FinderException;
}
```

Listing 1.14 Customer bean API.

The Cactus test (in Listing 1.15) for the Customer bean API is stuck in this pitfall. Notice that testLookupCustomer depends on testCreateCustomer being executed first. Also, the testSetAddress method relies on data being in the database from some external process (probably an SQL script). Here is the code.

```java
public class CustomerCactusTest extends ServletTestCase {
    private final String CUSTOMER_REF = "invoice.Customer";
    private final String ADDRESS_REF = "invoice.Address";
    private final String INVOICE_REF = "invoice.Invoice";

    private InvoiceHome iHome = null;
    private CustomerHome cHome = null;
    private Customer subject = null;
    private Address address = null;
    private AddressHome aHome = null;

    public CustomerCactusTest(String name) {
        super(name);
    }

    public static Test suite() {
        return new TestSuite(CustomerCactusTest.class);
    }
```

Listing 1.15 CustomerCactusTest. *(continues)*

```java
    }

    /**
     * This method tests that a newly created customer is in the
     * right state. The create method call will fail if the customer
     * named 'Elmer Fudd' is not deleted from the database
     * manually after each test run.
     * @throws Exception
     */
    public void testInitialCustomer() throws Exception {
        InitialContext ic = new InitialContext();
        cHome = (CustomerHome) ic.lookup(CUSTOMER_REF);
        CustomerPO custPO = new CustomerPO("Elmer", "Fudd");
        Customer customer = cHome.create(custPO);
        assertNotNull(customer);
        assertNotNull(customer.getId());
        assertNull(customer.getAddress());
        assertTrue(customer.getInvoices().size() == 0);
        assertEquals("Elmer", customer.getFirstName());
        assertEquals("Fudd", customer.getLastName());
    }

    /**
     * This method tests creating and adding an invoice. This method
     * will fail if the customer 'Elmer Fudd' is not in the
     * database already. There is an order dependency between this
     * method and testInitialCustomer.
     * @throws Exception
     */
    public void testAddInvoice() throws Exception {
        InitialContext ic = new InitialContext();
        cHome = (CustomerHome) ic.lookup(CUSTOMER_REF);
        iHome = (InvoiceHome) ic.lookup(INVOICE_REF);
        CustomerPO custPO = new CustomerPO("Elmer", "Fudd");
        Customer customer = cHome.lookupCustomer(custPO, null);
        Invoice inv = iHome.create(customer);
        assertTrue(customer.getInvoices().size() == 1);
    }

    /**
     * This method tests looking up a customer. This method requires
     * that the testInitialCustomer method has already been run or
     * that 'Elmer Fudd' is in the database.
     * @throws Exception
     */
    public void testLookupCustomer() throws Exception {
        InitialContext ic = new InitialContext();
        cHome = (CustomerHome) ic.lookup(CUSTOMER_REF);
        CustomerPO po = new CustomerPO("Elmer", "Fudd");
```

Listing 1.15 *(continued)*

```
        Customer customer = cHome.lookupCustomer(po, null);
        assertNotNull(customer);
        assertEquals("Elmer", customer.getFirstName());
        assertEquals("Fudd", customer.getLastName());
    }

    /**
     * This method tests setting the address on an existing customer.
     * It will fail if 'Pancho Villia' is not already in the database.
     * @throws Exception
     */
    public void testSetAddress() throws Exception {
        InitialContext ic = new InitialContext();
        cHome = (CustomerHome) ic.lookup(CUSTOMER_REF);
        aHome = (AddressHome) ic.lookup(ADDRESS_REF);
        Address address = aHome.create();
        address.setStreet("128 Wherever Ln.");
        address.setCity("Wizzleville");
        address.setState("CO");
        address.setZipCode("80345");
        CustomerPO po = new CustomerPO("Pancho", "Villia");
        Customer customer = cHome.lookupCustomer(po, null);
        customer.setAddress(address);
        assertNotNull(customer.getAddress());
    }

    public void setUp() throws Exception {
    }

    public void tearDown() throws Exception {
    }
}
```

Listing 1.15 *(continued)*

The order-dependent methods run on Sun's Windows JVM and Apple JVM in the correct order (probably because of their order in the file), but that is nothing to rely on. What will happen when the application is moved to big-iron servers and runs on IBM's JVM? Who knows?—that is the point. The tests might or might not be run in the correct order. Other JVMs might provide methods in different order than the Sun JVM, and that would cause the tests to fail.

On the surface, this might not look like much, just moving the methods around until they execute in the correct order. Or the really savvy JUnit developer might suggest creating a custom version of the test suite that will execute the tests in the order they are added and using the custom suite instead of the default reflection-based suite. While these workarounds are fine for a small project (say, one or two developers), they will not work on a bigger project. Members of the team other than the author of the test will come to hate this test over time because there will be failed tests unless they delete 'Elmer Fudd' from the database after each run of the tests. That manual step defeats the purpose of having repeatable, automatic unit tests. Tests must not be allowed to continue in this sorry state.

Solving Pitfall 1.5: Use setUp and tearDown and Introduce Test Decorators

There are two ways to solve this pitfall. The first is to use the setUp and tearDown methods that Cactus calls automatically before and after each test is run. The second, Introduce Test Decorators, is a twist on setUp and tearDown that can be used if the performance of having setUp and tearDown executed with each test becomes burdensome.

Better isolation (and better tests) is achieved by factoring out dependencies between tests. If the setUp method creates the subject and tearDown deletes the subject, then there is no opportunity for the tests to depend on each other. Each run of each test is starting over with a clean slate. If tests are isolated in this way, problems will be easier to pin on the subject code instead of some part of the testing apparatus. The failures need to be tied to the subject for the test to have value.

This solution also helps tests be more isolated from each other by getting rid of manual processes that are required for the tests to run. In small teams, manual processes are easy to communicate and are thus not as much of an issue, but in big teams manual processes are hard to communicate so that everyone on the team is completely comfortable with what needs to be done. Over time, the tests that require manual steps will be abandoned because when the manual process is not followed exactly, the tests fail. Unit tests should not have this kind of dependency. After all, they are supposed to be individual, independent, repeatable units.

The manual processes are usually captured well in test decorators. Whenever you have a manual process that you are building to support your tests, you should instead be building a test decorator to do all that you would do manually. Once the decorator is coded, the manual process is there for everyone else to use. We will see more about test decorators later in this solution.

Step-by-Step

1. Review the tests for creation, initialization, and deletion of subjects.
   a. Look especially for commonality between the initialization or creation.
   b. If the creation differs significantly, consider creating a new test class or custom setUp and tearDown methods that you can call manually.
2. Review the tests for order dependencies.
   a. Look for assumed instances.
3. Review manual processes needed to make the tests runnable.
   a. Look for SQL scripts that must be run or other external scripts required to make the tests pass.
4. Create a setUp and tearDown method pair.
   a. Consider using test decorators instead if the setUp and/or tearDown methods will take a long time to complete.
5. Add an instance variable to the test class for each distinct kind of subject.
   a. Each kind of subject will be used to test a different part of the API; for example, one subject could be useful for testing error response in the API, and another subject could be useful for testing the deletion behavior.
6. Move the create or initialization code from the tests to the setUp method.
   a. Initialize one subject for each distinct kind found in the first few steps.
   b. Find commonalities between the subjects, and initialize the subjects so that they can be reused in many tests.
   c. If there are many different sets of initialization code that must be built, consider creating a new test class for each kind of subject.
7. Move (or add) the delete code to the tearDown method.
8. Deploy and test.

Example

In this example, we will see applying the solution to the test class that we used to test the Customer bean earlier. As you will recall, the test is trapped in this pitfall and prone to unreliability. We will take that code through the steps and see how to fix the code so that it is more reliable and a better gauge of the quality of the test subject.

The first step in the process is to identify code that does creation and/or deletion in the tests. The testInitialCustomer method creates a Customer bean and then initializes it. The next step in the solution is to review the test for order dependencies. The testLookupCustomer method relies on the testInitialCustomer method being executed first so that the data is in the database. The third step is to look for manual steps that must be made for the tests to execute properly. The testSetAddress method relies on a preexisting customer being in the database. Now that we have reviewed the tests for candidate code for the setUp method, it is time to move that code into the setUp method.

The next step in the process is to add a setUp and tearDown method pair and then fill the setUp method with the code identified in the previous steps. For each distinct customer instance that will be tested, we need an instance variable. Two variables are added to the class, and the setUp method is changed to look like the code in Listing 1.16.

```java
public class CustomerCactusTest extends ServletTestCase {
    ...
    private Customer elmerFudd;
    private Customer panchoVillia;
    ...

    public void setUp() throws Exception {
        InitialContext ic = new InitialContext();
        cHome = (CustomerHome) ic.lookup(CUSTOMER_REF);
        aHome = (AddressHome) ic.lookup(ADDRESS_REF);
        iHome = (InvoiceHome) ic.lookup(INVOICE_REF);
        CustomerPO custPO = new CustomerPO("Elmer", "Fudd");
        elmerFudd = cHome.create(custPO);
        custPO.setFirstName("Pancho");
        custPO.setLastName("Villia");
        panchoVillia = cHome.create(custPO);
    }
```

Listing 1.16 New setUp method with initialization code.

```
    public void tearDown() throws Exception {
        elmerFudd.remove();
        indigoMontoya.remove();
        panchoVillia.remove();
    }
```

Listing 1.17 New tearDown method.

Notice that the setUp method in Listing 1.16 now creates all the data needed by the tests. No longer will the tests rely on an SQL script being run in order to pass. Notice also that the lookup for each of the homes is done here in the setUp method. Remember that putting this code in the setUp method does not save us any execution time—it is just convenient.

Because JNDI lookups can be expensive, you might consider a test decorator to do the JNDI lookup if the time to do the lookups in your test is prohibitively long (see Example 2, which follows). Also notice that in this code, the JNDI initial context does not require any initialization parameters. Remember that Cactus tests run on the server and because it is running on the server the InitialContext is able to root itself in the JNDI tree there.

The next step is to remove all this data created in the setUp in the tearDown method. Deleting the data is very important so that the tests can be repeatable. If the data is left in the database, all the create method calls in the setUp code will fail because there are customers with the same name already in the database (arguably, you would not want to build a real customer management system so that you could have only one customer per name; the point is that the tests need to clean up after themselves). The tearDown code is Listing 1.17.

The final step is to deploy and retest. Before we move on, though, let's take a look at some of the test methods and how they have changed. Specifically, let's look at the two test methods that had an order dependency. The initial code is Listing 1.18.

```
    public void testInitialCustomer() throws Exception {
        InitialContext ic = new InitialContext();
        cHome = (CustomerHome) ic.lookup(CUSTOMER_REF);
        CustomerPO custPO = new CustomerPO("Elmer", "Fudd");
        Customer customer = cHome.create(custPO);
        assertNotNull(customer);
        assertNotNull(customer.getId());
```

Listing 1.18 Original order-dependent test methods. *(continues)*

```
        assertNull(customer.getAddress());
        assertTrue(customer.getInvoices().size() == 0);
        assertEquals("Elmer", customer.getFirstName());
        assertEquals("Fudd", customer.getLastName());
    }

    public void testLookupCustomer() throws Exception {
        InitialContext ic = new InitialContext();
        cHome = (CustomerHome) ic.lookup(CUSTOMER_REF);
        CustomerPO po = new CustomerPO("Elmer", "Fudd");
        Customer customer = cHome.lookupCustomer(po, null);
        assertNotNull(customer);
        assertEquals("Elmer", customer.getFirstName());
        assertEquals("Fudd", customer.getLastName());
    }
```

Listing 1.18 *(continued)*

The new methods do not have the order dependency because they are able to rely on the beans created and destroyed by the setUp and tearDown methods. The new code is found in Listing 1.19.

The original method and the fixed method do not vary by many lines of code. The only real change is that the creation and JNDI lookup code was moved to the setUp method. This simple change makes all the difference. Now these two tests can run reliably and repeatably.

```
    public void testInitialCustomer() throws Exception {
        assertNotNull(elmerFudd);
        assertNotNull(elmerFudd.getId());
        assertNull(elmerFudd.getAddress());
        assertTrue(elmerFudd.getInvoices().size() == 0);
        assertEquals("Elmer", elmerFudd.getFirstName());
        assertEquals("Fudd", elmerFudd.getLastName());
    }

    public void testLookupCustomer() throws Exception {
        CustomerPO po = new CustomerPO("Elmer", "Fudd");
        Customer customer = cHome.lookupCustomer(po, null);
        assertNotNull(customer);
        assertEquals("Elmer", customer.getFirstName());
        assertEquals("Fudd", customer.getLastName());
    }
```

Listing 1.19 New order-independent test methods.

Example 2: Introduce Test Decorators

Test decorators have been mentioned a couple of times in this solution as something to look into if the setUp and tearDown methods are taking too long to execute. The nice thing about test decorators is that the setUp method is executed once, then the suite of test methods contained by the decorator is run and the test decorator's tearDown method is called. This approach allows the setUp and tearDown functionality to be executed only once for the whole set of tests. A decorator is introduced in the suite method on the test class. Here is the new code for that method.

```
public static Test suite() {
    return new CustomerBeanTestDecorator(
        new TestSuite(CustomerCactusTest.class));
}
```

The test decorator encapsulates the tests from the Cactus test class so that they are executed after the test decorator's setUp method is called. Then, after the last test is finished, the decorator's tearDown method is called. The code for the two methods is listed here.

```
public void setUp() throws Exception {
    Context ic = getInitialContext();
    CustomerHome cHome = (CustomerHome) ic.lookup(CUSTOMER_REF);
    CustomerPO custPO = new CustomerPO("Elmer", "Fudd");
    elmerFudd = cHome.create(custPO);
    custPO.setFirstName("Indigo");
    custPO.setLastName("Montoya");
    indigoMontoya = cHome.create(custPO);
    custPO.setFirstName("Pancho");
    custPO.setLastName("Villia");
    panchoVillia = cHome.create(custPO);
}

public void tearDown() throws Exception {
    elmerFudd.remove();
    indigoMontoya.remove();
    panchoVillia.remove();
}
```

With this decorator in place, the three Customer beans that are used in the tests will be created and removed only once per run of the test suite. The code was moved from the setUp and tearDown methods on the CustomerCactusTest class to the decorator for that purpose.

An important concept to make note of is that the decorator's setUp and tearDown methods are executed on the client side of Cactus, not on the server side. This means that the home and bean interface must be remote for this code to work. In this example, the Customer bean being tested was local only in the original code. The Customer bean must be redeployed with remote interfaces for this example to work.

Another way that decorator can be used is to automate the manual tasks required to prepare the environment for the tests to run. As stated earlier, the typical manual task loads test data into a database. That can easily be done from within a setUp method on a test decorator. Once the manual step is captured in a test decorator, the test will be more reliable and repeatable. The code on the Web site has an example of a test decorator that loads and removes data from the database by running an SQL script through JDBC into the database in the setUp and tearDown methods of a test decorator.

Listing 1.20 is an example test decorator that uses JDBC to load the content of a file and execute it against the database. This decorator could be used to eliminate the manual task of running an SQL script against the database. If you have a large data set, this way is probably more practical than using the create methods. The EJB create methods are not really intended to be used to do batch-oriented processing.

```java
public class CustomerLoaderTestDecorator extends TestSetup {
    private final String DB_URL =
            "jdbc:mysql://localhost/book?user=book";
    private final String DB_USER = "book";
    private final String DB_PASS = "book";
    //load the driver class
    private static final Class mySQLDriverClass = Driver.class;

    public CustomerLoaderTestDecorator(Test test) {
        super(test);
    }

    public void setUp() throws Exception {
        // AddData.sql is delimited by ';'
        InputStream is =
            getClass().getClassLoader().getResourceAsStream(
                "AddData.sql");
        executeBuffer(is);
    }

    public void tearDown() throws Exception {
        // RemoveData.sql is delimited by ';'
        InputStream is =
            getClass().getClassLoader().getResourceAsStream(
```

Listing 1.20 CustomerLoaderTestDecorator.

```
    "RemoveData.sql");
        executeBuffer(is);
    }

    private void executeBuffer(InputStream is) throws Exception {
        StringBuffer sql = new StringBuffer(128);
        DriverManager.registerDriver(new Driver());
        Connection conn = DriverManager.getConnection(DB_URL,
                DB_USER, DB_PASS);
        int nextChar = is.read();
        while(-1 != nextChar) {
            if(';' == nextChar) {
                Statement stmt = conn.createStatement();
                stmt.execute(sql.toString());
                stmt.close();
                stmt = null;
                sql.setLength(0);
            } else if('\n' != nextChar) { // skip new lines
                sql.append((char)nextChar);
            }
            nextChar = is.read();
        }
    }
}
```

Listing 1.20 *(continued)*

Applying this decorator to the test will remove the need to use the create calls and the remove calls from the tearDown method.

Pitfall 1.6: Failure to Isolate Subject

Test subjects that rely on other classes to function properly (which are most classes) are harder to test because the underlying classes might have bugs. Bugs in an underlying class might cause the test to fail even though the bug is not in the subject of the test. In a perfect world, no test failures would be caused by code other than the test subject. In that kind of scenario, the test would pass or fail based solely on the bugs (or lack of bugs) in the test subject. While the ideal scenario is hard to achieve, it is worth pursuing. Developers often don't even think about trying, and thus they end up in this pitfall.

Developers usually fall into this pitfall because they fail to understand that a unit test is just that; it's supposed to test a single unit of functionality at a time. Often tests end up testing the class under consideration and everything on which the test depends. That makes it very hard to isolate where the problem is and defeats part of the reason for having unit tests—essentially, the unit tests become integration tests. Instead, each of the underlying or support classes should have its own unit tests.

This pitfall usually shows itself as frequently broken tests, especially when a new version of a framework or library is incorporated. If the library is not being unit tested, then every user of the library is forced to debug it with his or her own tests. This is an inefficient process. The client code often looks broken when the underlying framework actually has the bug.

The form of this pitfall is seen in tests that work fine one day and then fail when some underlying .jar file is replaced. On small projects with one or two developers, this rarely happens because there is a lot of communication between the developers and very little happens that the whole team does not know about. On bigger teams, however, this is common. Developers for one part of the application need a later version of some class and upgrade and may not know the effect on others until after unit tests start failing. (One might argue that the unit tests should be run before checking in the new .jar file, but that is another pitfall for another time.)

The issue the developer faces is figuring out if the problem lies in the subject or the underlying classes from the new .jar file. Sometimes the developer does not even know about the new classes, just that the tests stop running properly. If the tests are properly isolated, then bugs in the subject will be exposed by the tests for the subject, and any bugs in the underlying classes will be exposed by unit tests for those classes.

> **DESIGNING WITH TESTING IN MIND**
>
> **Classes are more testable when they are designed with testing in mind. For example, imagine that a test subject relies on an instance of the java.util.Map interface in order to function and that the subject directly allocates an instance of my.great.coll.lib.HashMap to use in its implementation. Without thought to testing, this is a perfectly reasonable and typical practice. When we want to test the class and we do not want to rely on the custom map implementation (because we don't want bugs there to cause false test failures), we have no opportunity to replace the implementation of the custom map with one that we know works. If the test subject were slightly altered to allow the test to provide the implementation of the map, then the subject could be better isolated. If the subject can be better isolated, then test failures are more likely to be an indication of a bug in the subject instead of possibly being with the custom implementation of the map.**

There is value in integration tests, especially the integration between concurrent development teams. Cactus/JUnit is a great framework to use to build these kinds of tests. Problems arise when integration tests are used as unit tests. Bugs in the underlying code can mask problems in the subject and vice versa. Both kinds of tests are valuable and should be written.

Example

This pitfall is illustrated with tests for an Invoice class. The Invoice class provides the total dollar amount of the invoice by summing each line item. Here is the code for the Invoice class (Listing 1.21), followed by the code for the JUnit test for the invoice (Listing 1.22).

```java
public class Invoice {
    private List items;

    public Invoice() {
        super();
    }

    public void addLineItem(LineItem item) {
        getLineItems().add(item);
    }

    public void removeLineItem(LineItem item) {
        getLineItems().remove(item);
    }
```

Listing 1.21 Invoice. *(continues)*

```java
public Collection getLineItems() {
    if(null == items) {
        items = new ArrayList();
    }
    return items;
}

public void setLineItems(Collection items) {
    this.items = new ArrayList(items.size());
    Iterator itr = items.iterator();
    while(itr.hasNext()) {
        this.items.add(itr.next());
    }
}

public BigDecimal getInvoiceTotal() {
    Iterator itr = items.iterator();
    BigDecimal total = (new BigDecimal((double)0.0)).setScale(2);
    while(itr.hasNext()) {
        LineItem item = (LineItem)itr.next();
        total = total.add(item.getLineTotal());
    }
    return total;
}
}
```

Listing 1.21 *(continued)*

```java
public class InvoiceTest extends TestCase {
    private static final int QUANTITY = 3;
    private static final double COST = 12.34;
    private static final int COUNT = 10;

    private Invoice subject = null;

    public InvoiceTest(String name) {
        super(name);
    }

    public static Test suite() {
        return new TestSuite(InvoiceTest.class);
    }

    public void testInvoiceTotal() throws Exception {
        BigDecimal total = subject.getInvoiceTotal();
        BigDecimal expected = new BigDecimal(COUNT *
```

Listing 1.22 InvoiceTest.

```
        COST * QUANTITY);
        // setting up a value that can be used to assert the intent
        // of the API documented with the method.
        expected = expected.setScale(2, BigDecimal.ROUND_HALF_UP);
        // assert the intent
        assertEquals(expected, total);
    }

    public void setUp() throws Exception {
        subject = new Invoice();
        List items = new ArrayList();
        LineItem item = null;
        for(int i = 0;i < COUNT;i++) {
            item = new LineItem(subject);
            item.setUnitPrice(new BigDecimal(COST));
            item.setQuantity(new Integer(QUANTITY));
            items.add(item);
        }
        subject.setLineItems(items);
    }

    public void tearDown() throws Exception {
        subject = null;
    }
}
```

Listing 1.22 *(continued)*

The setUp method is creating a new invoice for the test and adding several line items to initialize the subject. This test indirectly tests the getLineTotal method from the LineItem class as well as the intended method on Invoice. It is important that the getLineTotal method is tested; however, that test needs to be in the unit test for the LineItem class, not in the test for Invoice. If the getLineTotal method has a bug, then the invoice test will fail—not due to a bug in the Invoice class, but rather due to the bug in the LineItem class.

Do not misunderstand—there is value in testing the interaction between classes like Invoice and LineItem. The integration tests should be run as such, so that any test failures can be attributed to the way that Invoice and LineItem interact instead of being falsely attributed to a bug in either class. With tests in place that are distinct, bugs like this are identified early and fixed more quickly, which is, of course, the whole point of doing testing.

Solving Pitfall 1.6: Introduce Mock Objects

The most common way to solve this pitfall is to use the Mock Objects Pattern. With Mock Objects, the tests become inside and outside tests. The Mock Objects become pseudo-tests on the inside, and the JUnit test body becomes the test from the outside. With this strategy, the interaction between the subject and the underlying objects can be tested as well as the results of that interaction on the subject itself. The basic idea is to replace the objects that the test subject depends on with Mock Objects that provide the same API but yield hard-coded data and simplified functionality to reduce the likelihood that a bug in the underlying code will affect the test.

Step-by-Step

1. Identify all the classes required to implement the subject.
2. For each class or interface, build a Mock Implementation.
3. For classes, write a subclass and override the required methods to return canned data.
   a. Make sure to provide initialization methods to specify what parameters to expect and what values to return when these values are provided.
4. In the test, initialize the Mock Object with the expected parameters and the values to return.
5. Initialize the subject with the Mock Object.
6. Call the method being tested.
7. Assert whatever state change is expected in the subject.
8. Assert state changes expected in the Mock Object.
9. Deploy and test.

Example

This example will test an Invoice class that is able to sum the line items it contains. The invoice asks each line item for its total value and sums these numbers to arrive at an order total. Because the invoice depends so heavily on the LineItem class, the test for the invoice will be testing the LineItem class even though it is not intended to do so. The InvoiceTest test class is stuck in this pitfall, as you can see in Listing 1.23, as it is testing both the invoice and, indirectly, the line item code.

```java
public class InvoiceTest extends TestCase {
    private static final int QUANTITY = 3;
    private static final double COST = 12.34;
    private static final int COUNT = 10;

    private Invoice subject = null;

    public InvoiceTest(String name) {
        super(name);
    }

    public static Test suite() {
        return new TestSuite(InvoiceTest.class);
    }

    public void testInvoiceTotal() throws Exception {
        BigDecimal total = subject.getInvoiceTotal();
        BigDecimal expected = new BigDecimal(COUNT * COST *
                QUANTITY);
        // setting up a value that can be used to assert the intent
        // of the API documented with the method.
        expected = expected.setScale(2, BigDecimal.ROUND_HALF_UP);
        // assert the intent
        assertEquals(expected, total);
    }

    public void setUp() throws Exception {
        subject = new Invoice();
        List items = new ArrayList();
        LineItem item = null;
        for(int i = 0;i < COUNT;i++) {
            BigDecimal total = (new BigDecimal(COST)).
                setScale(2, BigDecimal.ROUND_HALF_UP);
            BigDecimal quantity = (new BigDecimal(QUANTITY)).
                setScale(2, BigDecimal.ROUND_HALF_UP);
            total = total.multiply(quantity).
                setScale(2, BigDecimal.ROUND_HALF_UP);
            items.add(new MockLineItem(subject, total));
        }
        subject.setLineItems(items);
    }

    public void tearDown() throws Exception {
        subject = null;
    }
}
```

Listing 1.23 InvoiceTest.

64　Chapter 1

The testTotal method is testing what it should test in calling the get-InvoiceTotal method. Because the implementation of that method is so heavily dependent on the LineItem class, it is also testing, indirectly, the getLineTotal method on the LineItem class. Bugs in the LineItem class could show up as test failures in Invoice's tests.

The first step in solving this pitfall is to identify the underlying classes that Invoice needs for its implementation. We have identified the LineItem class already. ArrayList and Long are also used to implement the Invoice; however, because these two classes are part of the JDK we will assume they work and not try to replace them with Mock Objects.

The next step is to build a mock implementation of the LineItem class. Because LineItem is a class and not an interface, a subclass of LineItem is used that overrides the methods that Invoice uses. The implementation will return hard-coded data. If the Invoice class used an interface for LineItem instead, the mock implementation would simply implement that interface. Here is the code for the mock implementation of the LineItem class.

```java
public class MockLineItem extends LineItem {
    BigDecimal expected;

    public MockLineItem(Invoice invoice, BigDecimal expected) {
        super(invoice);
        this.expected = expected;
    }

    // this is the only method that actually does anything
    public BigDecimal getLineTotal() {
        return expected;
    }
}
```

The next step is to change the test so that it uses instances of the Mock Object instead of the actual object in the test. Because our test is creating LineItems in the setUp method, we modify that method to create MockLineItems instead. Here is the code for the changed setUp method.

```java
public void setUp() throws Exception {
    subject = new Invoice();
    List items = new ArrayList();
    LineItem item = null;
    for(int i = 0;i < COUNT;i++) {
        BigDecimal total = (new BigDecimal(COST)).
            setScale(2, BigDecimal.ROUND_HALF_UP);
        BigDecimal quantity = (new BigDecimal(QUANTITY)).
            setScale(2, BigDecimal.ROUND_HALF_UP);
        total = total.multiply(quantity);
```

```
            setScale(2, BigDecimal.ROUND_HALF_UP);
        items.add(new MockLineItem(subject, total));
    }
    subject.setLineItems(items);
}
```

The final step is to change the test methods to assert the correct state changes. The expected value has not changed since we populated our test subject with the same data, so the testInvoiceTotal method remains unchanged and looks like this.

```
    public void testInvoiceTotal() throws Exception {
        BigDecimal total = subject.getInvoiceTotal();
        BigDecimal expected = new BigDecimal(COUNT * COST * QUANTITY);
        // setting up a value that can be used to assert the intent
        // of the API documented with the method.
        expected = expected.setScale(2, BigDecimal.ROUND_HALF_UP);
        // assert the intent
        assertEquals(expected, total);
    }
```

Now the invoice test subject will be tested without reliance on the LineItem class. Any test failures can more easily be attributed to the Invoice class instead of the LineItem class. An interesting thing to note is that, in this example, none of the actual test methods had to change, only the setUp of the subject. Because we still expect the same behavior and we are initializing with the same data, the set of asserts in the original test is just what we want. This is often the case when putting Mock Objects in place if there was a good set of asserts to begin with.

CHAPTER 2

Struts ActionForms

ActionForm is an abstract JavaBean class that application developers subclass to act as a server-side representation of an HTML form on one or more Web pages. The Struts framework provides for automatic binding of values between ActionForm instances and HTML form fields. The cardinality of this relationship is defined by the developer, so a single ActionForm may correspond to several HTML forms.

ActionForms are intended to be used primarily as passive buffers for user interface values, so the code that developers create in their subclasses is generally for the purpose of manipulating these values on behalf of other portions of the application (for the most part, model objects). Inbound request values often require validation, and ActionForms inherit an empty method called by the framework explicitly for that purpose. Also, outbound values may need to be formatted for display in the user interface—for example, the value contained in a BigDecimal field in a value object might need to be displayed with thousands separators and a leading dollar sign. This would require conversion between the underlying Java type and a string value suitable for display in the user interface. The inverse operation would then have to be performed on values submitted in the request.

STRUTS ACTIONFORMS THE BIG PICTURE

One issue that developers struggle with when architecting Struts-based applications is the framework's inherent decoupling of type conversion and validation. When the framework receives a form submission, it invokes generic reflection functionality in the BeanUtils package (formerly part of the Struts codebase and now a subproject of the Jakarta Commons project) to bind the form values in the request to the associated ActionForm. The BeanUtils code is capable of converting string values to most common Java types (for example, Integer, BigDecimal, etc.) and is able to map nested and indexed properties (for example "address[0].city" would be mapped to a property named *city* in the first element of an array of JavaBeans contained in an ActionForm property named 'address').

These capabilities make it theoretically possible to place a graph of value objects directly in an ActionForm. (The Struts TagLib also avails itself of BeanUtils functionality, allowing properties to be mapped from the object graph into JSP tags during rendering.) If an exception is thrown during conversion of any of the inbound form values—as would happen, for example, if alphabetic characters were submitted in a form field bound to an Integer—Struts aborts processing of the request, returning control to the JSP. The result is that the user's input is lost, and no error message is provided.

Only if type conversion of all submitted form values succeeds is validation performed (when the framework calls the ActionForm's validate() method). While there are sufficient hooks in the Struts framework to allow an ambitious developer to alter the default inbound binding behavior to provide for more flexible error handling, no such hooks exist for modifying the outbound (that is, TagLib) binding behavior. The situation is problematic because the binding mechanism obviously has to work in both directions. Unfortunately, changing the outbound binding behavior requires modifying either the BeanUtils package or the Struts framework itself.

Therefore, most developers find it expedient to skirt the issue by coding String (or Boolean) properties in their ActionForms to represent each of the HTML form values expected in the request. This defers inbound type conversion until after validate() has been called, at the cost of making conversion an additional, separate step for which the developer is now responsible. The pitfalls described in this chapter assume that ActionForms follow this pattern.

Because the Struts framework doesn't provide built-in support for formatting, it doesn't provide a complete solution for type conversion and only recently added support for validation. Developers often resort to hand-coding the functionality wherever it is needed. This usually results in the scattering of formatting, type conversion, and validation code across a number of classes, and all too often leads to copying and pasting of functionality between methods, as described in the pitfalls in this chapter.

In other words, ActionForm functionality is usually limited to one or more of the following: performing type conversions, transferring values between objects, validating user input, and formatting values for presentation to the user. Because these areas are interrelated, their associated pitfalls, though potentially serious, are relatively few.

Three issues related to ActionForms can be major stumbling blocks. This chapter will focus on these three pitfalls and their solutions.

Pitfall 2.1: Copy/Paste Formatting describes the tendency to hard-code formatting logic in ActionForms and their associated value objects, copying the implementations wherever they are needed to format values for display in the user interface.

Pitfall 2.2: Copy/Paste Conversion details the common practice of hard-coding type conversion logic in ActionForms and their associated value objects, which usually results in a significant amount of duplicate code.

Pitfall 2.3: Copy/Paste Validation examines how the common practice of hand-coding validation logic in ActionForms leads to code duplication, as well as increased code complexity.

Pitfall 2.1: Copy/Paste Formatting

Ensuring that values displayed in the user interface are consistently and correctly formatted can be painstaking work. Unfortunately, Struts doesn't provide generic facilities to automate this task. The temptation is to code the required behavior directly in value object getter methods, which quickly leads to copying and pasting a particular formatting behavior to all the getter methods that need it.

This copy/paste formatting code is used to convert Java types (for example, BigDecimal, Date, etc.) into formatted strings suitable for display in the user interface, as well as to populate ActionForms with the values derived via this technique. This code often winds up being scattered among not only value objects, but also ActionForms, Actions, and helper classes. As the code base grows, such code becomes increasingly difficult to maintain, as a single formatting change may require modifying numerous methods. Over time, individual formatting implementations are often customized to provide for variations in the original behavior, making the task of applying global changes even more daunting.

This tendency is most common among developers under schedule constraints and/or new to the Struts framework, as they often find themselves applying brute-force design and coding techniques to ActionForms in the early stages of a project in order to get going. Unfortunately, once in place, the code tends to serve as a template for future development, leading to continuation of the same set of practices when user interface development ramps up.

The result on anything other than the smallest projects is that inordinate amounts of developer hours are spent implementing and maintaining formatting logic instead of core application functionality. This waste of development resources can ultimately lead to delays in implementing important business requirements.

> **FORMATTING AND THE STRUTS FRAMEWORK**
>
> The Struts framework provides handy facilities for many of the things a Web-based user interface needs to do. There are exceptions, however, and the absence of facilities for formatting values for display in the user interface is a notable one. The available Struts example applications also steer clear of this issue, leaving it an area that requires some design effort for all but the most trivial of Struts-based applications.

A typical manifestation of this pitfall is to code formatting behavior in a value object's getter methods, as in the following snippet:

```
public String getAmountAsString() {
    String amountString = "";

    try {
        if (amount != null) {
            amount = amount.setScale(CURRENCY_SCALE,
                                    BigDecimal.ROUND_HALF_UP);
            amountString = NumberFormat.getInstance().
                format(amount.doubleValue());
        }
    }
    catch (IllegalArgumentException e) {
        e.printStackTrace();
        throw new NumberFormatException("Unable to format value "
            + amount + " as BigDecimal");
    }

    return amountString;
}
```

This approach may seem harmless at first; however, it nearly always leads to wholesale copying and pasting of all or part of the implementation wherever formatting is required. Even if the formatting functionality is factored out into helper classes, the underlying assumption about how to format a given field is hard-coded into the value object's get...AsString() methods, which makes the formatting behavior relatively inflexible. For example, what if a given value was required to be formatted differently on two different pages in the user interface?

Also, the presence of an API such as this in an object that crosses the boundary between the presentation and business tiers is almost certain to lead to an unhealthy coupling between the layers. The result would be fragile code, as changes implemented to serve the needs of one tier break functionality that had been working correctly in the other.

In fact, the mere presence of the get...AsString() methods contributes to code bloat, which could serve only to obscure other, perhaps more important, details of a given class. In addition, as we shall see later, it can lead to a higher degree of coupling between the value objects and our Action subclasses, decreasing their flexibility and thus adding to the application's maintenance overhead.

Example

Let's take a look at a more comprehensive example of the Copy/Paste Formatting pitfall. Listing 2.1 is an example of a simple Invoice value class that contains formatting logic:

```java
package com.aboutobjects.pitfalls;

import java.io.Serializable;
import java.math.BigDecimal;
import java.text.FieldPosition;
import java.text.NumberFormat;
import java.text.SimpleDateFormat;
import java.util.Date;

public class InvoiceDO implements Serializable
{
    public final static int CURRENCY_SCALE = 2;
    public final static String DATE_FORMAT = "MM/dd/yyyy";

    private Integer invoiceNumber;
    private Date billingDate;
    private BigDecimal amount;

    public InvoiceDO(Integer invoiceNumber,
                    Date billingDate,
                    BigDecimal amount) {
        this.invoiceNumber = invoiceNumber;
        this.billingDate = billingDate;
        this.amount = amount;
    }

    public void setInvoiceNumber(Integer invoiceNumber) {
        this.invoiceNumber = invoiceNumber;
    }
    public Integer getInvoiceNumber() { return invoiceNumber; }

    public String getInvoiceNumberAsString() {
        return invoiceNumber.toString();
    }

    public void setBillingDate(Date billingDate) {
        this.billingDate = billingDate;
    }
    public Date getBillingDate() { return billingDate; }

    public String getBillingDateAsString() {
```

Listing 2.1 Invoice value class with formatting logic.

```
    StringBuffer dateBuf = new StringBuffer();

    if (billingDate != null) {
        SimpleDateFormat formatter =
            new SimpleDateFormat(DATE_FORMAT);
        formatter.setLenient(false);
        formatter.format(billingDate,
                         dateBuf,
                         new FieldPosition(0));
    }

    return dateBuf.toString();
}

public void setAmount(BigDecimal amount) {
    this.amount = amount;
}
public BigDecimal getAmount() { return amount; }

public String getAmountAsString() {
    String amountString = "";

    try {
        if (amount != null) {
            amount = amount.setScale(CURRENCY_SCALE,
                BigDecimal.ROUND_HALF_UP);
            amountString = NumberFormat.getInstance().format(
                amount.doubleValue());
        }
    }
    catch (IllegalArgumentException e) {
        throw new NumberFormatException("Unable to format value "
            + amount + " as BigDecimal");
    }

    return amountString;
}
}
```

Listing 2.1 *(continued)*

In order to access the formatting behavior of the InvoiceDO class, developers would have to add an extra line of code to the execute() methods of the appropriate Actions for each field to be formatted and populated in the ActionForm. Here's an example from a typical Action:

```
// Populate the InvoiceForm with values from the InvoiceDO
invoiceForm.setInvoiceNumber(invoiceDO.getInvoiceNumberAsString());
```

```
invoiceForm.setBillingDate(invoiceDO.getBillingDateAsString());
invoiceForm.setAmount(invoiceDO.getAmountAsString());
```

At first blush, this may not seem so bad. The get...AsString() methods are, after all, straightforward and fairly easy to code, and the ActionForm code is simple enough.

But the amount of code required to produce classes with a greater number of fields could be significant, and maintenance could become, at best, a chore, due to the increased coupling of the Action subclasses to the underlying details of the value objects used throughout the user interface.

Further, it is questionable whether formatting values to be displayed in the user interface is a proper responsibility of a value object that may be used in other contexts. Value objects are, by definition, simple data containers that can be safely passed between the tiers of an application, yet the formatting behavior defined here is defined in terms of the presentation tier. If developers later use these APIs in the business tier, changes to the presentation tier formatting logic could cause business-tier code to break. Therefore, it is generally safer to design value objects as pure data containers and leave formatting behavior to the user interface controller classes and their helpers.

We can accomplish this by creating Formatter helper classes and moving all the required formatting logic there. This approach can be extended to provide for flexible formatting behavior, as Formatters can be defaulted, based on the type of the underlying property, and overridden dynamically, based on developer-supplied criteria, as detailed in the solution that follows.

Solving Pitfall 2.1: Consolidate and Generalize Formatting Code

If you find yourself ensared in the Copy/Paste Formatting pitfall, you can apply Consolidate and Generalize Formatting Code to work your way out of it quickly and relatively painlessly. If, on the other hand, you have not yet begun coding your user interface, you may wish to adopt this design to preempt the pitfall altogether.

This solution allows you to isolate your formatting code, so that changes have to be applied only in one place and copy/paste implementations are no longer needed. It will also allow you to automate the selection of formatting behavior based on the Java type of each value object property, so that you need to provide code only when an alternative behavior is desired. For example, Date fields could be defaulted so that they would always be formatted as "mm/yy/dd" unless you add a line of code to specifically request a different formatting behavior.

As we discovered earlier, Struts is silent on the issue of formatting Java values for display in the user interface, so we need to take matters into our own hands. But that doesn't mean we're doomed to brute-force coding techniques. We can automate an otherwise tedious process and thus resolve the Copy/Paste Formatting pitfall.

This solution allows developers coding these classes to reuse common implementations, thus helping to avoid copy/paste errors and maintenance headaches while reducing the overhead involved in adding new functionality. In particular, moving to a shared implementation will make it far easier to accommodate changes in user interface requirements, as nearly any given change can now be implemented by modifying a single chunk of Formatter code, rather than by searching for all the copy/paste formatting implementations and modifying each one.

This solution also serves as the basis for the solution to Pitfall 2.2: Copy/Paste Conversion.

Step-by-Step

1. Hunt down copy/paste formatting code in value objects, helper classes, Actions, and ActionForms.
    a. Organize the collected methods and code snippets by class.
    b. Subcategorize the code by formatting type—for example, currency, percentage, etc.—where applicable.
2. Create a base class named Formatter to provide default formatting and to act as a factory for subclasses.
3. Create a Formatter subclass for each of the formatting types discovered.
    a. Add code to the base Formatter class's factory method for each subclass created.
    b. Move formatting code to format() methods in appropriate Formatter classes.
4. Create an abstract ActionForm subclass to act as a base class for all your ActionForms.
    a. Modify your existing ActionForms to inherit from the new base class.
    b. Add code to the base class to format and populate its property values.

5. Consider providing for customization of default formatting behavior and default values (that is, the value that is displayed when a null value of a given type is encountered in the underlying bean).

   a. Consider using wrapper classes for value classes such as BigDecimal to increase the available number of types.

   b. If necessary, add code to your ActionForm base class to handle customizations.

6. Clean up any remaining formatting code in Actions, ActionForms, value objects, and so on and test.

Example

The first step to solving Pitfall 2.1 is to create a simple Formatter base class, as shown in Listing 2.2.

```java
public class Formatter
{
    public static Formatter getFormatter(Class type) {
        return new Formatter();
    }

    protected String format(Object target) {
        return target == null ? "" : target.toString();
    }
}
```

Listing 2.2 A simple Formatter base class.

Now, find a candidate method containing formatting code that we can migrate to a Formatter subclass. For example:

```java
public String getAmountAsString() {
    String amountString = "";

    try {
        if (amount != null) {
            amount = amount.setScale(CURRENCY_SCALE,
                BigDecimal.ROUND_HALF_UP);
            amountString = NumberFormat.getInstance().
                format(amount.doubleValue());
        }
    }
    catch (IllegalArgumentException e) {
        e.printStackTrace();
        throw new NumberFormatException("Unable to format value "
```

```
            + amount + " as BigDecimal");
    }

    return amountString;
}
```

Then create a suitable Formatter subclass that overrides its parent's format() method, and move the code into the method implementation, as in the example in Listing 2.3.

```
... imports, etc.

public class CurrencyFormatter extends Formatter {
    /** The default scale for currency values */
    public final static int CURRENCY_SCALE = 2;
    /** The default format for currency values */
    public final static String CURRENCY_FORMAT = "#,##0.00";

    /**
     * Returns a string representation of its argument, formatted as a
     * currency value.
     *
     * @return a formatted String
     */
    protected String format(Object value) {
        if (value == null)
            return "";

        String stringValue = "";
        try {
            BigDecimal bigDecValue = (BigDecimal)value;
            bigDecValue = bigDecValue.setScale(CURRENCY_SCALE,
                BigDecimal.ROUND_HALF_UP);
            stringValue = NumberFormat.getInstance().
                format(bigDecValue.doubleValue());
        }
        catch (IllegalArgumentException iae) {
            throw new FormattingException("Unable to format " + value +
                "as a currency value", iae);
        }

        return stringValue;
    }
}
```

Listing 2.3 CurrencyFormatter.java.

Don't forget to add the new Formatter class to the base class's factory method, as in the snippet here.

```
public class Formatter
{
    public static Formatter getFormatter(Class type) {
        if (BigDecimal.class.isAssignableFrom(type))
            return new CurrencyFormatter();
        else
            return new Formatter();
    }
    ...
}
```

Now for the tricky part—to avoid scattering Formatter invocations throughout our code base, we need to automate the process of populating the ActionForm's fields. The goal is to localize calls to the formatting code in a single method. We can accomplish this by creating an abstract Action-Form base class containing a method that uses reflection to populate all of its fields, as in the pseudo-code shown here.

```
public void populate(Object bean) {
    // Get a Map representation of the bean, where the keys are
    // property names and the values are property values.
    Map valueMap = getMap(bean); // Create a Map representation of bean

    // Iterate the map's keys...
    while (iterate valueMap)) {
        ...
        // Use reflection to get type for current value;
        Class type = getType(current value);
        // Get Formatter for current type...
        Formatter formatter = getFormatter(key, type);
        // Use Formatter to format the value as a string...
        String formattedValue = formatter.format(the current value);
        // Use reflection to populate ActionForm property with
        // formatted value...
        setProperty(formattedValue);
    }
}
```

What follows is a simple version of a base class, *MyForm*, that provides formatting services to its subclasses. (Note: Obviously, MyForm is a terrible name for a class—you will no doubt substitute something more sensible.) The principal method, populate(), uses the facilities of the PropertyUtils class to provide the required reflection services.

PropertyUtils is one of several classes concerned with introspection in a library called *beanutils*, a package in the Apache Jakarta Commons subproject. These classes originated in Struts and were later moved to the Commons library because their functionality is so generally useful. Struts still depends on classes in the BeanUtils package to populate ActionForms from request values and to map values from ActionForms into JSP tags during rendering.

We can use the same facilities to help populate the ActionForm automatically, based on the properties of a given Java bean. The PropertyUtils describe() method extracts values from a bean (by using reflection to invoke the bean's getter methods) and presents them in a HashMap keyed by property name. MyForm's populate() method calls describe() to get a Map of the provided bean's values, and then iterates the HashMap. For each value in the HashMap, it calls another PropertyUtils method, getPropertyType(), to determine the value's class.

The populate() method then invokes the Formatter's factory method, getFormatter(), which returns the appropriate Formatter class for the given type. The value is converted by invoking the Formatter instance's format() method.

Listing 2.4 is the code for our initial version of MyForm. Note that at this stage the code isn't completely general in that it doesn't provide for handling nested ActionForms. Tips on how to make the solution more general can be found at the end of Pitfall 2.2.

```
package com.aboutobjects.pitfalls;

import java.lang.reflect.InvocationTargetException;
import java.util.Iterator;
import java.util.Map;

import org.apache.commons.beanutils.PropertyUtils;
import org.apache.struts.action.ActionForm;

/**
 * An abstract base class for ActionForms that adds support for
 * formatting of Java types, including Date, BigDecimal, and Integer.
 * The <code>populate()</code> method provides an entry point to
 * this functionality. The <code>keysToSkip()</code> method allows
 * subclasses to specify fields that should not be populated.
 */
public abstract class MyForm extends ActionForm {
    /**
     * Populates the MyForm instance by introspecting the specified
     * bean, converting any typed values to formatted strings, and
     * then using reflection to invoke its own String-based setter
     * methods.
     *
     * @param bean an object containing the values to be populated
     */
```

Listing 2.4 MyForm.java. *(continues)*

```java
    public void populate(Object bean) {
String errorMsg = "Unable to format values from bean: " + bean;
        Map valueMap = mapRepresentation(bean);
        Iterator keyIter = valueMap.keySet().iterator();

        while (keyIter.hasNext()) {
            String currKey = (String)keyIter.next();
            Object currValue = valueMap.get(currKey);

            try {
                // We can't use getClass() to get the type of currValue
                // because it could be null, so we call
                // callgetPropertyType() to introspect the bean instead.
                Class type = PropertyUtils.getPropertyType(bean,
                    currKey);
                Formatter formatter = Formatter.getFormatter(type);
                String value = formatter.format(currValue);
                // Populates the field corresponding to currKey
                // with value
                PropertyUtils.setSimpleProperty(this, currKey, value);
            }
            catch (IllegalAccessException iae) {
                throw new FormattingException(errorMsg, iae);
            }
            catch (InvocationTargetException ite) {
                throw new FormattingException(errorMsg, ite);
            }
            catch (NoSuchMethodException nsme) {
                throw new FormattingException(errorMsg, nsme);
            }
        }
    }

    /**
     * Returns a Map containing the values from the provided
     * Java bean, keyed by field name. Entries having keys
     * that match any of the strings returned by
     * <code>keysToSkip()</code> will be removed. Subclasses can
     * override <code>keysToSkip()</code> to customize its behavior.
     *
     * @param bean the Java bean from which to create the Map
     * @return a Map containing values from the provided bean
     */
    protected Map mapRepresentation(Object bean) {
        String errorMsg = "Unable to format values from bean: " + bean;
        Map valueMap = null;

        // PropertyUtils.describe() uses Introspection to generate a Map
        // of values from its argument, keyed by field name.
```

Listing 2.4 (continued)

```java
    try {
        valueMap = PropertyUtils.describe(bean);
    }
    catch (IllegalAccessException iae) {
        throw new FormattingException(errorMsg, iae);
    }
    catch (InvocationTargetException ite) {
        throw new FormattingException(errorMsg, ite);
    }
    catch (NoSuchMethodException nsme) {
        throw new FormattingException(errorMsg, nsme);
    }

    // Here we remove keys for values that shouldn't be populated.
    // Subclasses can override keysToSkip() to customize.
    Iterator keyIter = keysToSkip().iterator();
    while (keyIter.hasNext()) {
        String key = (String)keyIter.next();
        valueMap.remove(key);
    }

    return valueMap;
}

/**
 * Returns an array of keys, representing values that should not be
 * populated for the current form instance. Subclasses that override
 * this method to provide additional keys to be skipped should be
 * sure to call <code>super</code>
 *
 * @return an array of keys to be skipped
 */
protected ArrayList keysToSkip() {
    ArrayList keysToSkip = new ArrayList();
    // Don't populate "class" field inherited from Object
    keysToSkip.add("class");
    return keysToSkip;
}
```

Listing 2.4 *(continued)*

Now we extend MyForm in one of our ActionForm subclasses, as seen in Listing 2.5. We'll comment out all but one of the setter methods to isolate our initial testing. Of course, we need to make sure that the method we're testing is of the appropriate type—in this case BigDecimal. The Invoice-Form merely extends MyForm to take advantage of these new services:

```
package com.aboutobjects.pitfalls;

import java.io.Serializable;

public class InvoiceForm extends MyForm
{
    private String invoiceNumber;
    private String billingDate;
    private String amount;

/***
    public void setInvoiceNumber(String invoiceNumber) {
        this.invoiceNumber = invoiceNumber;
    }
    public String getInvoiceNumber() { return invoiceNumber; }

    public void setBillingDate(String billingDate) {
        this.billingDate = billingDate;
    }
    public String getBillingDate() { return billingDate; }
****/

    public void setAmount(String amount) {
        this.amount = amount;
    }
    public String getAmount() { return amount; }
}
```

Listing 2.5 InvoiceForm.java.

Once we have tested the new implementation and have it working correctly, we can begin moving additional formatting code to new Formatter classes, as we did with the CurrencyFormatter, and, of course, uncomment the associated form methods in order to test them. Listings 2.6 and 2.7 are the additional Formatters needed to complete our example.

```
package com.aboutobjects.pitfalls;

import java.text.SimpleDateFormat;
import java.text.ParsePosition;
import java.text.FieldPosition;

/**
 * A Formatter for date values
 */
public class DateFormatter extends Formatter {
```

Listing 2.6 DateFormatter.java.

```
    /**
     * The default date format string
     */
    public final static String DATE_FORMAT = "MM/dd/yyyy";

    /**
     * Unformats its argument and returns a java.util.Date instance
     * initialized with the resulting string.
     *
     * @return a java.util.Date intialized with the provided string
     */
    protected Object unformat(String string) {
        if (string == null || string.trim().length() < 1)
            return null;

        SimpleDateFormat formatter = new SimpleDateFormat(DATE_FORMAT);
        formatter.setLenient(false);

        return formatter.parse(string, new ParsePosition(0));
    }

    /**
     * Returns a string representation of its argument, formatted as a
     * date with the "MM/dd/yyyy" format.
     *
     * @return a formatted String
     */
    protected String format(Object value) {
        if (value == null)
            return "";

        StringBuffer buf = new StringBuffer();
        SimpleDateFormat formatter = new SimpleDateFormat(DATE_FORMAT);
        formatter.setLenient(false);
        formatter.format(value, buf, new FieldPosition(0));

        return buf.toString();
    }
}
```

Listing 2.6 *(continued)*

```
package com.aboutobjects.pitfalls;

/**
 * A Formatter for integer values
 */
```

Listing 2.7 IntegerFormatter.java. *(continues)*

```
public class IntegerFormatter extends Formatter
{
    /**
     * Returns an object representation of its argument.
     *
     * @return an object
     */
    protected Object unformat(String string) {
        if (string == null || string.trim().length() < 1)
            return null;

        return new Integer(string);
    }

    /**
     * Returns a formatted version of its argument.
     *
     * @return a formatted String
     */
    protected String format(Integer anInteger) {
        return (anInteger == null ? "" : anInteger.toString());
    }
}
```

Listing 2.7 *(continued)*

The next step is to clean up the Actions. Formerly our Action subclasses populated the values in our ActionForm one field at a time. (The other alternative is to pass a long list of parameters, which is even more fragile; for example, mixing up two parameters of the same type introduces a bug that can be quite subtle.) The following code

```
invoiceDO.setInvoiceNumberAsString(invoiceForm.getInvoiceNumber());
invoiceDO.setBillingDateAsString(invoiceForm.getBillingDate());
invoiceDO.setAmountAsString(invoiceForm.getAmount());
```

can now be replaced by a single line:

```
invoiceForm.populate(invoice);
```

Note, however, that if you don't currently have an error page hooked up to display uncaught exceptions (which you should, but that's another story), you will probably want to add a try/catch block to catch runtime exceptions thrown in the lower levels.

```
try {
    invoiceForm.populate(invoiceBean, Formatter.STRING_TO_OBJECT);
}
```

```
catch (FormattingException fe) {
    fe.printStackTrace();
}
```

Listing 2.8 details the code for the RuntimeException subclass thrown by MyForm and by the Formatter classes.

```java
package com.aboutobjects.pitfalls;

/**
 * The exception thrown when a formatting error occurs, usually
 * in user interface code.
 */
public class FormattingException extends RuntimeException
{
    private Throwable cause;

    public FormattingException(String message) {
        super(message);
    }

    public FormattingException(String message, Throwable cause) {
        super(message);
        this.cause = cause;
    }

    public void setCause(Throwable cause) { this.cause = cause; }
    public Throwable getCause() { return cause; }

    public String toString() {
        return super.toString() + (cause == null ? "" :
            "\nOriginal Cause:\n" + cause.toString();
    }

    public void printStackTrace() {
        super.printStackTrace();
        if (cause != null) {
            System.out.println("\nOriginal Cause:\n");
            cause.printStackTrace();
        }
    }
}
```

Listing 2.8 FormattingException.java.

Once all the required Formatters have been created, we can double check to ensure that any remaining formatting code in our value objects has been removed. For example, we can put the class in Listing 2.9 on a diet.

```java
package com.aboutobjects.pitfalls;

import java.io.Serializable;
import java.math.BigDecimal;
import java.text.FieldPosition;
import java.text.NumberFormat;
import java.text.SimpleDateFormat;
import java.util.Date;

public class InvoiceDO implements Serializable
{
    public final static int CURRENCY_SCALE = 2;
    public final static String DATE_FORMAT = "MM/dd/yyyy";

    private Integer invoiceNumber;
    private Date billingDate;
    private BigDecimal amount;

    public InvoiceDO(Integer invoiceNumber,
                    Date billingDate,
                    BigDecimal amount) {
        this.invoiceNumber = invoiceNumber;
        this.billingDate = billingDate;
        this.amount = amount;
    }

    public void setInvoiceNumber(Integer invoiceNumber) {
        this.invoiceNumber = invoiceNumber;
    }
    public Integer getInvoiceNumber() { return invoiceNumber; }

    public String getInvoiceNumberAsString() {
        return invoiceNumber.toString();
    }

    public void setBillingDate(Date billingDate) {
        this.billingDate = billingDate;
    }
    public Date getBillingDate() { return billingDate; }

    public String getBillingDateAsString() {
        StringBuffer dateBuf = new StringBuffer();

        if (billingDate != null) {
            SimpleDateFormat formatter =
                new SimpleDateFormat(DATE_FORMAT);
            formatter.setLenient(false);
            formatter.format(billingDate, dateBuf,
                new FieldPosition(0));
```

Listing 2.9   InvoiceDO.java before refactoring.

```
        }
            return dateBuf.toString();
        }

        public void setAmount(BigDecimal amount) {
            this.amount = amount;
        }
        public BigDecimal getAmount() { return amount; }

        public String getAmountAsString() {
            String amountString = "";

            try {
                if (amount != null) {
                    amount = amount.setScale(CURRENCY_SCALE,
                        BigDecimal.ROUND_HALF_UP);
                    amountString = NumberFormat.getInstance().format(
                        amount.doubleValue());
                }
            }
            catch (IllegalArgumentException e) {
                    throw new NumberFormatException("Unable to format value "
                        + amount + " as BigDecimal");
            }

            return amountString;
        }
    }
```

Listing 2.9 *(continued)*

After stripping out the formatting code, we're left with the slimmed-down version shown in Listing 2.10.

```
package com.aboutobjects.pitfalls;

import java.io.Serializable;
import java.math.BigDecimal;
import java.util.Date;

public class InvoiceDO extends AbstractDO implements Serializable
{
    private Integer invoiceNumber;
    private Date billingDate;
    private BigDecimal amount;

    public void setInvoiceNumber(Integer invoiceNumber) {
```

Listing 2.10 InvoiceDO.java after refactoring. *(continues)*

```
            this.invoiceNumber = invoiceNumber;
    }
    public Integer getInvoiceNumber() { return invoiceNumber; }

    public void setBillingDate(Date billingDate) {
        this.billingDate = billingDate;
    }
    public Date getBillingDate() { return billingDate; }

    public void setAmount(BigDecimal amount) { this.amount = amount; }
    public BigDecimal getAmount() { return amount; }
}
```

Listing 2.10 *(continued)*

That represents a 3 to 1 reduction in lines of code (from 78 to 25) for a class containing only 3 fields. Obviously, for larger classes, the reduction would likely be proportionally greater (unless the values were principally strings and integers), especially if more complex formatting rules were to be implemented.

In addition, this means that in the future when fields are added, removed, or renamed, we won't have to modify the code in any of our Action subclasses to reflect the changes.

Figures 2.1 and 2.2 provide an overview of how the solution changes the calling sequence for our example. Figure 2.1 shows how the sequence would have looked prior to the solution.

The new sequence looks like the one shown in Figure 2.2.

Our current implementation of MyForm leaves a couple of issues unresolved, both of which relate to the issue of flexibility raised by the Copy/Paste Formatting pitfall. One is that developers may want to override the default formatting behavior. For example, suppose we added a BigDecimal salesTaxRate field to our model. In our current design, all BigDecimal values are formatted as currency amounts, but the salesTaxRate field represents a percentage.

Let's further suppose that the user interface requirements state that percentage values must be formatted with a trailing "%" sign. How are we going to get our two BigDecimal values formatted differently?

Developers may also be required to provide varying default values (that is, the value to display when the underlying bean field is null) for fields that share a single datatype. For example, suppose an item's ship date is required to default to a blank string, while the invoice date must default to today's date.

The solution to both these problems involves making a couple of small changes in the populate() method. We will also add two new methods: getFormatter(), to allow for overriding the default Formatter class for the given type, and setFormatterType(), to allow overrides to be specified dynamically. In addition, we will add a new method, setDefaultString(), to allow developers to specify the default value to display when a property's value is null. The specified values will be cached in HashMap fields added to MyForm.

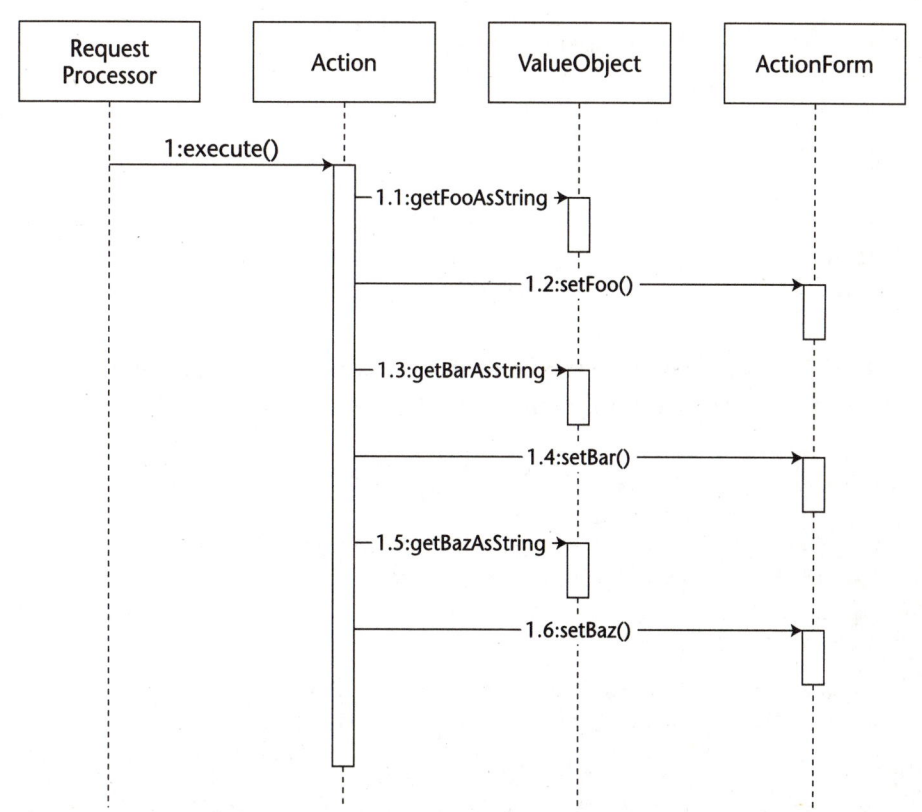

Figure 2.1 Calling sequence before the solution.

Chapter 2

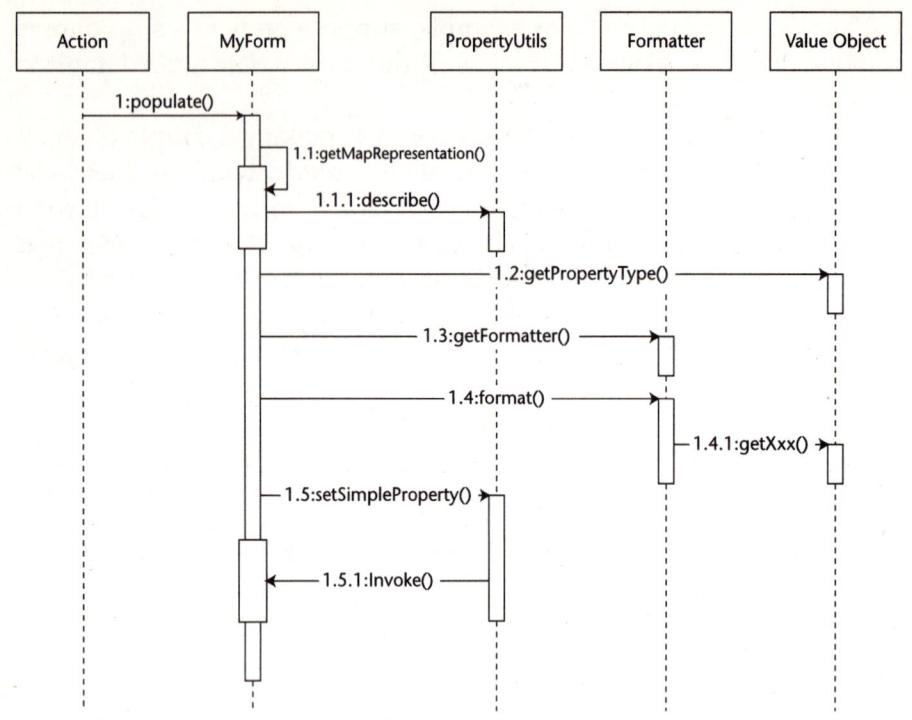

Figure 2.2 Calling sequence after the solution.

Listing 2.11 is an example implementation of MyForm, modified to provide for overriding of default values and formats.

```
package com.aboutobjects.pitfalls;

import java.lang.reflect.InvocationTargetException;
import java.util.Iterator;
import java.util.Map;
import java.util.HashMap;

import org.apache.commons.beanutils.PropertyUtils;
import org.apache.struts.action.ActionForm;

/**
 * An abstract base class for ActionForms that adds support for
 * automatic formatting and unformatting of string values, and for the
 * transfer of the resulting values between itself and the given bean.
 * The <code>populate()</code> method provides an entry point to
 * this functionality, while the <code>keysToSkip()</code> method allows
 * subclasses to specify fields that should not be populated.
 * <p>
```

Listing 2.11 MyForm.java modified to allow for runtime customization.

```
 * Additional methods are provided to allow subclasses to override
 * formatting defaults. The <code>setDefaultString()</code> method
 * allows callers to specify overrides for the default string used
 * to represent a <code>null</code> for a given property. Similarly, the
 * <code>setFormatterType()</code> method allows callers to specify a
 * formatting type other than the default for a given property.
 */
public abstract class MyForm extends ActionForm {
    /** The default string representation of null percentage values. */
    public final static String DEFAULT_PERCENTAGE_STRING = "0%";

    /** The percentage format key */
    public final static String PERCENTAGE_FORMAT = "percentageFormat";

    /**
     * The strings to display when null values are encountered.
     * Keys correspond to fields in the Form. The presence of a given
     * key indicates that the value provided in the map should be used
     * instead of the normal default string.
     */
    private Map defaultStringMap = new HashMap();

    /**
     * The format to use instead of the default format
     * for a given type.
     */
    private Map formatMap = new HashMap();

    /**
     * Populates the instance by introspecting the specified bean,
     * converting any typed values to formatted strings, and
     * then using reflection to invoke its own String-based setter
     * methods.
     * <p>
     * If null values are encountered in the bean, MyForm will
     * be populated with the default string associated with the given
     * type. The default null values can be overridden by calling
     * <code>setdefaultString(String key, String value)</code> and
     * providing an alternative string.
     *
     * @param bean an object containing the values to be populated
     */
    public void populate(Object bean) {
        String errorMsg = "Unable to format values from bean: " + bean;
        Map valueMap = mapRepresentation(bean);
        Iterator keyIter = valueMap.keySet().iterator();

        while (keyIter.hasNext()) {
```

Listing 2.11 *(continued)*

```
            String currKey = (String)keyIter.next();
            Object currValue = valueMap.get(currKey);

            try {
                Class type = PropertyUtils.getPropertyType(bean,
                    currKey);
                // Applies any overrides for the type of formatting
                // to use and the default string for null values.
                String value = null;
                if (currValue == null) {
                    value = (String) defaultStringMap.get(key);
                else {
                    Formatter formatter = getFormatter(currKey, type);
                    value = formatter.format(currValue);
                }
                PropertyUtils.setSimpleProperty(this, currKey, value);
            }
            catch (IllegalAccessException iae) {
                throw new FormattingException(errorMsg, iae);
            }
            catch (InvocationTargetException ite) {
                throw new FormattingException(errorMsg, ite);
            }
            catch (NoSuchMethodException nsme) {
                throw new FormattingException(errorMsg, nsme);
            }
        }
    }

    /**
     * Sets the default value to display for the given key when the
     * property value in the associated bean is <code>null</code>.
     *
     * @param key the name of the property
     * @parm value the value to display
     */
    public void setDefaultString(String key, String value) {
        defaultStringMap.put(key, value);
    }

    /**
     * Sets the default Formatter class to use for the given key
     *
     * @param key the name of the property
     * @param value the value to display
     */
    public void setFormatterType(String key, Class type) {
        if (!Formatter.class.isAssignableFrom(type))
            throw new FormattingException(type + "must be a Formatter");
```

Listing 2.11 *(continued)*

```java
            formatMap.put(key, type);
}

/**
 * Returns a Map containing the values from the provided
 * Java bean, keyed by field name. Entries having keys
 * that match any of the strings returned by
 * <code>keysToSkip()</code> will be removed. Subclasses can
 * override <code>keysToSkip()</code> to customize its behavior.
 *
 * @param bean the Java bean from which to create the Map
 * @return a Map containing values from the provided bean
 */
protected Map mapRepresentation(Object bean) {
    String errorMsg = "Unable to format values from bean: " + bean;
    Map valueMap = null;

    // PropertyUtils.describe() uses Introspection to generate a Map
    // of values from its argument, keyed by field name.
    try {
        valueMap = PropertyUtils.describe(bean);
    }
    catch (IllegalAccessException iae) {
        throw new FormattingException(errorMsg, iae);
    }
    catch (InvocationTargetException ite) {
        throw new FormattingException(errorMsg, ite);
    }
    catch (NoSuchMethodException nsme) {
        throw new FormattingException(errorMsg, nsme);
    }

    // Remove keys for values that shouldn't be populated.
    Iterator keyIter = keysToSkip().iterator();
    while (keyIter.hasNext()) {
        String key = (String)keyIter.next();
        valueMap.remove(key);
    }

    return valueMap;
}

/**
 * Returns an array of keys, representing values that should not be
 * populated for the current form instance. Subclasses that override
 * this method to provide additional keys to be skipped should be
 * sure to call <code>super</code>
 *
 * @return an array of keys to be skipped
```

Listing 2.11 *(continued)*

```
    */
    protected ArrayList keysToSkip() {
        ArrayList keysToSkip = new ArrayList();
        // Don't populate "class" field inherited from Object
        keysToSkip.add("class");
        return keysToSkip;
    }

    /**
     * Returns a Formatter for the provided type. If the provided key
     * matches an entry in the formatMap, the Formatter type indicated
     * by the entry is used instead of the default for the given type.
     *
     * @param key The name of the property to be formatted
     * @param type The type of the property to be formatted
     * @return A Formatter
     */
    protected Formatter getFormatter(String key, Class type) {
        Class formatType = (Class) formatMap.get(key);
        if (formatType == null)
            return Formatter.getFormatter(type);

        if (formatType.isAssignableFrom(PercentageFormatter.class)) {
            if (!BigDecimal.class.isAssignableFrom(type))
                throw new FormattingException("Unable to format value "
                    + "of type " + type + " as a percentage.");

            return new PercentageFormatter();
        }

        return null;
    }
}
```

Listing 2.11 *(continued)*

WRAPPING JAVA VALUE CLASSES

If customizing default values is a relatively unimportant issue in your application, you may be able to take advantage of a simpler technique to provide customized formatting behavior: simply create wrapper classes for certain Java types. For example, to format currency values and percentage values differently, create a Percentage and a Currency class to wrap BigDecimal. This will suffice to allow the Formatter class's factory method, getFormatter(), to return different Formatters for the two classes. This approach lacks the flexibility of the solution detailed here, so apply it only if your user interface requirements are fairly stable.

We can now add code to InvoiceForm's default constructor to customize its behavior.

```
public final static String SALES_TAX_RATE_KEY = "salesTaxRate";

public InvoiceForm() {
    setFormatterType(SALES_TAX_RATE_KEY, PercentageFormatter.class);
    setDefaultString(SALES_TAX_RATE_KEY,
                MyForm.DEFAULT_PERCENTAGE_STRING);
}
```

Note that Action classes can also invoke these methods if more dynamic customization is required.

Pitfall 2.2: Copy/Paste Conversion

If you find yourself scratching your head at the rapid growth of the code size for the user interface, and if you have trouble remembering all the user interface-related files that have to be modified whenever there's a change to classes representing the model, you're probably experiencing Pitfall 2.2: Copy/Paste Conversion.

As noted in Pitfall 2.1, many developers have a tendency to code with one eye on the nearest available example. If the designers of the early prototype of an application employ brute-force coding to transfer values to and from ActionForm instances, chances are that when full-scale development begins, other developers will employ the same techniques in developing production code.

Unfortunately, this is often the beginning of a self-perpetuating cycle, wherein less experienced developers contribute to a rapidly growing, increasingly complex code base. It's hard to fault them for mimicking existing project code.

Copy/Paste Conversion occurs when developers need to transfer values from their string representations in fields on ActionForm instances to corresponding properties on value objects used to transmit the data to the business tier. In most cases, at least some of the fields on the value objects contain Java types other than String, so that additional code is required to convert the values to the appropriate type.

Likewise, if any special formatting characters were applied when presenting the data in the user interface (for example, commas as thousands separators in currency values), they would need to be removed before the conversions could take place.

This pitfall usually becomes apparent in development when code bloat makes it increasingly hard to get work done. Developers may become frustrated, as each change to the underlying model requires modifications to multiple methods in a number of highly coupled classes. Coding mistakes become hard to spot, and subtle bugs may begin to creep in, as copy/paste code is pasted incorrectly or is not maintained consistently.

> **FRAMEWORK BEAN POPULATION FACILITIES**
>
> **The Struts framework doesn't directly provide facilities for transferring values from ActionForm instances to JavaBeans, and unfortunately there are few nontrivial examples available to developers to guide them in how to accomplish this. Though it may be far from obvious for those new to the Struts framework, the Jakarta Commons BeanUtils package contains a number of methods that are quite helpful in this regard, as we will see.**

The Copy/Paste Conversion pitfall takes a number of forms, though all of them are similar in nature. We will focus here on one of the typical variants. In this scenario, additional setter methods are added to convert from String to the underlying type as necessary, as in the following example:

```
// String-based Constructor.
public InvoiceDO(String invoiceNumberString,
                 String billingDateString,
                 String amountString) {
    super();
    setInvoiceNumberAsString(invoiceNumberString);
    setBillingDateAsString(billingDateString);
    setAmountAsString(amountString);
}

...

// Setter that converts from String to BigDecimal
public void setAmountAsString(String string) {
    String errorMsg = "Unable to parse a currency value from " +
        string;
    BigDecimal value = null;

    if (string != null && string.trim().length() > 0) {
        try {
            DecimalFormat formatter =
                    new DecimalFormat(CURRENCY_FORMAT);
            Number parsedNumber = formatter.parse(string.trim());
            value = new BigDecimal(parsedNumber.doubleValue());
        }
        catch (NumberFormatException nfe) {
            throw new NumberFormatException(errorMsg);
        }
        catch (ParseException pe) {
            throw new NumberFormatException(errorMsg);
        }
    }

    setAmount(value);
}
```

Instances can be initialized by adding a line of code to the appropriate Action subclass for each field to be transferred, as shown in the code that follows. (This may look familiar, as it closely resembles the code used to populate the InvoiceForm in Pitfall 2.1.)

```
// Populate the InvoiceDO with values from the InvoiceForm
invoiceDO.setInvoiceNumberAsString(invoiceForm.getInvoiceNumber());
invoiceDO.setBillingDateAsString(invoiceForm.getBillingDate());
invoiceDO.setAmountAsString(invoiceForm.getAmount());
```

Alternatively, we could have implemented a bulk setter method on the InvoiceDO, taking as many parameters as necessary to replace the multiple lines of code above with a single API call accompanied by a laundry list of arguments—pick your poison.

Example

Listing 2.12 is a modified version of the InvoiceDO class from Pitfall 2.1, which has now ballooned in size from 78 to 122 lines of code. Note that if we stripped it of its formatting and conversion code, it would weigh in at a sprightly 25 lines.

```
package com.aboutobjects.pitfalls;

import java.io.Serializable;
import java.math.BigDecimal;
import java.text.*;
import java.util.Date;

public class InvoiceDO implements Serializable
{
    public final static int CURRENCY_SCALE = 2;
    public final static String CURRENCY_FORMAT = "#,##0.00";
    public final static String DATE_FORMAT = "MM/dd/yyyy";

    private Integer invoiceNumber;
    private Date billingDate;
    private BigDecimal amount;

    public InvoiceDO(String invoiceNumberString,
                     String billingDateString,
                     String amountString) {
        super();
        setInvoiceNumberAsString(invoiceNumberString);
        setBillingDateAsString(billingDateString);
        setAmountAsString(amountString);
    }

    public void setInvoiceNumber(Integer invoiceNumber) {
        this.invoiceNumber = invoiceNumber;
    }
    public Integer getInvoiceNumber() { return invoiceNumber; }

    public void setInvoiceNumberAsString(String string) {
        if (string == null || string.trim().length() < 1)
            invoiceNumber = null;
```

Listing 2.12 InvoiceDO with conversion and formatting code.

```java
        else
            invoiceNumber = new Integer(string);
    }

    public String getInvoiceNumberAsString() {
        return invoiceNumber.toString();
    }

    public void setBillingDate(Date billingDate) {
        this.billingDate = billingDate;
    }
    public Date getBillingDate() { return billingDate; }

    public String getBillingDateAsString() {
        StringBuffer dateBuf = new StringBuffer();

        if (billingDate != null) {
            SimpleDateFormat formatter =
                new SimpleDateFormat(DATE_FORMAT);
            formatter.setLenient(false);
            formatter.format(billingDate, dateBuf,
                new FieldPosition(0));
        }

        return dateBuf.toString();
    }

    public void setBillingDateAsString(String string) {
        Date dateValue = null;

        if (string != null && string.trim().length() > 0) {
            SimpleDateFormat formatter =
                new SimpleDateFormat(DATE_FORMAT);
            formatter.setLenient(false);
            dateValue = formatter.parse(string, new ParsePosition(0));
        }

        setBillingDate(dateValue);
    }

    public void setAmount(BigDecimal amount) {
        this.amount = amount;
    }
    public BigDecimal getAmount() { return amount; }

    public void setAmountAsString(String string) {
        String errorMsg = "Unable to parse a currency value from " +
            string;
        BigDecimal value = null;
```

Listing 2.12 *(continued)*

```java
        if (string != null && string.trim().length() > 0) {
            try {
                DecimalFormat formatter =
                        new DecimalFormat(CURRENCY_FORMAT);
                Number parsedNumber = formatter.parse(string.trim());
                value = new BigDecimal(parsedNumber.doubleValue());
            }
            catch (NumberFormatException nfe) {
                throw new NumberFormatException(errorMsg);
            }
            catch (ParseException pe) {
                throw new NumberFormatException(errorMsg);
            }
        }

        setAmount(value);
    }

    public String getAmountAsString() {
        String amountString = "";

        try {
            if (amount != null) {
                amount = amount.setScale(CURRENCY_SCALE,
                    BigDecimal.ROUND_HALF_UP);
                amountString = NumberFormat.getInstance().
                    format(amount.doubleValue());
            }
        }
        catch (IllegalArgumentException e) {
            e.printStackTrace();
            throw new NumberFormatException("Unable to format value "
                + amount + " as BigDecimal");
        }

        return amountString;
    }
}
```

Listing 2.12 *(continued)*

Again, this may not look so bad given that we're dealing with only three fields. Increase that number to a more realistic level, though, and we can end up with quite a bit of fairly useless code, which unfortunately would have to be hand-maintained whenever the corresponding model objects changed.

Note that our JavaBean class contains formatting rules that are specifically for our Struts-based user interface. It is, however, quite possible that our application will have other interfaces and that those interfaces, particularly if they are system-to-system interfaces, might have quite different formatting rules from those required by the user interface. It is even possible (though less likely) that different types of user interfaces (for example. Swing versus Web-based) might have different formatting requirements.

Unfortunately, once they have coded these rules into a bean class that crosses over into the business tier, developers are likely to be tempted to reuse the existing formatting implementation by adding customizations for their particular interface, thus coupling the various presentations and introducing added complexity to the formatting code.

Solving Pitfall 2.2: Consolidate and Generalize Bean Population Code

This solution borrows from and builds on the solution to Pitfall 2.1, in which we implemented an abstract base class for our ActionForms that included a reflection-based populate() method. In essence, we want to do the same thing in reverse to automate the processes of converting the ActionForm's string values to the appropriate types, then populating the corresponding bean fields with the converted values.

When we applied the solution in the preceding section, we were able to dispense with only half of the offending copy/paste code. This should allow us to do away with the remainder. The resulting decoupling of Actions, ActionForms, and value objects yields increased design and coding flexibility and makes the code more robust. Eliminating redundant code eases maintenance, simplifying tasks that would otherwise be tedious (and, at times, downright bewildering), while reducing the number of potential points of failure.

Pitfall 2.1 is a corollary to this pitfall, in that it solves the inverse problem—converting String values to Java types. In fact, the following example solution includes code from its solution, thus demonstrating a complete, bidirectional approach to resolving both pitfalls.

Step-by-Step

1. Hunt for copy/paste bean population and type conversion code in value objects, Actions, ActionForms, and helper classes.
    a. Organize the methods and snippets according to the Java type being converted/populated.
2. Add unformat() method to the base Formatter class.

3. Begin moving code to Formatter classes.
   a. Match up with existing Formatter classes where possible and move to overridden unformat() method.
   b. Create new Formatter classes if necessary.
4. Modify MyForm's populate() method to make it bidirectional.
5. Add fields inherited from ActionForm to the keysToSkip() array to avoid runtime errors.
6. Deploy and test.

Example

Once we have identified and cataloged the copy/paste type conversion and bean population code, we can begin the process of moving it to the appropriate Formatters. The first step is to add a default unformat() implementation to the base Formatter class.

```
protected Object unformat(String target) {
    return target;
}
```

Now we can override this method in subclasses. Let's start with an offending method from the InvoiceDO class:

```
public void setAmountAsString(String string) {
    String errorMsg = "Unable to parse a currency value from " +
        string;
    BigDecimal value = null;

    if (string != null && string.trim().length() > 0) {
        try {
            DecimalFormat formatter =
                    new DecimalFormat(CURRENCY_FORMAT);
            Number parsedNumber = formatter.parse(string.trim());
            value = new BigDecimal(parsedNumber.doubleValue());
        }
        catch (NumberFormatException nfe) {
            throw new NumberFormatException(errorMsg);
        }
        catch (ParseException pe) {
            throw new NumberFormatException(errorMsg);
        }
    }

    setAmount(value);
}
```

After moving the above code to the new unformat() implementation, our CurrencyFormatter should look like the code in Listing 2.13.

```java
package com.aboutobjects.pitfalls;

import java.text.NumberFormat;
import java.text.ParseException;
import java.text.DecimalFormat;
import java.math.BigDecimal;

/**
 * A Formatter for currency values.
 */
public class CurrencyFormatter extends Formatter {
    /** The default scale for currency values */
    public final static int CURRENCY_SCALE = 2;

    /** The default format for currency values */
    public final static String CURRENCY_FORMAT = "#,##0.00";

    /**
     * Unformats its argument and returns a BigDecimal instance
     * initialized with the resulting string value
     *
     * @return a BigDecimal initialized with the provided string
     */
    protected Object unformat(String target) {
        if (target == null || target.trim().length() < 1)
            return null;

        String errorMsg = "Unable to parse a currency value from " +
            target;
        BigDecimal value;
        try {
            DecimalFormat formatter =
                new DecimalFormat(CURRENCY_FORMAT);
            Number parsedNumber = formatter.parse(target.trim());
            value = new BigDecimal(parsedNumber.doubleValue());
        }
        catch (NumberFormatException nfe) {
            throw new FormattingException(errorMsg, nfe);
        }
        catch (ParseException pe) {
            throw new FormattingException(errorMsg, pe);
        }

        return value;
```

Listing 2.13 CurrencyFormatter.java with unformat() method added. *(continues)*

```java
    }

    /**
     * Returns a string representation of its argument, formatted as a
     * currency value.
     *
     * @return a formatted String
     */
    protected String format(Object value) {
        if (value == null)
            return "";

        String stringValue = "";
        try {
            BigDecimal bigDecValue = (BigDecimal)value;
            bigDecValue = bigDecValue.setScale(CURRENCY_SCALE,
                BigDecimal.ROUND_HALF_UP);
            stringValue = NumberFormat.getInstance().
                format(bigDecValue.doubleValue());
        }
        catch (IllegalArgumentException iae) {
            throw new FormattingException("Unable to format " + value +
                "as a currency value", iae);
        }

        return stringValue;
    }
}
```

Listing 2.13 (continued)

The next step is to make MyForm's populate() method bidirectional. In the solution to Pitfall 2.1, we were creating formatted string representations of Java value objects and populating them in MyForm. Now we want to implement the inverse operation, taking formatted strings from the user interface, removing any extraneous formatting (such as comma thousands separators in currency values), coercing the unformatted strings to the appropriate Java types, and populating the corresponding bean property with the resulting value. We do that in Listing 2.14 by modifying the populate() method to include the new behavior and adding a *mode* parameter to gate it.

Note that we had to add a couple of keys to the list returned by keysToSkip() to avoid accessing the servletWrapper and multipartRequestHandler properties inherited from ActionForm.

```java
package com.aboutobjects.pitfalls;

import java.lang.reflect.InvocationTargetException;
import java.util.Iterator;
import java.util.Map;
import java.util.HashMap;
import java.math.BigDecimal;

import org.apache.commons.beanutils.PropertyUtils;
import org.apache.struts.action.ActionForm;

/**
 * An abstract base class for ActionForms that adds support for
 * automatic formatting and unformatting of string values and for the
 * transfer of the resulting values between itself and the given bean.
 * The <code>populate()</code> method provides an entry point to
 * this functionality, while the <code>keysToSkip()</code> method allows
 * subclasses to specify fields that should not be populated.
 * <p>
 * Additional methods are provided to allow subclasses to override
 * formatting defaults. The <code>setDefaultString()</code> method
 * allows callers to specify overrides for the default string used
 * to represent a <code>null</code> for a given property. Similarly, the
 * <code>setFormatterType()</code> method allows callers to specify a
 * formatting type other than the default for a given property.
 */
public abstract class MyForm extends ActionForm {
    /** The default string representation of null percentage values. */
    public final static String DEFAULT_PERCENTAGE_STRING = "0%";
    /** The percentage format key */
    public final static String PERCENTAGE_FORMAT = "percentageFormat";
    /** Indicates that conversion is from string to object */
    public final static int TO_OBJECT = 0;
    /** Indicates that conversion is from object to string */
    public final static int TO_STRING = 1;

    /**
     * The strings to display when null values are encountered.
     * Keys correspond to fields in the Form. The presence of a given
     * key indicates that the value provided in the map should be used
     * instead of the normal default string.
     */
    private Map defaultStringMap = new HashMap();

    /**
     * The format to use instead of the default format
     * for a given type.
     */
```

Listing 2.14 Bidirectional version of MyForm.java. *(continues)*

```java
    private Map formatMap = new HashMap();

    /**
     * Transfers values to and from the given bean, depending on the
     * value of <code>mode</code>. If the given mode is
     * <code>TO_STRING</code>, populates
     * the instance by introspecting the specified bean,
     * converting any typed values to formatted strings, and
     * then using reflection to invoke its own String-based setter
     * methods. If the mode is <code>TO_OBJECT</code>, performs the
     * inverse operation, unformatting and converting properties of
     * the MyForm instance and populating the resulting values in the
     * given bean.
     * <p>
     * If null values are encountered in the bean, MyForm will
     * be populated with the default string associated with the given
     * type. The default null values can be overridden by calling
     * <code>setdefaultString(String key, String value)</code> and
     * providing an alternative string.
     *
     * @param bean an object containing the values to be populated
     * @param mode Whether conversion is to String or to Java type
     */
    public void populate(Object bean, int mode) {
        String errorMsg = "Unable to format values from bean: " + bean;
        Object source = (mode == TO_STRING ? bean : this);
        Object target = (mode == TO_STRING ? this : bean);
        Map valueMap = mapRepresentation(source);
        Iterator keyIter = valueMap.keySet().iterator();

        while (keyIter.hasNext()) {
            String currKey = (String)keyIter.next();
            Object currValue = valueMap.get(currKey);

            try {
                Class type =
                    PropertyUtils.getPropertyType(bean, currKey);
                Formatter formatter = getFormatter(currKey, type);
                Object value = null;

                switch (mode) {
                case TO_OBJECT:
                    value = formatter.unformat((String)currValue);
                    break;
                case TO_STRING:
                    if (currValue == null)
                        value = (String) defaultStringMap.get(currkey);
                    else
                        value = formatter.format(currValue);
```

Listing 2.14 *(continued)*

```
                    break;
                default:
                    throw new RuntimeException("Unknown mode: " +
                        mode);
            }

            PropertyUtils.setSimpleProperty(target, currKey, value);
        }
        catch (IllegalAccessException iae) {
            throw new FormattingException(errorMsg, iae);
        }
        catch (InvocationTargetException ite) {
            throw new FormattingException(errorMsg, ite);
        }
        catch (NoSuchMethodException nsme) {
            throw new FormattingException(errorMsg, nsme);
        }
    }
}

/**
 * Sets the default value to display for the given key when the
 * property value in the associated bean is <code>null</code>.
 *
 * @param key the name of the property
 * @parm value the value to display
 */
public void setDefaultString(String key, String value) {
    defaultStringMap.put(key, value);
}

/**
 * Sets the default Formatter class to use for the given key
 *
 * @param key the name of the property
 * @param value the value to display
 */
public void setFormatterType(String key, Class type) {
    if (!Formatter.class.isAssignableFrom(type))
        throw new FormattingException(type + "must be a Formatter");
    formatMap.put(key, type);
}

/**
 * Returns a Map containing the values from the provided
 * Java bean, keyed by field name. Entries having keys
 * that match any of the strings returned by
 * <code>keysToSkip()</code> will be removed.
 *
```

Listing 2.14 *(continued)*

```
     * @param bean the Java bean from which to create the Map
     * @return a Map containing values from the provided bean
     */
    protected Map mapRepresentation(Object bean) {
        String errorMsg = "Unable to format values from bean: " + bean;
        Map valueMap = null;

        // PropertyUtils.describe() uses Introspection to generate a Map
        // of values from its argument, keyed by field name.
        try {
            valueMap = PropertyUtils.describe(bean);
        }
        catch (IllegalAccessException iae) {
            throw new FormattingException(errorMsg, iae);
        }
        catch (InvocationTargetException ite) {
            throw new FormattingException(errorMsg, ite);
        }
        catch (NoSuchMethodException nsme) {
            throw new FormattingException(errorMsg, nsme);
        }

        // Remove keys for values that shouldn't be populated.
        // Subclasses can override keysToSkip() to customize.
        Iterator keyIter = keysToSkip().iterator();
        while (keyIter.hasNext()) {
            String key = (String)keyIter.next();
            valueMap.remove(key);
        }

        return valueMap;
    }

    /**
     * Returns an array of keys, representing values that should not be
     * populated for the current form instance. Subclasses that override
     * this method to provide additional keys to be skipped should be
     * sure to call <code>super</code>
     *
     * @return an array of keys to be skipped
     */
    protected ArrayList keysToSkip() {
        ArrayList keysToSkip = new ArrayList();
        // Don't populate "class" field inherited from Object
        keysToSkip.add("class");
        return keysToSkip;
    }

    /**
```

Listing 2.14 *(continued)*

```
     * Returns a Formatter for the provided type. If the provided key
     * matches an entry in the formatMap, the Formatter type indicated
     * by the entry is used instead of the default for the given type.
     *
     * @param key The name of the property to be formatted
     * @param type The type of the property to be formatted
     * @return A Formatter
     */
    protected Formatter getFormatter(String key, Class type) {
        Class formatType = (Class) formatMap.get(key);
        if (formatType == null)
            return Formatter.getFormatter(type);

        if (formatType.isAssignableFrom(PercentageFormatter.class)) {
            if (!BigDecimal.class.isAssignableFrom(type))
                throw new FormattingException("Unable to format value "
                    + "of type " + type + " as a percentage.");

            return new PercentageFormatter();
        }

        return null;
    }
}
```

Listing 2.14 *(continued)*

The next step is to replace the bean population code in the affected Action classes with a call to the new version of populate(). The following code, for example, would be a candidate for replacement.

```
// Populate the InvoiceDO with values from the InvoiceForm
invoiceDO.setInvoiceNumberAsString(invoiceForm.getInvoiceNumber());
invoiceDO.setBillingDateAsString(invoiceForm.getBillingDate());
invoiceDO.setAmountAsString(invoiceForm.getAmount());
```

The preceding code can now be replaced by a single line of code:

```
invoiceForm.populate(invoiceBean, MyForm.TO_OBJECT);
```

Again, if you don't have an error-handling page that will print a stack trace if a runtime exception is thrown, add a try/catch block; it will likely prove a timesaver.

```
        try {
            invoiceForm.populate(invoiceBean, MyForm.TO_OBJECT);
        }
        catch (FormattingException fe) {
```

```
                fe.printStackTrace();
        }
```

Once the first Formatter is working, we can move the remaining conversion/population code, as in Listings 2.15 and 2.16.

```
package com.aboutobjects.pitfalls;

/**
 *  A Formatter for integer values
 */
public class IntegerFormatter extends Formatter
{
    /**
     * Returns an object representation of its argument.
     *
     * @return an object
     */
    protected Object unformat(String string) {
        if (string == null || string.trim().length() < 1)
            return null;

        return new Integer(string);
    }

    /**
     * Returns a formatted version of its argument.
     *
     * @return a formatted String
     */
    protected String format(Integer anInteger) {
        return (anInteger == null ? "" : anInteger.toString());
    }
}
```
Listing 2.15 IntegerFormatter.java.

```
package com.aboutobjects.pitfalls;

import java.text.SimpleDateFormat;
import java.text.ParsePosition;
import java.text.FieldPosition;

/**
```
Listing 2.16 DateFormatter.java.

```java
 * A Formatter for date values
 */
public class DateFormatter extends Formatter {
    /**
     * The default date format string
     */
    public final static String DATE_FORMAT = "MM/dd/yyyy";

    /**
     * Unformats its argument and returns a java.util.Date instance
     * initialized with the resulting string.
     *
     * @return a java.util.Date initialized with the provided string
     */
    protected Object unformat(String string) {
        if (string == null || string.trim().length() < 1)
            return null;

        SimpleDateFormat formatter = new SimpleDateFormat(DATE_FORMAT);
        formatter.setLenient(false);

        return formatter.parse(string, new ParsePosition(0));
    }

    /**
     * Returns a string representation of its argument, formatted as a
     * date with the "MM/dd/yyyy" format.
     *
     * @return a formatted String
     */
    protected String format(Object value) {
        if (value == null)
            return "";

        StringBuffer buf = new StringBuffer();
        SimpleDateFormat formatter = new SimpleDateFormat(DATE_FORMAT);
        formatter.setLenient(false);
        formatter.format(value, buf, new FieldPosition(0));

        return buf.toString();
    }
}
```

Listing 2.16   *(continued)*

HANDLING NESTED ACTIONFORMS

Nearly every Web application contains pages that need to display lists of values in a table. An easy way to model the value list is by creating an ActionForm property that contains an array of ActionForms, where each item represents a table row. It can also be convenient to directly nest an ActionForm within another ActionForm (for example, it might be handy to stick a reusable AddressForm inside several different forms, such as InvoiceForm, CompanyForm, ContactForm, etc.).

While this in itself is simple enough to achieve, our current formatting and type conversion infrastructure would need to be enhanced a bit to work with this slightly more complex structure. To achieve this increased generality, we will need to add a bit of code to MyForm's populate() method, as well as adding several entirely new, albeit small methods. What follows in Listing 2.17 is a new version of the populate() method that accommodates both of the desired types of nesting. New or modified code is set in italics.

```
public void populate(Object bean, int mode) {
    String errorMsg = "Unable to format values from bean: "
        + bean;
    Object source = (mode == TO_STRING ? bean : this);
    Object target = (mode == TO_STRING ? this : bean);
    Map valueMap = mapRepresentation(source, mode);
    Iterator keyIter = valueMap.keySet().iterator();

    while (keyIter.hasNext()) {
        String currKey = (String)keyIter.next();
        Object currValue = valueMap.get(currKey);
        Object value = null;
        try {
            Class type = PropertyUtils.getPropertyType(bean,
                currKey);
            boolean isNestedObject = isNestedObject(type);
            boolean isListOfNestedObjects =
                isListOfNestedObjects(currValue, type);
            if (isNestedObject)
                value = populateNestedObject(currValue, mode);
            if (isListOfNestedObjects)
                value = populateList((List) currValue, mode);
            if (!(isNestedObject || isListOfNestedObjects)) {
                Formatter formatter = getFormatter(currKey,
                    type);
                switch (mode) {
                case TO_OBJECT:
                    value =
                        formatter.unformat((String)currValue);
```

Listing 2.17 New version of the MyForm populate() method.

```
                        break;
                    case TO_STRING:
                        if (currValue == null)
                            value = (String)
                                defaultStringMap.get(currkey);
                        else
                            value = formatter.format(currValue);
                        break;
                    default:
                        throw new RuntimeException("Unknown mode: " +
                            mode);
                }
            }

            PropertyUtils.setSimpleProperty(target, currKey,
                value);
        }
        catch (InstantiationException ie) {
            throw new FormattingException(errorMsg, ie);
        }
        catch (IllegalAccessException iae) {
            throw new FormattingException(errorMsg, iae);
        }
        catch (InvocationTargetException ite) {
            throw new FormattingException(errorMsg, ite);
        }
        catch (NoSuchMethodException nsme) {
            throw new FormattingException(errorMsg, nsme);
        }
    }
}
```

Listing 2.17 *(continued)*

Listing 2.18 demonstrates the new methods called from the modified version of populate():

```
/**
 * Returns a class corresponding to the provided class. Used by
 * the infrastructure to determine the binding between
 * ActionForms and their associated JavaBean classes. This method
```

Listing 2.18 New methods called from the modified version of populate(). *(continues)*

(continued)

HANDLING NESTED ACTIONFORMS *(Continued)*

```
 * must be overridden by subclasses that contain nested objects
 * to return the appropriate types.
 *
 * @param type The given class
 * @return The Class corresponding to the provided type
 */
public Class mappedType(Class type) { return null; }
/**
 * Returns <code>true</code> if the provided object is a List
 * containing nested objects; false otherwise.
 *
 * @param object The potential List
 * @param type The class of the provided object
 * @return boolean
 */
public static boolean isListOfNestedObjects(Object object,
                                            Class type) {
    if (type == null)
        return false;
    if (List.class.isAssignableFrom(type)) {
        Iterator listIter = ((List) object).iterator();
        if (listIter.hasNext()) {
            Object obj = listIter.next();
            if (isNestedObject(obj.getClass()))
                return true;
        }
    }
    return false;
}

/**
 * Returns <code>true</code> if an object of the provided type
 * should be considered a nested object, false otherwise.
 *
 * @param type The type to be tested
 * @return boolean
 */
public static boolean isNestedObject(Class type) {
    if (type == null)
        return false;
    if (AbstractDO.class.isAssignableFrom(type) ||
        MyForm.class.isAssignableFrom(type))
            return true;
```

Listing 2.18 *(continued)*

```
        return false;
}

/**
 * If the provided List is non-null, returns a List of objects
 * populated with the values of the objects in the provided List.
 *
 * @param source The original list of objects
 * @param mode The direction in which binding is taking place
 * @return A List of objects
 */
protected List populateList(List source, int mode)
    throws InstantiationException, IllegalAccessException {
    if (source == null)
        return null;
    ArrayList target = new ArrayList();

    Iterator sourceIter = source.iterator();
    while (sourceIter.hasNext()) {
        Object currObj = sourceIter.next();
        if (currObj instanceof AbstractDO ||
            currObj instanceof MyForm) {
            Object newObj = populateNestedObject(currObj, mode);
            target.add(newObj);
        }
    }
    return target;
}

/**
 * If the provided object is non-null, returns a new object
 * populated with values from the provided object. The new object
 * will be of the type returned by a call to the
 * <code>mappedType()</code> method, which subclasses should
 * override to return an appropriate type.
 *
 * @param source The nested object
 * @param mode The direction in which binding is taking place
 * @return An object populated with values from the nested
 * object.
 */
```

Listing 2.18 *(continued)*

(continued)

HANDLING NESTED ACTIONFORMS *(Continued)*

```
    protected Object populateNestedObject(Object source, int mode)
        throws InstantiationException, IllegalAccessException {
        if (source == null)
            return null;
        Class sourceClass = source.getClass();
        Class targetClass = mappedType(sourceClass);
        if (targetClass == null)
            throw new FormattingException(
                "No target class defined for " + sourceClass);
        Object target = targetClass.newInstance();
        if (target instanceof MyForm)
            ((MyForm) target).populate(source , mode);
        else
            ((MyForm) source).populate(target, mode);
        return target;
    }
```

Listing 2.18 *(continued)*

We can refactor the populate() method to improve readability and maintainability by splitting it into several methods, as in Listing 2.19:

```
public void populate(Object bean, int mode) {
    String errorMsg = "Unable to format values from bean: "
        + bean;
    Object target = (mode == TO_STRING ? bean : this);
    Map valueMap = mapRepresentation(target, mode);

    Iterator keyIter = valueMap.keySet().iterator();
    while (keyIter.hasNext()) {
        String currKey = (String)keyIter.next();
        Object currValue = valueMap.get(currKey);
        try {
            populateProperty(bean, currKey, currValue, mode);
        }
        catch (InstantiationException ie) {
            throw new FormattingException(errorMsg, ie);
        }
        catch (IllegalAccessException iae) {
            throw new FormattingException(errorMsg, iae);
        }
        catch (InvocationTargetException ite) {
```

Listing 2.19 Populate() method split into several methods.

```java
                    throw new FormattingException(errorMsg, ite);
        }
        catch (NoSuchMethodException nsme) {
            throw new FormattingException(errorMsg, nsme);
        }
    }
}

/**
 * Populates the property identified by the provided key.
 * Handling is provided for nested properties and Lists of
 * nested properties.
 *
 * @param bean The Java bean that contains the property
 * @param key The name of the property
 * @param obj The new value for the property
 * @param mode Whether to populate the bean or the form
 */
protected void populateProperty(Object bean,
                                String key,
                                Object obj,
                                int mode)
    throws InstantiationException, IllegalAccessException,
        NoSuchMethodException, InvocationTargetException {

    Object target = (mode == TO_STRING ? this : bean);
    Class type = PropertyUtils.getPropertyType(bean, key);
    Object value = null;

    boolean isNestedObject = isNestedObject(type);
    boolean isListOfNestedObjects =
        isListOfNestedObjects(obj, type);
    if (isNestedObject)
        value = populateNestedObject(obj, mode);
    if (isListOfNestedObjects)
        value = populateList((List) obj, mode);
    if (!(isNestedObject || isListOfNestedObjects))
        value = convert(type, key, obj, mode);
    PropertyUtils.setSimpleProperty(target, key, value);
}
/**
```

Listing 2.19 *(continued)*

(continued)

HANDLING NESTED ACTIONFORMS *(Continued)*

```
 * Converts the provided object either from a String to a Java
 * type or vice versa, depending on the value of
 * <code>mode</code>.
 *
 * @param type The class of the associated bean property
 * @param key The name of the associated bean property
 * @param obj The object to convert
 * @param mode Whether conversion is to String or to Java type
 * @return The converted object
 */
protected Object convert(Class type,
                        String key,
                        Object obj,
                        int mode)
    throws InstantiationException, IllegalAccessException,
        NoSuchMethodException, InvocationTargetException {

    Object convertedObj = null;
    Formatter formatter = getFormatter(key, type);
    switch (mode) {
        case TO_OBJECT:
            convertedObj = formatter.unformat((String)obj);
            break;
        case TO_STRING:
            if (currValue == null)
                value = (String) defaultStringMap.get(currkey);
            else
                value = formatter.format(currValue);
            break;
        default:
            throw new RuntimeException("Unknown mode: " + mode);
    }
    return convertedObj;
}
```

Listing 2.19 *(continued)*

Pitfall 2.3: Copy/Paste Validation

Struts provides a simple hook, the empty validate() method in the ActionForm class, as a starting point for validation of HTML form values submitted in the request. Your subclasses can override this method to provide the necessary validation logic. While it may be tempting simply to hand-code whatever logic is needed on a case-by-case basis, there are a number of problems with this approach.

The most obvious problem is the proliferation of copy/paste code across all of the ActionForms that perform validation, and even within individual ActionForms. For example, simply checking that a required field has been set involves testing to see if the value is null or an empty string, as shown here:

```
if (amount == null || amount.trim().equals("")) {
    errors.add("amount", new ActionError("error.required"));
}
```

In some applications (particularly those of the business-to-business variety) a single ActionForm may have dozens of required fields, so these checks can add up to quite a bit of code. Matters get much worse if we have to perform more complex validations on the values. For instance, to check whether the amount in the preceding example is within a given range, we might be forced to add a block of code like this:

```
BigDecimal value = null;
try {
    DecimalFormat formatter =
        new DecimalFormat(CURRENCY_FORMAT);
    Number number = formatter.parse(amount.trim());
    value = new BigDecimal(number.doubleValue());
}
catch (NumberFormatException nfe) {
    errors.add("amount", new ActionError("error.currency"));
}
catch (ParseException pe) {
    errors.add("amount", new ActionError("error.currency"));
}

if (value != null &&
    (value.compareTo(new BigDecimal(MIN_AMOUNT)) < 0 ||
     value.compareTo(new BigDecimal(MAX_AMOUNT)) > 0)) {
        errors.add("amount", new ActionError("error.range"));
}
```

It's not hard to imagine a validate() method growing to hundreds of lines of code in a large ActionForm if thrown together in this slapdash manner. While that would be bad enough, there are other, more subtle downsides to this pitfall. As you can see in the preceding block of code, we had to convert the string value submitted in the request to a BigDecimal in order to perform the range comparisons. This also served to ensure that the string could be parsed as a BigDecimal.

Unfortunately, we will have to convert this same BigDecimal property again later, when it is transferred to the associated value object. That means that there is a redundant block of conversion code somewhere else that must be kept in sync with the code in all of our validate() methods that contain similar logic.

Another problem is that we have no default validation rules, so a rule must be hand-coded for every field. That makes our codebase a lot more fragile, in that adding, renaming, or changing the type of any variable requires changes not only to the property fields, but also to the validation code in every case.

While aspects of this pitfall can be partially mitigated by abstracting common functionality out into helper classes, such as the Formatters presented earlier in this chapter, the problems remain fundamentally unchanged. And while the pitfall example presented represents the worst-case scenario, code of this sort is unfortunately all too common in actual Struts-based applications.

One way to avoid this pitfall is to use the ValidatorForm, added in Struts 1.1. ValidatorForm is a subclass of ActionForm that implements the inherited validate() method to invoke generic validation functionality in the Jakarta Commons Validator framework. The Validator framework provides a comprehensive mechanism for declarative specification of validation rules in XML, and most of the existing literature on Struts offers explanations and examples of its usage. While this is quite useful, there are some potential downsides.

The Validator framework in some cases (depending on the rules you specify) performs a redundant type conversion step, leaving the door open for a potential mismatch between its conversion code and yours. And while the Validator solution also provides for validation via regex masks, if a mask is specified incorrectly or if there is a discrepancy in the conversion code bases, a value could pass validation but then fail later during type conversion, leading to runtime errors.

Then, too, Validator doesn't provide default validation based on type, so you have to explicitly bind every field that requires validation to one or more rules. This means that any change to ActionForm properties requires modifying the XML validation spec to add, delete, or modify the corresponding entries.

Example

The example in Listing 2.20 illustrates the worst-case scenario of this pitfall—hard-coded validation. The InvoiceForm class that follows contains a validate() method that performs validation on only two fields: amount and billingDate. There are only two rules associated with the fields—each is a required field, and each must be within a given range. That is, the amount has to be within a minimum and maximum value, and the billingDate cannot be later than today.

```java
package com.aboutobjects.pitfalls;

import java.math.BigDecimal;
import java.text.DecimalFormat;
import java.text.ParseException;
import java.text.ParsePosition;
import java.text.SimpleDateFormat;
import java.util.ArrayList;
import java.util.Date;

import javax.servlet.http.HttpServletRequest;

import org.apache.struts.action.Action;
import org.apache.struts.action.ActionForm;
import org.apache.struts.action.ActionError;
import org.apache.struts.action.ActionErrors;
import org.apache.struts.action.ActionMapping;
import org.apache.struts.action.ActionMessage;
import org.apache.struts.action.ActionMessages;

public class InvoiceForm extends ActionForm
{
    /**  The default format for currency values */
    public final static String CURRENCY_FORMAT = "#,##0.00";
    /** The default format for date values */
    public final static String DATE_FORMAT = "MM/dd/yyyy";
    /** The minimum allowable currency amount*/
    public final static String MIN_AMOUNT = "0.00";
    /** The maximum allowable currency amount*/
    public final static String MAX_AMOUNT = "9999.99";

    private String invoiceNumber;
    private String billingDate;
    private String amount;

    public ActionErrors validate(ActionMapping mapping,
                       HttpServletRequest request) {
```

Listing 2.20 InvoiceForm.java with hard-coded validation. *(continues)*

```java
ActionErrors errors = new ActionErrors();

// amount must be set and must be between 0 and 9,999.99.
if (amount == null || amount.trim().equals("")) {
    errors.add("amount", new ActionError("error.required"));
}
else {
    BigDecimal value = null;
    try {
        DecimalFormat formatter =
            new DecimalFormat(CURRENCY_FORMAT);
        Number number = formatter.parse(amount.trim());
        value = new BigDecimal(number.doubleValue());
    }
    catch (NumberFormatException nfe) {
        errors.add("amount", new ActionError("error.currency"));
    }
    catch (ParseException pe) {
        errors.add("amount", new ActionError("error.currency"));
    }

    if (value != null &&
        (value.compareTo(new BigDecimal(MIN_AMOUNT)) < 0 ||
         value.compareTo(new BigDecimal(MAX_AMOUNT)) > 0)) {
            errors.add("amount",
                new ActionError("error.range"));
    }
}

// billingDate must be set and must not be later than today.
if (billingDate == null || billingDate.trim().equals("")) {
    errors.add("billingDate",
        new ActionError("error.required"));
}
else {
    Date date = null;
    SimpleDateFormat formatter =
        new SimpleDateFormat(DATE_FORMAT);
    formatter.setLenient(false);
    ParsePosition position = new ParsePosition(0);
    date = formatter.parse(billingDate.trim(), position);

    if (position.getErrorIndex() != -1) {
        errors.add("billingDate",
            new ActionError("error.billingDate"));
    }
    else if (date.after(new Date())) {
        errors.add("billingDate",
            new ActionError("error.range"));
```

Listing 2.20 *(continued)*

```
            }
        }

        // Post a global message instructing user to clean up
        // validation errors and resubmit
        if (errors.size() > 0) {
            ActionMessage message =
                new ActionMessage("message.validation");
            ActionMessages messages = new ActionMessages();
            messages.add(ActionMessages.GLOBAL_MESSAGE, message);
            request.setAttribute(Action.MESSAGE_KEY, messages);
        }

        return errors;
    }

    public String getInvoiceNumber() { return invoiceNumber; }
    public void setInvoiceNumber(String invoiceNumber) {
        this.invoiceNumber = invoiceNumber;
    }

    public String getBillingDate() { return billingDate; }
    public void setBillingDate(String billingDate) {
        this.billingDate = billingDate;
    }

    public String getAmount() { return amount; }
    public void setAmount(String amount) {
        this.amount = amount;
    }
}
```

Listing 2.20 *(continued)*

Solving Pitfall 2.3: Consolidate and Generalize Validation Code

As noted previously, the Formatter classes we designed for the solutions to the earlier pitfalls in this chapter could be helpful in resolving the current pitfall. For example, in the validate() method, we could have used a CurrencyFormatter and a DateFormatter to convert the amount and billingDate values. That alone would ensure consistency and simplify maintenance significantly because the code for any given conversion would be in only one place. Although conversion might be called twice on each field, we would be guaranteed that precisely the same conversion would be performed. Any changes to a given conversion would be applied to only one method, so we wouldn't have to worry about keeping copy/paste implementations in sync.

It would be even better if we could leverage the reflection mechanism we added to MyForm in the previous solutions to aid not only in formatting and type conversion, but in validation as well, especially because we have already noted how validation and type conversion are so closely intertwined. In fact, from an architectural perspective, it makes little sense to decouple these related processes.

On further reflection, we can surmise that MyForm's populate() method could be made to serve our purpose in combining type conversion and validation in a single step. The refactored solution that follows demonstrates how to implement this approach. We will use as our basis a simplified version of the populate() code presented at the end of Pitfall 2.2, where we refactored it into three separate methods, as in Listing 2.21.

```java
public void populate(Object bean, int mode) {
    String errorMsg = "Unable to format values from bean: " + bean;
    Object target = (mode == TO_STRING ? bean : this);
    Map valueMap = mapRepresentation(target, mode);

    Iterator keyIter = valueMap.keySet().iterator();
    while (keyIter.hasNext()) {
        String currKey = (String)keyIter.next();
        Object currValue = valueMap.get(currKey);
        try {
            populateProperty(bean, currKey, currValue, mode);
        }
        catch (InstantiationException ie) {
            throw new FormattingException(errorMsg, ie);
        }
        catch (IllegalAccessException iae) {
            throw new FormattingException(errorMsg, iae);
        }
        catch (InvocationTargetException ite) {
            throw new FormattingException(errorMsg, ite);
        }
        catch (NoSuchMethodException nsme) {
            throw new FormattingException(errorMsg, nsme);
        }
    }
}

/**
 * Converts the provided object either from a String to a Java type or
```

Listing 2.21 MyForm's populate() method refactored into three separate methods.

```java
 * vice versa, depending on the value of <code>mode</code>.
 *
 * @param type The class of the associated bean property
 * @param key The name of the associated bean property
 * @param obj The object to convert
 * @param mode Whether conversion is to String or to Java type
 * @return The converted object
 */
protected Object convert(Class type, String key, Object obj, int mode)
    throws InstantiationException, IllegalAccessException,
        NoSuchMethodException, InvocationTargetException {

    Object convertedObj = null;
    Formatter formatter = Formatter.getFormatter(type);
    switch (mode) {
        case TO_OBJECT:
            convertedObj = formatter.unformat((String)obj);
            break;
        case TO_STRING:
            if (obj == null) {
                convertedObj =
                    (String) defaultStringMap.get(key);
            }
            else {
                convertedObj = formatter.format(obj);
            }
            break;
        default:
            throw new RuntimeException("Unknown mode: " + mode);
    }
    return convertedObj;
}

/**
 * Populates the property identified by the provided key.
 *
 * @param bean The Java bean that contains the property
 * @param key The name of the property
 * @param obj The new value for the property
 * @param mode Whether to populate the bean or the form
 */
protected void populateProperty(Object bean,
                                String key,
                                Object obj,
                                int mode)
    throws InstantiationException, IllegalAccessException,
```

Listing 2.21 *(continued)*

```
                NoSuchMethodException, InvocationTargetException {

    Object target = (mode == TO_STRING ? this : bean);
    Class type = PropertyUtils.getPropertyType(bean, key);
    Object value = null;

    value = convert(type, key, obj, mode);

    PropertyUtils.setSimpleProperty(target, key, value);
}
```

Listing 2.21 *(continued)*

Step-by-Step

1. Implement type-based validation in your ActionForm base class as follows:

    a. Add a bean property to store a reference to the value object associated with the ActionForm.

    b. Add a Formatter property to the FormattingException class from the previous pitfall, to transmit state required in the next step.

    c. Add code to the base class's populate() method to generate an error message if a FormattingException is thrown by a Formatter's unformat() method.

    d. Implement a validate() method that automatically invokes populate().

    e. Modify Action classes to get and set the bean on the ActionForm as necessary. Remove any type conversion and bean population code.

2. Test the new functionality to ensure that it works properly. Once it is working, proceed to the next step.

3. Catalog the types of validation that are currently being performed in your ActionForms.

4. Pick one of the types of validation that is not currently handled by the new validation code, and add code to your ActionForm base class to implement it generically, as follows:

    a. First add a validationMap property.

    b. Now create an addValidationRule() method to add entries to the validationMap.

c. Add a convenience method for the specific type of validation you are implementing.

d. Add code to populate() to execute the validation rule.

e. Remove the corresponding validation code from the validate() implementations in all subclasses.

f. Be sure to add a call to super() in all subclass implementations of validate().

5. Once the the new validation code is working correctly, repeat for each additional type of validation that needs to be performed. (Note that you may have some validation code that doesn't easily lend itself to generalization. Leave such code in place for now.)

6. Deploy and test.

Example

We'll begin solving this pitfall by modifying the MyForm class from Pitfall 2.2's solution to treat exceptions thrown by Formatter's unformat() method as validation errors. First we'll add a bean property:

```
/** The value object associated with this form */
private transient Object bean;

public Object getBean() { return bean; }
public void setBean(Object bean) { this.bean = bean; }
```

We will need to add a property to the FormattingException class to maintain a reference to the Formatter instance that threw it, as shown here:

```
private Formatter formatter;
public Formatter getFormatter() { return formatter; }
public void setFormatter(Formatter formatter) {
    this.formatter = formatter;
}
```

Next, we'll modify the convert() method to catch FormattingException and call setFormatter() on it before rethrowing it.

```
protected Object convert(Class type, String key, Object obj, int mode)
    throws InstantiationException, IllegalAccessException,
        NoSuchMethodException, InvocationTargetException {

    Object convertedObj = null;
    Formatter formatter = getFormatter(key, type);
    try {
        switch (mode) {
```

```
            case TO_OBJECT:
                convertedObj = formatter.unformat((String) obj);
                break;
            case TO_STRING:
                if (obj == null) {
                    convertedObj =
                        (String) defaultStringMap.get(key);
                }
                else {
                    convertedObj = formatter.format(obj);
                }
                break;
            default:
                throw new RuntimeException("Unknown mode: "
                    + mode);
        }
    }
    catch (FormattingException e) {
        e.setFormatter(formatter);
        throw e;
    }

    return convertedObj;
}
```

Now we can add code to populateProperty() to catch any FormattingExceptions thrown during attempts to convert strings to Java types, and we can generate corresponding ActionError instances, as shown here:

```
protected ActionErrors populateProperty(Object bean,
                                        String key,
                                        Object obj,
                                        int mode)
    throws InstantiationException, IllegalAccessException,
        NoSuchMethodException, InvocationTargetException {

    Object target = (mode == TO_STRING ? this : bean);
    Class type = PropertyUtils.getPropertyType(bean, key);
    ActionErrors errors = new ActionErrors();
    Object value = null;

    if (mode == TO_STRING) {
        value = convert(type, key, obj, mode);
    }
    else {
        try {
            String errorKey = null;
            value = convert(type, key, obj, mode);
        }
        catch (FormattingException e) {
            String errorKey =
```

```
                e.getFormatter().getErrorKey();
            errors.add(key, new ActionError(errorKey));
        }
    }

    PropertyUtils.setSimpleProperty(target, key, value);
    return errors;
}
```

The populate() method can now return the ActionErrors collected during its execution. Note that we are caching the associated value object, so that it will be available when the corresponding HTML form is submitted. We need to do this because we are going to be calling populate() from MyForm's validate() method, which is invoked by the framework prior to the corresponding Action's execute() method. (Formerly, we depended on the execute() method to populate the bean.)

```
protected ActionErrors populate(Object bean, int mode) {
    String errorMsg = "Unable to format values from bean: " + bean;
    Object target = (mode == TO_STRING ? bean : this);
    Map valueMap = mapRepresentation(target, mode);
    ActionErrors errors = new ActionErrors();

    if (mode == TO_STRING)
        setBean(bean);

    Iterator keyIter = valueMap.keySet().iterator();
    while (keyIter.hasNext()) {
        String currKey = (String)keyIter.next();
        Object currValue = valueMap.get(currKey);
        try {
            ActionErrors currErrors =
                populateProperty(bean, currKey, currValue, mode);
            errors.add(currErrors); // requires Struts 1.1b3 or later
        }
        catch (InstantiationException ie) {
            throw new FormattingException(errorMsg, ie);
        }
        catch (IllegalAccessException iae) {
            throw new FormattingException(errorMsg, iae);
        }
        catch (InvocationTargetException ite) {
            throw new FormattingException(errorMsg, ite);
        }
        catch (NoSuchMethodException nsme) {
            throw new FormattingException(errorMsg, nsme);
        }
    }
    return errors;
}
```

Finally, we will add a validate() implementation to MyForm:

```
public ActionErrors validate(ActionMapping mapping,
                             HttpServletRequest request) {
    ActionErrors errors = populate(this.bean, TO_OBJECT);
    return errors;
}
```

We should now be almost ready to test our new implementation. Before we do that, though, we need to remove the old validation code from InvoiceForm. Note the call to super() in the new version of validate():

```
public ActionErrors validate(ActionMapping mapping,
                             HttpServletRequest request) {

    ActionErrors errors = super.validate(mapping, request);

    // Post a global message instructing user to clean up
    // validation errors and resubmit
    if (errors.size() > 0) {
        ActionMessage message =
            new ActionMessage("message.validation");
        ActionMessages messages = new ActionMessages();
        messages.add(ActionMessages.GLOBAL_MESSAGE, message);
        request.setAttribute(Globals.MESSAGE_KEY, messages);
    }

    return errors;
}
```

There is one last little detail. As long as the action mapping in struts-config.xml contains validate="true", the validate() method will be called when the form is submitted, and the corresponding bean will be populated automatically. In the relatively rare circumstances where this is not the case, the corresponding Action will still have to call populate() directly, as before, to transfer values from the ActionForm to the bean. Otherwise, though, such calls are now unnecessary and, in fact, redundant and should therefore be removed.

Once we have tested our solution and gotten it working correctly, we can begin to add support for additional types of validation. First we will add a generic mechanism for capturing validation rules, which will be contained in a validationMap field.

```
/** The validation rules for this form */
private Map validationMap = new HashMap();
```

Note that at this point we won't be needing accessor methods for the validationMap. You can, of course, add them if you wish. This would allow

Actions to modify the Map dynamically, giving your application greater runtime flexibility. It is up to you whether you want to allow this.

A new method, addValidationRule(), will be responsible for adding rules to the Map. Note that each entry is a Map of rules, keyed by property name.

```
public void addValidationRule(String key, String rule, Object value) {
    Map values = (Map) validationMap.get(key);
    if (values == null) {
        values = new HashMap();
        validationMap.put(key, values);
    }
    values.put(rule, value);
}
```

Now we're ready to add validation rules. Let's begin by adding a simple rule for required fields. Each time we add a new rule type, we implement two new methods on MyForm, one to add the rule to the validation Map and the other to execute the rule:

```
public void addRequiredFields(String[] keys) {
    for (int i = 0; i < keys.length; i++) {
        addValidationRule(keys[i], "required", Boolean.TRUE);
    }
}

protected boolean validateRequired(String key, String value) {
    Map rules = (Map) validationMap.get(key);
    if (rules == null)
        return true;
    Boolean required = (Boolean) rules.get("required");
    if (required == null)
        return true;
    boolean isRequired = required.booleanValue();
    boolean isBlank = (value == null || value.trim().equals(""));

    return !(isRequired && isBlank);
}
```

Finally, we need to modify the populateProperty() method so that it will call the new validateRequired() method:

```
protected ActionErrors populateProperty(Object bean,
                                        String key,
                                        Object obj,
                                        int mode)
    throws InstantiationException, IllegalAccessException,
        NoSuchMethodException, InvocationTargetException {
```

```
        Object target = (mode == TO_STRING ? this : bean);
        Class type = PropertyUtils.getPropertyType(bean, key);
        ActionErrors errors = new ActionErrors();
        Object value = null;

        if (mode == TO_STRING) {
            value = convert(type, key, obj, mode);
        }
        else {
            try {
                String errorKey = null;
                value = convert(type, key, obj, mode);

                if (!validateRequired(key,(String)obj))
                    errorKey = "error.required";
                if (errorKey != null)
                    errors.add(key, new ActionError(errorKey));
            }
            catch (FormattingException e) {
                String errorKey =
                    e.getFormatter().getErrorKey();
                errors.add(key, new ActionError(errorKey));
            }
        }

        PropertyUtils.setSimpleProperty(target, key, value);
        return errors;
    }
```

We can now add code to InvoiceForm's constructor to set up the required fields rule:

```
public InvoiceForm() {
    ...
    addRequiredFields(new String[] { "billingDate", "amount" });
}
```

Once we have tested our rule, we can add another. For example, to add a range check, we can follow the same procedure. In this case, though, we will create a new helper class, Range, to make things a bit easier. Range simply represents a range of objects that implement the Comparable interface. Note that a Range may be unbounded, if one of its two values is null. The isInRange() Boolean method provides a simple means of determining if a given object falls within the range, as shown in Listing 2.22.

```java
package com.aboutobjects.pitfalls;

import java.io.Serializable;

public class Range implements Serializable {
    Comparable minValue;
    Comparable maxValue;

    public Range(Comparable minValue, Comparable maxValue) {
        setMinValue(minValue);
        setMaxValue(maxValue);
    }

    public Comparable getMinValue() { return minValue; }
    public void setMinValue(Comparable minValue) {
        this.minValue = minValue;
    }

    public Comparable getMaxValue() { return maxValue; }
    public void setMaxValue(Comparable maxValue) {
        this.maxValue = maxValue;
    }

    boolean isInRange(Comparable value) {
        if (value == null)
            return false;
        if ((minValue == null || value.compareTo(minValue) >= 0) &&
            (maxValue == null || value.compareTo(maxValue) <= 0))
                return true;
        return false;
    }
}
```

Listing 2.22 Range.java.

Here is the pair of new methods to be added to MyForm to implement range validation:

```java
protected boolean validateRange(String key, Object value) {
    Map rules = (Map) validationMap.get(key);
    if (rules == null)
        return true;
    Range range = (Range) rules.get("range");
    return range == null || range.isInRange((Comparable) value);
}

protected boolean validateRequired(String key, String value) {
    Map rules = (Map) validationMap.get(key);
```

```java
        if (rules == null)
            return true;
        Boolean required = (Boolean) rules.get("required");
        if (required == null)
            return true;
        boolean isRequired = required.booleanValue();
        boolean isBlank = (value == null || value.trim().equals(""));

        return !(isRequired && isBlank);
    }
```

We then need to modify the populateProperty() method to call validateRequired(), as shown here:

```java
    protected ActionErrors populateProperty(Object bean,
                                            String key,
                                            Object obj,
                                            int mode)
        throws InstantiationException, IllegalAccessException,
            NoSuchMethodException, InvocationTargetException {

        Object target = (mode == TO_STRING ? this : bean);
        Class type = PropertyUtils.getPropertyType(bean, key);
        ActionErrors errors = new ActionErrors();
        Object value = null;

        if (mode == TO_STRING) {
            value = convert(type, key, obj, mode);
        }
        else {
            try {
                String errorKey = null;
                value = convert(type, key, obj, mode);

                if (!validateRequired(key,(String)obj))
                    errorKey = "error.required";
                else if (!validateRange(key, value))
                    errorKey = "error.range";

                if (errorKey != null)
                    errors.add(key, new ActionError(errorKey));
            }
            catch (FormattingException e) {
                String errorKey =
                    e.getFormatter().getErrorKey();
                errors.add(key, new ActionError(errorKey));
            }
        }

        PropertyUtils.setSimpleProperty(target, key, value);
        return errors;
    }
```

Now all we need to do is to add code to InvoiceForm's constructor to set up the rules for validating ranges, and we'll be ready to test the new code:

```java
public InvoiceForm() {
    ...
    addRequiredFields(new String[] { "billingDate", "amount" });
    addRange("billingDate", (Comparable) null, new Date());
    addRange("amount",
            new BigDecimal(MIN_AMOUNT),
            new BigDecimal(MAX_AMOUNT));
}
```

Listings 2.23 and 2.24 show the complete, refactored implementations of MyForm and InvoiceForm, respectively.

```java
package com.aboutobjects.pitfalls;

import java.lang.reflect.InvocationTargetException;
import java.math.BigDecimal;
import java.util.ArrayList;
import java.util.HashMap;
import java.util.Iterator;
import java.util.Map;

import javax.servlet.http.HttpServletRequest;

import org.apache.commons.beanutils.PropertyUtils;
import org.apache.struts.action.ActionError;
import org.apache.struts.action.ActionErrors;
import org.apache.struts.action.ActionForm;
import org.apache.struts.action.ActionMapping;

/**
 * An abstract base class for ActionForms that adds support for
 * automatic formatting and unformatting of string values and for the
 * transfer of the resulting values between itself and the given bean.
 * The <code>populate()</code> method provides an entry point to
 * this functionality, while the <code>keysToSkip()</code> method allows
 * subclasses to specify fields that should not be populated.
 * <p>
 * Additional methods are provided to allow subclasses to override
 * formatting defaults. The <code>setDefaultString()</code> method
 * allows callers to specify overrides for the default string used
 * to represent a <code>null</code> for a given property. Similarly, the
 * <code>setFormatterType()</code> method allows callers to specify a
 * formatting type other than the default for a given property.
 * <p>
```

Listing 2.23 MyForm.java refactored to support generic validation. *(continues)*

136   Chapter 2

```
 * Developers can also specify validation rules by invoking
 * <code>addRange()</code> to add a range validation or
 * <code>addRequiredFields() to add required field validations for an
 * array of property names.
 */
public abstract class MyForm extends ActionForm {
    /** Indicates that conversion is from string to object */
    public final static int TO_OBJECT = 0;
    /** Indicates that conversion is from object to string */
    public final static int TO_STRING = 1;
    /** Formatter class to use for given property. Overrides default. */
    private Map formatMap = new HashMap();
    /** The value object associated with this form */
    private transient Object bean;
    /** The validation rules for this form */
    private Map validationMap = new HashMap();
    /**
     * The strings to display when null values are encountered.
     * Keys correspond to fields in the Form. The presence of a given
     * key indicates that the value provided in the map should be used
     * instead of the normal default string.
     */
    private Map defaultStringMap = new HashMap();

    /**
     * Populates the bean associated with this form and returns an
     * ActionErrors populated with validation errors, if any.
     * @return Validation errors.
     */
    public ActionErrors validate(ActionMapping mapping,
                                 HttpServletRequest request) {
        ActionErrors errors = populate(this.bean, TO_OBJECT);
        return errors;
    }

    /**
     * Populates the form with values from the given bean,
     * converting Java types to formatted string values suitable
     * for presentation in the user interface. Conversions are
     * applied automatically by introspecting the type of each
     * property and finding the appropriate Formatter class to use
     * based on the type information.
     * <p>
     * This behavior can be customized by calling
     * <code>setFormatterType(String key, Class type)</code>
     * with an alternative Formatter class for a given property name.
     * <p>
     * If null values are encountered in the bean, MyForm will
```

Listing 2.23   (continued)

```java
     * be populated with the default string supplied by the
     * Formatter, unless the default has been overridden by calling
     * to <code>setDefaultString(String key, String value)</code> with
     * an alternative string.
     *
     * @param bean The bean to populate
     * @return Validation errors
     */
    public ActionErrors populate(Object bean) {
        return populate(bean, TO_STRING);
    }

    /**
     * Adds an entry for the provided rule to the validation map.
     * @param key The name of the property to which the rule applies
     * @param rule The name of the rule
     * @param value A value or values used in executing the rule
     */
    public void addValidationRule(String key, String rule, Object value)
{
        Map values = (Map) validationMap.get(key);
        if (values == null) {
            values = new HashMap();
            validationMap.put(key, values);
        }
        values.put(rule, value);
    }

    /**
     * Associates the "required field" rule with the provided keys
     * @param keys The names of the required fields
     */
    public void addRequiredFields(String[] keys) {
        for (int i = 0; i < keys.length; i++) {
            addValidationRule(keys[i], "required", Boolean.TRUE);
        }
    }

    /**
     * Adds a range rule for the provided key
     * @param key The name of the property to which the rule applies
     * @param min The minimum allowable value
     * @param max The maximum allowable value
     */
    public void addRange(String key, Comparable min, Comparable max) {
        Range range = new Range(min, max);
        addValidationRule(key, "range", range);
```

Listing 2.23 (continued)

```java
}

/**
 * Sets the default value to display for the given key when the
 * property value in the associated bean is <code>null</code>.
 *
 * @param key the name of the property
 * @param value the value to display
 */
public void setDefaultString(String key, String value) {
    defaultStringMap.put(key, value);
}


/**
 * Sets the default Formatter class to use for the given key
 *
 * @param key the name of the property
 * @param value the value to display
 */
public void setFormatterType(String key, Class type) {
    if (!Formatter.class.isAssignableFrom(type))
        throw new FormattingException(type + "must be a Formatter");
    formatMap.put(key, type);
}

public Object getBean() { return bean; }
public void setBean(Object bean) { this.bean = bean; }

/**
 * Transfers values to and from the given bean, depending on the
 * value of <code>mode</code>. If the given mode is
 * <code>TO_STRING</code>, populates
 * the instance by introspecting the specified bean,
 * converting any typed values to formatted strings, and
 * then using reflection to invoke its own String-based setter
 * methods. If the mode is <code>TO_OBJECT</code>, performs the
 * inverse operation, unformatting and converting properties of
 * the MyForm instance and populating the resulting values in the
 * given bean.
 * <p>
 * If null values are encountered in the bean, MyForm will
 * be populated with the default string associated with the given
 * type. The default null values can be overridden by calling
 * <code>setDefaultString(String key, String value)</code> with
 * an alternative string. The default Formatter to use can be
 * overridden by calling
 * <code>setFormatterType(String key, Class type)</code> with an
 * alternative Formatter class.
```

Listing 2.23 *(continued)*

```
     * <p>
     * You ordinarily don't call this method directly; it is called
     * automatically by <code>validate()</code>.
     *
     * @param bean An object containing the values to be populated
     * @param mode Whether conversion is to String or to Java type
     * @return Validation errors
     */
    protected ActionErrors populate(Object bean, int mode) {
        String errorMsg = "Unable to format values from bean: " + bean;
        Object target = (mode == TO_STRING ? bean : this);
        Map valueMap = mapRepresentation(target, mode);
        ActionErrors errors = new ActionErrors();

        if (mode == TO_STRING)
            setBean(bean);

        Iterator keyIter = valueMap.keySet().iterator();
        while (keyIter.hasNext()) {
            String currKey = (String)keyIter.next();
            Object currValue = valueMap.get(currKey);
            try {
                ActionErrors currErrors =
                    populateProperty(bean, currKey, currValue, mode);
                errors.add(currErrors);
            }
            catch (InstantiationException ie) {
                throw new FormattingException(errorMsg, ie);
            }
            catch (IllegalAccessException iae) {
                throw new FormattingException(errorMsg, iae);
            }
            catch (InvocationTargetException ite) {
                throw new FormattingException(errorMsg, ite);
            }
            catch (NoSuchMethodException nsme) {
                throw new FormattingException(errorMsg, nsme);
            }
        }
        return errors;
    }

    /**
     * Converts the provided object either from a String to a Java type
     * or vice versa, depending on the value of <code>mode</code>.
     *
     * @param type The class of the associated bean property
     * @param key The name of the associated bean property
```

Listing 2.23 (continued)

```
     * @param obj The object to convert
     * @param mode Whether conversion is to String or to Java type
     * @return The converted object
     */
    protected Object convert(Class type,
                             String key,
                             Object obj,
                             int mode)
        throws InstantiationException, IllegalAccessException,
            NoSuchMethodException, InvocationTargetException {

        Object convertedObj = null;
        Formatter formatter = getFormatter(key, type);
        try {
            switch (mode) {
                case TO_OBJECT:
                    convertedObj = formatter.unformat((String) obj);
                    break;
                case TO_STRING:
                    if (obj == null) {
                        convertedObj =
                            (String) defaultStringMap.get(key);
                    }
                    else {
                        convertedObj = formatter.format(obj);
                    }
                    break;
                default:
                    throw new RuntimeException("Unknown mode: "
                        + mode);
            }
        }
        catch (FormattingException e) {
            e.setFormatter(formatter);
            throw e;
        }

        return convertedObj;
    }

    /**
     * Populates the property identified by the provided key. Handling
     * is provided for nested properties and Lists of nested properties.
     *
     * @param bean The Java bean that contains the property
     * @param key The name of the property
     * @param obj The new value for the property
     * @param mode Whether to populate the bean or the form
     */
```

Listing 2.23 *(continued)*

```java
    protected ActionErrors populateProperty(Object bean,
                                            String key,
                                            Object obj,
                                            int mode)
        throws InstantiationException, IllegalAccessException,
               NoSuchMethodException, InvocationTargetException {

        Object target = (mode == TO_STRING ? this : bean);
        Class type = PropertyUtils.getPropertyType(bean, key);
        ActionErrors errors = new ActionErrors();
        Object value = null;

        if (mode == TO_STRING) {
            value = convert(type, key, obj, mode);
        }
        else {
            try {
                String errorKey = null;
                value = convert(type, key, obj, mode);

                if (!validateRequired(key,(String)obj))
                    errorKey = "error.required";
                else if (!validateRange(key, value))
                    errorKey = "error.range";
                if (errorKey != null)
                    errors.add(key, new ActionError(errorKey));
            }
            catch (FormattingException e) {
                String errorKey =
                    e.getFormatter().getErrorKey();
                errors.add(key, new ActionError(errorKey));
            }
        }

        PropertyUtils.setSimpleProperty(target, key, value);
        return errors;
}

/**
 * Returns <code>false</code> if there is a rule corresponding to
 * the provided key and the given value does not fall within it;
 * <code>true</code> otherwise.
 * @param key The key under which the rule is stored
 * @param value The value to be validated
 * @return The result of the validation
 */
protected boolean validateRange(String key, Object value) {
    Map rules = (Map) validationMap.get(key);
```

Listing 2.23 *(continued)*

Chapter 2

```java
        if (rules == null)
            return true;
        Range range = (Range) rules.get("range");
        return range == null || range.isInRange((Comparable) value);
    }

    /**
     * Returns <code>false</code> if the provided value is a required
     * field and is blank or null; <code>true</code> otherwise.
     * @param key The name of the field to be validated
     * @param value The value to be validated
     * @return The result of the validation
     */
    protected boolean validateRequired(String key, String value) {
        Map rules = (Map) validationMap.get(key);
        if (rules == null)
            return true;
        Boolean required = (Boolean) rules.get("required");
        if (required == null)
            return true;
        boolean isRequired = required.booleanValue();
        Boolean isBlank = (value == null || value.trim().equals(""));

        return !(isRequired && isBlank);
    }

    /**
     * Returns a Map containing the values from the provided
     * Java bean, keyed by field name. Entries having keys
     * that match any of the strings returned by
     * <code>keysToSkip()</code> will be removed.
     *
     * @param bean the Java bean from which to create the Map
     * @return a Map containing values from the provided bean
     */
    protected Map mapRepresentation(Object bean, int mode) {
        String errorMsg = "Unable to format values from bean: " + bean;
        Map valueMap = null;

        // PropertyUtils.describe() uses Introspection to generate a Map
        // of values from its argument, keyed by field name.
        try {
            valueMap = PropertyUtils.describe(bean);
        }
        catch (IllegalAccessException iae) {
            throw new FormattingException(errorMsg, iae);
        }
        catch (InvocationTargetException ite) {
```

Listing 2.23 *(continued)*

```
            throw new FormattingException(errorMsg, ite);
        }
        catch (NoSuchMethodException nsme) {
            throw new FormattingException(errorMsg, nsme);
        }

        // Remove keys for properties that shouldn't be populated.
        Iterator keyIter = keysToSkip(mode).iterator();
        while (keyIter.hasNext()) {
            String key = (String)keyIter.next();
            valueMap.remove(key);
        }

        return valueMap;
    }

    /**
     * Returns an array of keys, representing values that should not be
     * populated for the current form instance. Subclasses that override
     * this method to provide additional keys to be skipped should be
     * sure to call <code>super</code>
     *
     * @return an array of keys to be skipped
     */
    protected ArrayList keysToSkip(int mode) {
        ArrayList keysToSkip = new ArrayList();
        keysToSkip.add("class");
        keysToSkip.add("servletWrapper");
        keysToSkip.add("multipartRequestHandler");
        keysToSkip.add("bean");
        return keysToSkip;
    }

    /**
     * Returns a Formatter for the provided type. If the provided key
     * matches an entry in the formatMap, the Formatter type indicated
     * by the entry is used instead of the default for the given type.
     *
     * @param key The name of the property to be formatted
     * @param type The type of the property to be formatted
     * @return A Formatter
     */
    protected Formatter getFormatter(String key, Class type) {
        Class formatType = (Class) formatMap.get(key);
        if (formatType == null)
            return Formatter.getFormatter(type);

        if (formatType.isAssignableFrom(PercentageFormatter.class)) {
```

Listing 2.23 *(continued)*

```
                if (!BigDecimal.class.isAssignableFrom(type))
                    throw new FormattingException("Unable to format value "
                        + "of type " + type + " as a percentage.");

                return new PercentageFormatter();
        }

        return null;
    }
}
```

Listing 2.23 *(continued)*


```
package com.aboutobjects.pitfalls;

import java.math.BigDecimal;
import java.util.ArrayList;
import java.util.Date;

import javax.servlet.http.HttpServletRequest;

import org.apache.struts.Globals;
import org.apache.struts.action.ActionErrors;
import org.apache.struts.action.ActionMapping;
import org.apache.struts.action.ActionMessage;
import org.apache.struts.action.ActionMessages;

public class InvoiceForm extends MyForm
{
    private String invoiceNumber;
    private String billingDate;
    private String amount;
    private String salesTaxRate;

    public InvoiceForm() {
        addRequiredFields(new String[] { "billingDate", "amount" });
        addRange("billingDate", (Comparable) null, new Date());
        addRange("amount",
                new BigDecimal("0.00"),
                new BigDecimal("9999.99"));
    }

    public ActionErrors validate(ActionMapping mapping,
                                HttpServletRequest request) {
        ActionErrors errors = super.validate(mapping, request);
        // Post a global message instructing user to clean up
```

Listing 2.24 InvoiceForm.java refactored to use generic validation in MyForm.

```
        // validation errors and resubmit
    if (errors.size() > 0) {
        ActionMessage message =
            new ActionMessage("message.validation");
        ActionMessages messages = new ActionMessages();
        messages.add(ActionMessages.GLOBAL_MESSAGE, message);
        request.setAttribute(Globals.MESSAGE_KEY, messages);
    }
    return errors;
}

public String getInvoiceNumber() { return invoiceNumber; }
public void setInvoiceNumber(String invoiceNumber) {
    this.invoiceNumber = invoiceNumber;
}

public String getBillingDate() { return billingDate; }
public void setBillingDate(String billingDate) {
    this.billingDate = billingDate;
}

public String getAmount() { return amount; }
public void setAmount(String amount) {
    this.amount = amount;
}
```

Listing 2.24 *(continued)*

Once you have tested the new code, you can look for additional validation rules to abstract out from your existing code base. As mentioned earlier, you may find some validation that doesn't lend itself to this type of generalization. This code can simply be left in place, though it should be examined carefully to ensure that it doesn't implement logic that properly belongs to the business tier.

Although it may take a bit of extra time to code and test the infrastructure code presented in this chapter, the time saved in writing, debugging, and maintaining your ActionForms should make it well worth the investment.

CHAPTER 3

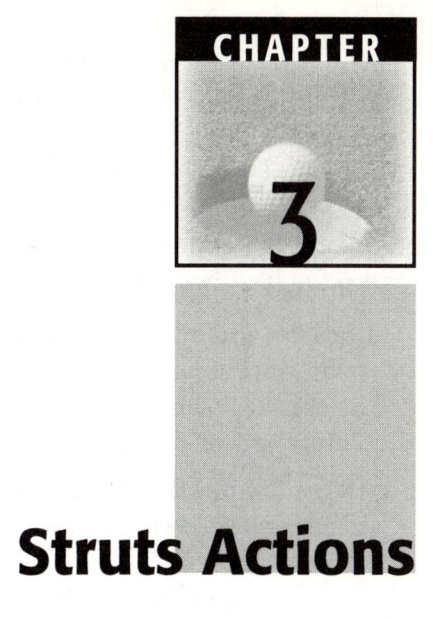

Struts Actions

Actions embody an application's user interface logic. Struts defines the Action class as a controller component; therefore, Action implementations should not contain business logic, which properly belongs in model objects. Instead, Actions should confine themselves to responding to user requests, requesting services from the business tier, managing the associated responses, and handling system events.

Positioned at the nexus of all these activities, Actions often contain complex functionality. Because their only framework-defined functionality is the empty execute() method (perform() in Struts 1.1), the door is left open for developers to trip over a number of significant pitfalls in designing and implementing their functionality. Owing to their fine-grained nature, Actions also tend to proliferate, magnifying the ill effects of poor design practices that often lead to redundant code, coupling to the business tier, and other pathologies.

Much time can be wasted dealing with such a code base, as a single change or addition may affect numerous Action classes containing similar (sometimes nearly identical) functionality. Just locating all the bits of code affected by a given change can prove tedious under these circumstances.

This chapter covers several significant pitfalls that developers fall prey to when working with Actions. The provided solutions are designed to help keep the complexity of Actions to a manageable level and to help reduce the likelihood of runtime errors.

Pitfall 3.1: Business-Tier Code in Actions occurs as a result of hard-coding whatever logic is needed and can cause business-tier code to be sprinkled liberally through a number of Action classes, making your application inflexible and difficult to maintain.

Pitfall 3.2: Copy/Paste Code in Actions describes the tendency for redundant code to proliferate throughout a project's Action classes. Resolving it can lead to dramatic improvements in the readability and maintainability of Actions.

Pitfall 3.3: Accessing ActionForms in the Session occurs when one or more of the techniques that developers use to locate ActionForms at runtime lead to errors. Strange, intermittent bugs in your user interface usually result.

Pitfall 3.4: Overloaded ActionMappings occurs when developers write Actions that both navigate to a page and handle forms submitted from that page. Extra care must taken when defining the ActionMappings that correspond to such Actions, or the application may begin to exhibit some odd and befuddling quirks.

Pitfall 3.1: Business-Tier Code in Actions

Given that most nontrivial Actions manipulate or at least access model data, it is not surprising that developers often mistakenly code functionality that ought to be located in the business-tier in their Actions. Actions are typically employed to locate data for a given set of selection criteria, store modified data, and the like. Because the Action is the application's entry point for the request cycle, containing the method that the framework invokes when the user clicks a hyperlink or a button, it is handy simply to place there whatever code is necessary to satisfy the user's request.

Often, project managers don't provide sufficient time and resources for the type of up-front architecture work required to start development on the right track, leaving developers to improvise as best they can. Without infrastructure, best-practices guidelines, and sound example code, developers often resort to ad hoc techniques, coding the required functionality in their Action classes with minimal design effort in order to meet schedule deadlines.

Actions are particularly seductive in this regard because they are both stateless and atomic—atomic because each subclass usually represents the system's response to a single, specific request by the user and stateless because they are pooled and subsequently reused to service new requests. As a consequence, developers may feel that the design of the code in any given Action is relatively unimportant. In a microcosmic sense, this is true because a flaw in the design of an individual Action is unlikely to have an adverse effect on the design of other components.

When viewed from the perspective of their role in the overall architecture of the system, the design of Actions in general is essential because they embody most of the controller logic that defines the application's functionality. Actions generally have important interactions with the business tier and manage navigational flow and user interface behavior. Without proper design, Actions are likely to become coupled to business-tier objects, leading to inflexibility and increased maintenance overhead.

Once development proceeds along these lines, changing course can be difficult because developers tend to follow precedent (that is, the existing codebase serves as example code for new development) and because managers are often loathe to incur the risk involved in reworking the code once it has passed its system test.

This pitfall usually emerges during development when developers notice that it is taking far too much schedule time to produce the required user interface code. Action subclasses start to become increasingly large and unwieldy, making it difficult to extend their behavior and to track down bugs. The additional overhead of hand-coding, testing, and debugging business-tier functionality in each new Action eats into the schedule. Changes in the business tier often trigger wholesale modifications to Action subclasses because their implementations are tightly coupled.

The general form of this pitfall is to find business-tier code sprinkled liberally through a number of Action classes. For example, developers implementing an EJB-based application might, in the absence of clear guidelines to the contrary, code home interface lookups and direct calls to Session Beans or even to Entity Beans in their Actions, as in this execute() method:

```
...
    public ActionForward execute(ActionMapping mapping,
                                 ActionForm form,
                                 HttpServletRequest request,
                                 HttpServletResponse response)
        throws IOException, ServletException {
    ...
    String url = bundle.getString("jndi.provider.url");
    String factory = bundle.getString("jndi.initial.context.factory");
    Properties properties = new Properties();
    properties.put(Context.INITIAL_CONTEXT_FACTORY, factory);
    properties.put(Context.PROVIDER_URL, url);
    boolean exception = false;
    invoiceDO invoice = null;
    try {
        InitialContext initialContext = new InitialContext(properties);
        Object obj = initialContext.lookup("InvoiceSession");
        Class type = InvoiceSessionHome.class;
        InvoiceSessionHome sessionHome = (InvoiceSessionHome)
                PortableRemoteObject.narrow(obj,type);
        InvoiceSession session = sessionHome.create();
        invoice = session.findInvoice(invoiceNumber);
    }
    catch (NamingException e) {
        ...
    }
    catch (RemoteException e) {
        ...
    }
    catch (CreateException e) {
        ...
    }
    catch (FinderException e) {
        ...
    }

    ((InvoiceForm) form).setInvoice(invoice);
    ...
}
```

In a similar vein, developers often make the mistake of implementing business logic directly in Actions, as in the following snippet:

```
// Apply discount, if any
BigDecimal amount = invoice.getAmount();
if (amount.compareTo(DISCOUNT_THRESHOLD) > 0) {
    BigDecimal discountedAmount = amount.multiply(DISCOUNT_FACTOR);
    invoice.setAmount(discountedAmount);
}
```

Such code usually winds up being copied and pasted in numerous places in the presentation tier. If the same logic is required by back-end components, it may be copied and pasted there as well (or written from scratch by business-tier developers, who may not be aware of the existence of the presentation-tier version). It is quite easy for these separate implementations to get out of sync with one another, opening the door to runtime errors. When requirements change, it can be a tedious and time-consuming process to track down and update all these separate implementations.

Example

Here's an Action that directly accesses a stateless Session Bean in order to find an invoice. Note that the code that follows contains a number of static strings that would ordinarily be replaced with constants in production code, but they have been left in place in order to make the example easier to follow. We'll continue this practice throughout the rest of the code examples in this chapter. Note also that the example makes use of the populate() method from the MyForm class in the previous chapter.

The problem with this Action is that its functionality is all over the map, first getting the application's resource bundle to look up property settings, then getting the JNDI context to look up a Session Bean's home interface, creating a Session Bean instance, and invoking its finder method, in addition to performing more typical Action functionality—managing Action-Forms and returning an ActionForward.

Following this approach will lead to a proliferation of redundant code because many other Actions will need identical functionality to perform JNDI lookups and access Session Beans. In addition, the Action code depends on implementation details of the business tier, making it vulnerable to breakage and increased maintenance overhead as that code base evolves. It also leaves us without a central place to implement performance optimizations, such as caching the Session Bean and the JNDI context, as can be seen in Listing 3.1.

```java
package com.aboutobjects.pitfalls;

import java.rmi.RemoteException;
import java.util.MissingResourceException;
import java.util.Properties;
import java.util.ResourceBundle;
import javax.ejb.CreateException;
import javax.ejb.FinderException;
import javax.naming.Context;
import javax.naming.InitialContext;
import javax.naming.NamingException;
import javax.rmi.PortableRemoteObject;
import javax.servlet.http.HttpServletRequest;
import javax.servlet.http.HttpServletResponse;

import com.aboutobjects.pitfalls.ejb.InvoiceSession;
import com.aboutobjects.pitfalls.ejb.InvoiceSessionHome;
import org.apache.struts.action.*;

/**
 * An Action that attempts to save an invoice. If the invoice is saved,
 * we forward to the Confirmation page. Otherwise, we return to the
 * Save Invoice page and display an appropriate error message.
 */
public class FindInvoiceAction extends Action
{
    public ActionForward execute(ActionMapping mapping,
                                 ActionForm form,
                                 HttpServletRequest request,
                                 HttpServletResponse response)
        throws Exception
    {
        ResourceBundle bundle = null;
        try {
            bundle = ResourceBundle.getBundle("ApplicationResources");
        }
        catch (MissingResourceException e) {
            e.printStackTrace();
            ActionErrors errors = new ActionErrors();
            ActionError error = new ActionError("error.system");
            errors.add(error);
            saveErrors(request, errors);
            return mapping.findForward("findInvoicePage");
        }

        FindInvoiceForm findInvoiceForm = (FindInvoiceForm) form;
        FindInvoiceBean bean =
            (FindInvoiceBean) findInvoiceForm.getBean();
```

Listing 3.1 A find Action containing business-tier code.

```
        Integer invoiceNumber = bean.getInvoiceNumber();

    InvoiceDO invoice = null;
    String url = bundle.getString("jndi.provider.url");
    String factory =
        bundle.getString("jndi.initial.context.factory");
    Properties properties = new Properties();
    properties.put(Context.INITIAL_CONTEXT_FACTORY, factory);
    properties.put(Context.PROVIDER_URL, url);
    boolean exception = false;

    try {
        InitialContext initialContext =
            new InitialContext(properties);
        Object obj = initialContext.lookup("InvoiceSession");
        Class type = InvoiceSessionHome.class;
        InvoiceSessionHome sessionHome = (InvoiceSessionHome)
                PortableRemoteObject.narrow(obj,type);
        InvoiceSession session = sessionHome.create();
        invoice = session.findInvoice(invoiceNumber);
    }
    catch (NamingException e) {
        e.printStackTrace();
        exception = true;
    }
    catch (RemoteException e) {
        e.printStackTrace();
        exception = true;
    }
    catch (CreateException e) {
        e.printStackTrace();
        exception = true;
    }
    catch (FinderException e) {
        ActionError error =
            new ActionError("error.find", invoiceNumber);
        ActionErrors errors = new ActionErrors();
        errors.add(ActionErrors.GLOBAL_ERROR, error);
        saveErrors(request, errors);
        return mapping.findForward("findInvoicePage");
    }

    if (exception) {
        ActionError error = new ActionError("error.system");
        ActionErrors errors = new ActionErrors();
        errors.add(ActionErrors.GLOBAL_ERROR, error);
        saveErrors(request, errors);
        return mapping.findForward("findInvoicePage");
    }
```

Listing 3.1 *(continued)*

```
        else {
                // We need to get the InvoiceForm instance from the session
                // and populate it with values from the InvoiceDO we just
                // found so that the values will be available to the JSP.
                // Note: this contains a bug we'll explore later.
                InvoiceForm invoiceForm = (InvoiceForm)
                    request.getSession().getAttribute("invoiceForm");

                // Pre-populate the InvoiceForm so that the values will be
                // available to the JSP we are forwarding to.
                invoiceForm.populate(invoice);
                return mapping.findForward("saveInvoicePage");
        }
    }
}
```

Listing 3.1 *(continued)*

The next example, a related Action from the same application, serves two purposes: First, it illustrates the degree of redundancy that this pitfall leads to, in that it contains much of the same code as the previous example Action; second, it also contains a bit of business logic, pointing up another aspect of this pitfall.

The new Action (in Listing 3.2) is responsible for persisting a modified invoice. In addition to the lookup and access code seen in the previous example, this class contains business logic that calculates and applies a discount. Obviously, placing the code here makes it impossible for back-end components (not to mention other Actions) to reuse the functionality, thus encouraging copying and pasting of the implementation.

You may notice that the code looks remarkably similar to the previous example—in fact, the code for looking up the Session Bean is identical, which should be an immediate tip that something is wrong. One thing that distinguishes the two Actions, however, is the snippet of business logic that applies a discount to invoice amounts over a certain threshold.

One concern with placing the code here is that although we can see that some business logic is executed, we can never be sure that all the necessary business logic is being applied to this invoice because the logic is not grouped inside a model object that represents the totality of an Invoice's behavior. Another concern is that this functionality may already exist elsewhere, either in other UI components or in the business tier. Hence we incur the risks and potential overhead of maintaining multiple implementations of the same functionality.

```java
package com.aboutobjects.pitfalls;

import java.math.BigDecimal;
import java.rmi.RemoteException;
import java.util.MissingResourceException;
import java.util.Properties;
import java.util.ResourceBundle;
import javax.ejb.CreateException;
import javax.ejb.FinderException;
import javax.naming.Context;
import javax.naming.InitialContext;
import javax.naming.NamingException;
import javax.rmi.PortableRemoteObject;
import javax.servlet.http.HttpServletRequest;
import javax.servlet.http.HttpServletResponse;

import com.aboutobjects.pitfalls.ejb.InvoiceSession;
import com.aboutobjects.pitfalls.ejb.InvoiceSessionHome;
import org.apache.struts.action.*;

/**
 * An Action that attempts to save an invoice. If the invoice is saved,
 * we forward to the Confirmation page. Otherwise, we return to the
 * Save Invoice page and display an appropriate error message.
 */
public class SaveInvoiceAction extends Action
{
    public final static BigDecimal DISCOUNT_FACTOR =
        new BigDecimal(".90");
    public final static BigDecimal DISCOUNT_THRESHOLD =
        new BigDecimal("999.99");

    public ActionForward execute(ActionMapping mapping,
                                 ActionForm form,
                                 HttpServletRequest request,
                                 HttpServletResponse response)
        throws Exception
    {
        // Get an invoice bean, which will be used
        // to transfer the values to the Business Tier.
        InvoiceForm invoiceForm = (InvoiceForm)form;
        InvoiceDO invoice = (InvoiceDO) invoiceForm.getBean();

        // Apply discount, if any
        BigDecimal amount = invoice.getAmount();
        if (amount.compareTo(DISCOUNT_THRESHOLD) > 0) {
            BigDecimal discountedAmount =
                amount.multiply(DISCOUNT_FACTOR);
```

Listing 3.2 A save Action containing business-tier code. *(continues)*

```java
            invoice.setAmount(discountedAmount);
    }

    ResourceBundle bundle = null;
    try {
        bundle = ResourceBundle.getBundle("ApplicationResources");
    }
    catch (MissingResourceException e) {
        e.printStackTrace();
        ActionError error = new ActionError("error.save");
        ActionErrors errors = new ActionErrors();
        errors.add(ActionErrors.GLOBAL_ERROR, error);
        saveErrors(request, errors);
        return mapping.findForward("saveInvoicePage");
    }

    String url = bundle.getString("jndi.provider.url");
    String factory =
        bundle.getString("jndi.initial.context.factory");
    Properties properties = new Properties();
    properties.put(Context.INITIAL_CONTEXT_FACTORY, factory);
    properties.put(Context.PROVIDER_URL, url);
    Integer invoiceNumber = invoice.getInvoiceNumber();
    boolean exception = false;

    try {
        InitialContext initialContext =
            new InitialContext(properties);
        Object obj = initialContext.lookup("InvoiceSession");
        Class type = InvoiceSessionHome.class;
        InvoiceSessionHome sessionHome = (InvoiceSessionHome)
                PortableRemoteObject.narrow(obj,type);
        InvoiceSession session = sessionHome.create();
        session.saveInvoice(invoice);
    }
    catch (NamingException e) {
        e.printStackTrace();
        exception = true;
    }
    catch (RemoteException e) {
        e.printStackTrace();
        exception = true;
    }
    catch (CreateException e) {
        e.printStackTrace();
        exception = true;
    }
    catch (FinderException e) {
        ActionError error =
```

Listing 3.2 *(continued)*

```
                new ActionError("error.find", invoiceNumber);
            ActionErrors errors = new ActionErrors();
            errors.add(ActionErrors.GLOBAL_ERROR, error);
            saveErrors(request, errors);
            return mapping.findForward("saveInvoicePage");
        }

        if (exception) {
            ActionError error = new ActionError("error.save");
            ActionErrors errors = new ActionErrors();
            errors.add(ActionErrors.GLOBAL_ERROR, error);
            saveErrors(request, errors);
            return mapping.findForward("saveInvoicePage");
        }
        else {
            invoiceForm.populate(invoice);
            ActionMessage message =
                new ActionMessage("message.confirm");
            ActionMessages messages = new ActionMessages();
            messages.add(ActionMessages.GLOBAL_MESSAGE, message);
            saveMessages(request, messages);
            return mapping.findForward("confirmInvoicePage");
        }
    }
}
```

Listing 3.2 *(continued)*

There are two approaches to avoiding this pitfall, and they are not mutually exclusive. One is to spend time early in the project, usually during the prototyping stage, experimenting with architectural approaches that allow the presentation-tier and business-tier components to be loosely coupled. For larger projects, it is particularly important to provide good working example code at this stage, so that developers have it for reference in the early stages of development.

The other approach is to strongly encourage continuous refactoring. Using the latter approach without the former may not work terribly well on larger projects because once coding is well underway it can be expensive to introduce new, reusable artifacts if their adoption would require significant changes to the existing code base. The best time to get at least a preliminary design in place is before coding officially begins.

Solving Pitfall 3.1: Move Business-Tier Code to BusinessDelegate

This is the primary solution to Pitfall 3.1. (A related solution is found in Pitfall 3.2.)

The potential for coupling between application tiers is not unique to Struts; rather, it is an area of general concern for any Java Enterprise application. Because there are well-known, general solutions for this class of problems, our solution will focus on applying them in the context of Struts-based development. In particular, we will apply the BusinessDelegate and ServiceLocator patterns outlined in the book *Core J2EE Patterns*.*

Moving the copy/paste business-tier code out of our Action classes into a BusinessDelegate will allow our Actions to share implementations of business logic, lookup, and access code. This will help to ensure consistent behavior while simplifying maintenance. At the same time, by hiding the business tier behind a façade, the user interface layer will be meaningfully shielded from changes to the objects in that tier.

This approach will also allow us to code caching behavior and other optimizations at the appropriate levels, in central, shared locations, while simplifying the code of our Actions, making them easier to modify and debug.

Step-by-Step

1. Hunt down business-tier code in Actions, ActionForms, and helpers.
   a. Organize the collected methods and code snippets according to the model objects on which they operate.
   b. Determine how many BusinessDelegates are required.
   c. Map the functionality to the BusinessDelegates and model objects you wish to target.
2. Find the business logic located in Actions.
   a. See if there are existing business-tier methods to provide the same functionality. If there are, modify the Action code to call those methods.
   b. If the needed methods don't exist, create them, moving the implementation from the Actions to the appropriate classes in the business tier.
3. Create a ServiceLocator class if you are using Session Beans or message-driven beans.
   a. If you are not using EJBs, create the necessary data access objects.
   b. Move lookup code to the ServiceLocator class.

---

* Deepak Alur, John Crupi, Dan Malks, *Core J2EE Patterns: Best Practices and Design Strategies* (Upper Saddle River, NJ: Prentice Hall, 2001).

4. Create the required BusinessDelegate classes.
    a. Move access code to the appropriate classes.
    b. Insert calls to the new BusinessDelegate methods in Actions to replace the relocated code.
    c. Move business logic code to the model objects.
5. Deploy and test.

Example

The pair of diagrams in Figures 3.1 and 3.2 illustrate how the calling sequence looks before and after we apply the solution to this pitfall, which should help to give you a clearer picture of how the new classes and APIs we are introducing relate to one another.

Our first step in implementing this solution is to create a ServiceLocator class. We will migrate any JNDI lookup code found in our Actions to this new class. Note that the ServiceLocator could later be extended to support other JNDI lookups your application needs to perform. Here's an example of a block of code that needs to be moved to the ServiceLocator.

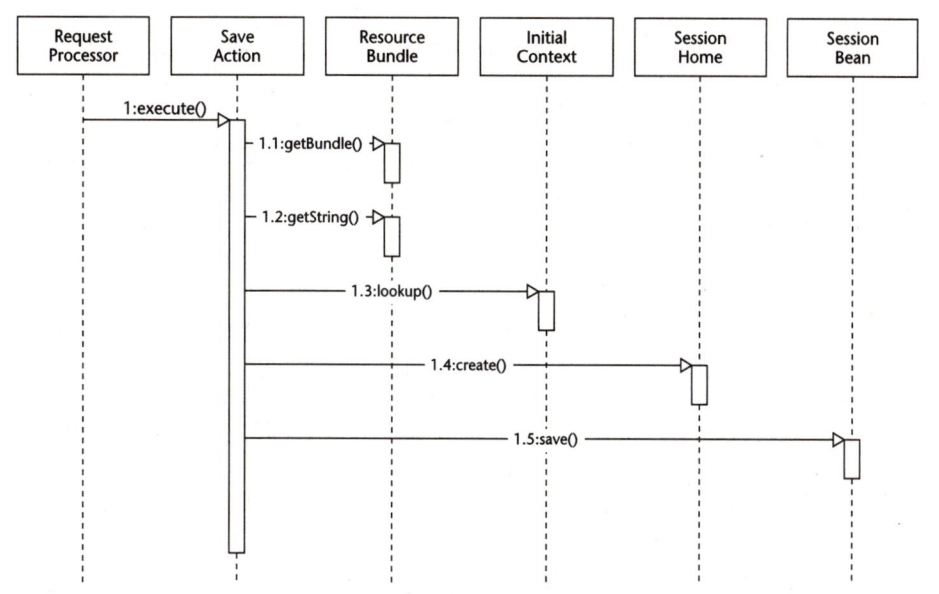

Figure 3.1 Action calling sequence without BusinessDelegate.

160 Chapter 3

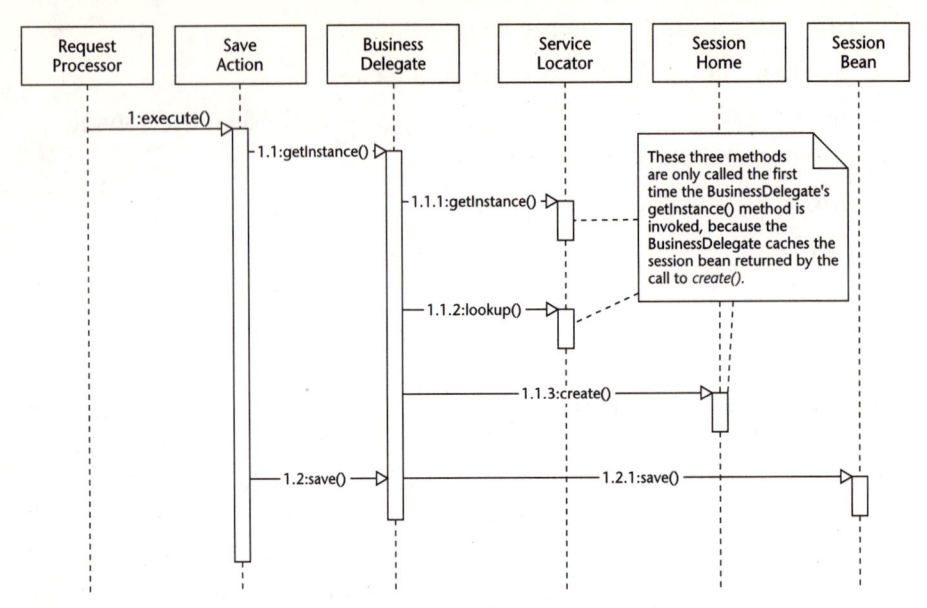

Figure 3.2 Action calling sequence after adding BusinessDelegate.

Note (on diagram): These three methods are only called the first time the BusinessDelegate's getInstance() method is invoked, because the BusinessDelegate caches the session bean returned by the call to *create()*.

```
...
ResourceBundle bundle = null;
try {
    bundle = ResourceBundle.getBundle("ApplicationResources");
}
catch (MissingResourceException e) {
    e.printStackTrace();
    ActionError error = new ActionError("error.system");
    request.setAttribute("error", error);
    return mapping.findForward("findInvoicePage");
}
...
String url = bundle.getString("jndi.provider.url");
String factory =
    bundle.getString("jndi.initial.context.factory");
Properties properties = new Properties();
properties.put(Context.INITIAL_CONTEXT_FACTORY, factory);
properties.put(Context.PROVIDER_URL, url);
boolean exception = false;

try {
    InitialContext initialContext =
        new InitialContext(properties);
    Object obj = initialContext.lookup("InvoiceSession");
```

```
            Class type = InvoiceSessionHome.class;
            InvoiceSessionHome sessionHome = (InvoiceSessionHome)
                    PortableRemoteObject.narrow(obj,type);
            ...
    }
    catch (NamingException e) {
        ...
```

Listing 3.3 shows how the code would look after being moved to the ServiceLocator class.

```
package com.aboutobjects.pitfalls.delegate;

import java.util.MissingResourceException;
import java.util.Properties;
import java.util.ResourceBundle;
import javax.ejb.EJBHome;
import javax.naming.Context;
import javax.naming.InitialContext;
import javax.naming.NamingException;
import javax.rmi.PortableRemoteObject;

/**
 * A locator of EJBHome interfaces. Caches the initial context to save
 * lookup overhead.
 */
public class ServiceLocator
{
    /** The JNDI provider URL key */
    public final static String JNDI_PROVIDER_URL = "jndi.provider.url";
    /** The JNDI initial context factory class  key */
    public final static String JNDI_INITIAL_CONTEXT_FACTORY =
        "jndi.initial.context.factory";
    /** The singleton instance */
    private static ServiceLocator uniqueInstance = new ServiceLocator();
    /** The cached initial context */
    private InitialContext initialContext;

    /**
     * An exception indicating that the requested service was not found.
     */
    public class LocatorException extends DelegateException {
        public LocatorException(String message, Throwable cause) {
            super(message, cause);
        }
    }

    // Make the constructor private since this is a Singleton.
    private ServiceLocator()
```

Listing 3.3 ServiceLocator.java. *(continues)*

```java
        throws LocatorException {
        // Note: the ResourceBundle-related code below could be moved
        // to a helper class.
        ResourceBundle bundle = null;
        try {
            bundle = ResourceBundle.getBundle("ApplicationResources");
        }
        catch (MissingResourceException e) {
            e.printStackTrace();
            throw new LocatorException("Unable to read " +
                "ApplicationResources resource bundle", e);
        }

        String url = bundle.getString(JNDI_PROVIDER_URL);
        String factory = bundle.getString(JNDI_INITIAL_CONTEXT_FACTORY);
        Properties properties = new Properties();
        properties.put(Context.INITIAL_CONTEXT_FACTORY, factory);
        properties.put(Context.PROVIDER_URL, url);
        try {
            // Note that the initialContext is now cached, saving
            // the lookup overhead on subsequent calls.
            initialContext = new InitialContext(properties);
        }
        catch (NamingException e) {
            throw new DelegateException("Can't create initial context",
                e);
        }
    }

    /**
     * Returns the ServiceLocator singleton instance.
     * @return the singleton instance
     */
    public static ServiceLocator getInstance() {
        return uniqueInstance;
    }

    /**
     * Returns the EJBHome for the provided service name. Throws a
     * <code>ServiceLocator.LocatorException</code> if the lookup fails.
     *
     * @param serviceName the name of the Session Bean to look up
     * @param type the class of the Session Bean's home interface
     * @return the home interface for the given service name
     */
    public EJBHome lookup(String serviceName, Class type)
        throws ServiceLocator.LocatorException {
        try {
            Object objref = initialContext.lookup(serviceName);
```

Listing 3.3 *(continued)*

```
            return (EJBHome) PortableRemoteObject.narrow(objref, type);
        }
        catch (NamingException e) {
            throw new LocatorException(
                "Lookup failed for service named " + serviceName, e);
        }
    }
}
```

Listing 3.3 *(continued)*

Now we can create a BusinessDelegate and move any code that accesses Session Bean services there. You will probably want to pick out a single Action to begin with to minimize the number of concurrent changes. Once you have a single access method working, you can begin transferring others one by one, replacing their implementations in the Actions with calls to the new BusinessDelegate methods.

For example, let's start by moving the following code from the FindInvoiceAction.

```
...
InvoiceDO invoice = null;
try {
    ...
    InvoiceSession session = sessionHome.create();
    invoice = session.findInvoice(invoiceNumber);
}
catch (RemoteException e) {
...
```

Here's the corresponding method we'll need to create in our new BusinessDelegate implementation, the InvoiceDelegate class:

```
...
private InvoiceSession invoiceSession;
...
InvoiceDO findInvoice(FindInvoiceBean bean)
    throws DelegateException, InvoiceDelegate.NotFoundException {
    Integer invoiceNumber = bean.getInvoiceNumber();
    InvoiceDO invoice = null;
    try {
        invoice = invoiceSession.findInvoice(invoiceNumber);
    }
    catch (FinderException e) {
        throw new NotFoundException();
    }
    catch (RemoteException e) {
```

```
            throw new DelegateException("Exception occurred while trying"
                + "to find invoice number" + invoiceNumber, e);
    }
    return invoice;
}
...
```

The code in FindInvoiceAction now becomes this:

```
...
InvoiceDO invoice = null;
try {
    InvoiceDelegate delegate = InvoiceDelegate.getInstance();
    invoice = delegate.findInvoice(bean);
}
catch (InvoiceDelegate.NotFoundException e) {
    ...
}
catch(DelegateException e) {
    ...
}
...
}
```

Once you have an initial version working, continue migrating code from your other Actions. You may want to consider creating several Business-Delegates if there are distinct portions of your user interface that work with different sets of model objects. Our InvoiceDelegate ends up looking like Listing 3.4.

```
package com.aboutobjects.pitfalls.delegate;

import java.rmi.RemoteException;
import javax.ejb.CreateException;
import javax.ejb.DuplicateKeyException;
import javax.ejb.FinderException;

import com.aboutobjects.pitfalls.FindInvoiceBean;
import com.aboutobjects.pitfalls.InvoiceDO;
import com.aboutobjects.pitfalls.ejb.InvoiceSession;
import com.aboutobjects.pitfalls.ejb.InvoiceSessionHome;

/**
 * A BusinessDelegate to proxy calls to the invoice Session Bean.
 */
public class InvoiceDelegate
{
    /* The singleton instance. */
```

Listing 3.4 InvoiceDelegate.java.

```java
    private static InvoiceDelegate uniqueInstance =
        new InvoiceDelegate();
/* The cached InvoiceSession instance. */
private InvoiceSession invoiceSession;

/**
 * An exception thrown by findInvoice() and saveInvoice() to
 * indicate that the invoice was not found.
 */
public class NotFoundException extends Exception { }

/**
 * An exception thrown by insertInvoice() to indicate that the
 * invoice already exists.
 */
public class DuplicateException extends Exception { }

// Make the constructor private because this is a Singleton.
// Note that the InvoiceSession is cached during construction,
// saving overhead for subsequent service invocations.
private InvoiceDelegate() {
    String exceptionMsg = "Unable to create InvoiceSession";
    try {
        ServiceLocator locator = ServiceLocator.getInstance();
        InvoiceSessionHome home = (InvoiceSessionHome)
            locator.lookup("InvoiceSession",
                           InvoiceSessionHome.class);
        invoiceSession = home.create();
    }
    catch (CreateException e) {
        throw new DelegateException(exceptionMsg, e);
    }
    catch (RemoteException e) {
        throw new DelegateException(exceptionMsg, e);
    }
    catch (ServiceLocator.LocatorException e) {
        throw new DelegateException(exceptionMsg, e);
    }
}

/**
 * Returns the Singleton instance.
 * @return the unique InvoiceDelegate instance.
 */
public static InvoiceDelegate getInstance() {
    return uniqueInstance;
}

/**
```

Listing 3.4 *(continued)*

```
     * Returns an invoice that matches criteria in the provided bean.
     * Throws an <code>InvoiceDelegate.NotFoundException</code> if no
     * matching invoice is found. Throws a
     * <code>DelegateException</code> if a lower-level exception
     * is encountered.
     *
     * @param bean a bean containing criteria used to find an invoice
     * @return an InvoiceDO matching the provided bean
     */
    public InvoiceDO findInvoice(FindInvoiceBean bean)
        throws DelegateException, InvoiceDelegate.NotFoundException {
        Integer invoiceNumber = bean.getInvoiceNumber();
        InvoiceDO invoice = null;
        try {
            invoice = invoiceSession.findInvoice(invoiceNumber);
        }
        catch (FinderException e) {
            throw new NotFoundException();
        }
        catch (RemoteException e) {
            throw new DelegateException("Exception occurred while " +
                "trying to find invoice number" + invoiceNumber, e);
        }
        return invoice;
    }

    /**
     * Saves the provided invoice.
     * Throws a <code>InvoiceDelegate.NotFoundException</code> if no
     * matching invoice is found. Throws a
     * <code>DelegateException</code> if the save attempt fails.
     *
     * @param the invoice to be saved
     */
    public void saveInvoice(InvoiceDO invoice)
        throws DelegateException, InvoiceDelegate.NotFoundException {
        try {
            invoiceSession.saveInvoice(invoice);
        }
        catch (FinderException e) {
            throw new NotFoundException();
        }
        catch (RemoteException e) {
            throw new DelegateException("Unable to save invoice "
                                        + invoice);
        }
    }

    /**
```

Listing 3.4 *(continued)*

```java
 * Inserts the provided invoice.
 * Throws a <code>InvoiceDelegate.DuplicateException</code> if an
 * invoice is found with the same primary key. Throws a
 * <code>DelegateException</code> if the attempted insert fails.
 *
 * @param the invoice to be inserted
 */
public void insertInvoice(InvoiceDO invoice)
    throws DelegateException, InvoiceDelegate.DuplicateException {
    String exceptionMsg = "Unable to create invoice " + invoice;
    try {
        invoiceSession.insertInvoice(invoice);
    }
    catch (DuplicateKeyException e) {
        throw new DuplicateException();
    }
    catch (CreateException e) {
        throw new DelegateException(exceptionMsg, e);
    }
    catch (RemoteException e) {
        throw new DelegateException(exceptionMsg, e);
    }
}

/**
 * Applies any available discounts to the provided invoice.
 * Throws a <code>DelegateException</code> if the
 * attempted operation fails.
 *
 * @return the modified invoice
 * @param the invoice to which the discount is to be applied
 */
public InvoiceDO applyDiscount(InvoiceDO invoice)
    throws DelegateException {
    String exceptionMsg = "Unable to apply discount to " + invoice;
    try {
        return invoiceSession.applyDiscount(invoice);
    }
    catch (RemoteException e) {
        throw new DelegateException(exceptionMsg, e);
    }
}
}
```

Listing 3.4 *(continued)*

Finally, we'll move code that implements non-UI-level business logic to the appropriate model classes. In this case, we'll take the snippet of code that calculates and applies the discount and move it to the InvoiceSession-Bean. (You may have noticed that we have already provided a proxy method in the InvoiceDelegate class source listing.)

```
public final static BigDecimal DISCOUNT_FACTOR = new BigDecimal(".90");
public final static BigDecimal DISCOUNT_THRESHOLD =
    new BigDecimal("999.99");

protected static BigDecimal getDiscount(BigDecimal amount) {
    return (amount.compareTo(DISCOUNT_THRESHOLD) > 0 ?
            amount.multiply(DISCOUNT_FACTOR) :
            amount);
}

public InvoiceDO applyDiscount(InvoiceDO invoice)
    throws RemoteException {
    invoice.setAmount(getDiscount(invoice.getAmount()));
    return invoice;
}
```

Here are new versions of the two Actions. Note that we have again left static strings in a number of places where we would ordinarily use constants in production code in order to make the example code a bit easier to follow.

As you can see, our Actions have become a good bit simpler and easier to read, and their dependencies have been significantly reduced, as witnessed by the reduction in import statements. We have dramatically reduced the coupling between the presentation and business tiers.

Our InvoiceDelegate and ServiceLocator now provide appropriate caching for the Session Bean and the home interface. Finally, all of our business logic is now grouped together in one centralized, universally accessible place, as noted in Listing 3.5, so that it can be shared by all components of our system. Note that keeping the business logic methods clustered in this fashion also makes it considerably easier to compare them against the requirements.

```
package com.aboutobjects.pitfalls;

import javax.servlet.ServletException;
import javax.servlet.http.HttpServletRequest;
import javax.servlet.http.HttpServletResponse;

import com.aboutobjects.pitfalls.delegate.DelegateException;
import com.aboutobjects.pitfalls.delegate.InvoiceDelegate;
```

Listing 3.5 A FindInvoiceAction that collaborates with the InvoiceDelegate.

```java
import org.apache.struts.action.*;

/**
 * An Action that attempts to find an InvoiceDO. If one is found,
 * the InvoiceForm in the session is initialized with its values, and
 * we forward to the Save Invoice page. Otherwise, we return to the
 * Find Invoice page and display an appropriate error message.
 */
public class FindInvoiceAction extends Action
{
    public ActionForward execute(ActionMapping mapping,
                                 ActionForm form,
                                 HttpServletRequest request,
                                 HttpServletResponse response)
        throws Exception
    {
        FindInvoiceForm findInvoiceForm = (FindInvoiceForm) form;
        FindInvoiceBean bean = (FindInvoiceBean)
            findInvoiceForm.getBean();
        Integer invoiceNumber = bean.getInvoiceNumber();

        // Use the InvoiceDelegate to find the invoice
        InvoiceDO invoice = null;
        try {
            InvoiceDelegate delegate = InvoiceDelegate.getInstance();
            invoice = delegate.findInvoice(bean);
        }
        catch (InvoiceDelegate.NotFoundException e) {
            ActionError error =
                new ActionError("error.find", invoiceNumber);
            ActionErrors errors = new ActionErrors();
            errors.add(ActionErrors.GLOBAL_ERROR, error);
            saveErrors(request, errors);
            return mapping.findForward("findInvoicePage");
        }
        catch (DelegateException e) {
            e.printStackTrace();
            ActionError error = new ActionError("error.system");
            ActionErrors errors = new ActionErrors();
            errors.add(ActionErrors.GLOBAL_ERROR, error);
            saveErrors(request, errors);
            return mapping.findForward("findInvoicePage");
        }

        // We need to get the InvoiceForm instance from the session
        // and populate it with values from the InvoiceDO we just found
        // so that the values will be available to the next JSP.
        // Note: the following line contains a bug we'll explore later.
        InvoiceForm invoiceForm = (InvoiceForm)
```

Listing 3.5 (continued)

```
                    request.getSession().getAttribute("invoiceForm");

            // Pre-populate the InvoiceForm so that the values will be
            // available to the JSP we are forwarding to.
            invoiceForm.populate(invoice);
            return mapping.findForward("saveInvoicePage");
        }
    }
```

Listing 3.5 *(continued)*

Listing 3.6 shows the body of a SaveInvoiceAction that shares the InvoiceDelegate.

```
// Imports, javadoc, etc.
...
public class SaveInvoiceAction extends Action
{
    public ActionForward execute(ActionMapping mapping,
                                 ActionForm form,
                                 HttpServletRequest request,
                                 HttpServletResponse response)
        throws Exception
    {

        InvoiceForm invoiceForm = (InvoiceForm)form;
        InvoiceDO invoice = (InvoiceDO) invoiceForm.getBean();

        // Use the InvoiceDelegate to save the invoice
        try {
            InvoiceDelegate delegate = InvoiceDelegate.getInstance();
            invoice = delegate.applyDiscount(invoice);
            delegate.saveInvoice(invoice);
        }
        catch (InvoiceDelegate.NotFoundException e) {
            ActionError error =
                new ActionError("error.find",
                    invoice.getInvoiceNumber());
            ActionErrors errors = new ActionErrors();
            errors.add(ActionErrors.GLOBAL_ERROR, error);
            saveErrors(request, errors);
            return mapping.findForward("saveInvoicePage");
        }
        catch (DelegateException e) {
            ActionError error = new ActionError("error.save");
            ActionErrors errors = new ActionErrors();
            errors.add(ActionErrors.GLOBAL_ERROR, error);
```

Listing 3.6 A SaveInvoiceAction that collaborates with the InvoiceDelegate.

```
            saveErrors(request, errors);
            return mapping.findForward("saveInvoicePage");
        }

        invoiceForm.populate(invoice);

        ActionMessage message = new ActionMessage("message.confirm");
        ActionMessages messages = new ActionMessages();
        messages.add(ActionMessages.GLOBAL_MESSAGE, message);
        saveMessages(request, messages);
        return mapping.findForward("confirmInvoicePage");
    }
}
```

Listing 3.6 *(continued)*

Pitfall 3.2: Copy/Paste Code in Actions

Pitfall 3.1 explored the problems associated with copy/paste business-tier code in Actions. In that case, we were dealing with code such as business logic and JNDI lookups that clearly did not belong in the presentation tier. Unlike that pitfall, though, the Copy/Paste Code in Actions pitfall deals with code that does belong in the presentation tier but that nevertheless end up being copied and pasted.

While this pitfall may seem relatively minor in terms of its potential negative consequences, resolving it can lead to dramatic improvements in the readability and maintainability of Actions. The issue here is that the code contained in most Actions tends to be quite similar. For example, posting an error (or other) message to be displayed on a succeeding Web page generally requires a snippet of code more or less like the following:

```
ActionError error = new ActionError("error.save");
ActionErrors errors = new ActionErrors();
errors.add(ActionErrors.GLOBAL_ERROR, error);
saveErrors(request, errors);
```

If a great deal of this kind of code is copied, it can become a burden to maintain, while at the same time obscuring the more significant bits of code in a given method.

Example

The excerpt that follows is from the SaveInvoiceAction Listing (Listing 3.2) found in Pitfall 3.1. You'll notice that it contains several blocks of nearly identical code to post messages to the user interface. Although this code is fairly trivial, it constitutes a substantial portion of the code of the entire method and thus serves to obscure the more important application logic. Over time, as the method gets larger, the noise level increases, making the code more difficult to read. Changes to the error-handling code may require visiting numerous classes, resulting in increased maintenance overhead.

```
...
try {
    InvoiceDelegate delegate = InvoiceDelegate.getInstance();
    delegate.saveInvoice(invoice);
}
```

```
    catch (InvoiceDelegate.NotFoundException e) {
        ActionError error =
            new ActionError("error.find", invoice.getInvoiceNumber());
        ActionErrors errors = new ActionErrors();
        errors.add(ActionErrors.GLOBAL_ERROR, error);
        saveErrors(request, errors);
        return mapping.findForward("saveInvoicePage");
    }
    catch (DelegateException e) {
        ActionError error = new ActionError("error.save");
        ActionErrors errors = new ActionErrors();
        errors.add(ActionErrors.GLOBAL_ERROR, error);
        saveErrors(request, errors);
        return mapping.findForward("saveInvoicePage");
    }

    invoiceForm.populate(invoice,);

    ActionMessage message = new ActionMessage("message.confirm");
    ActionMessages messages = new ActionMessages();
    messages.add(ActionMessages.GLOBAL_MESSAGE, message);
    saveMessages(request, messages);
    return mapping.findForward("confirmInvoicePage");
    ...
```

Solving Pitfall 3.2: Move Common Code to Base Class

The first question we have to answer once we have decided to abstract common functionality out of our Actions is where to move the code. One perfectly acceptable alternative is to migrate the code to helper classes. Because the functionality involved in this case is fairly specific to Actions, it will be more straightforward to create an Action base class and move the code there. As your application grows in complexity, you will find additional uses for this base class. (See Pitfall 3.3: Accessing ActionForms in the Session for another example of the use of an Action base class method.)

The main thing we want to accomplish is the elimination of as much redundant code as possible. Doing so will clean up our Actions, making them easier to read and therefore easier to maintain. It will also reduce or eliminate the need to search through countless Actions to migrate a given to all the ones that have the same bit of copy/paste code (sometimes in multiple places in the same file). This will also help keep bugs from creeping into our Actions as the result of botched attempts to propagate or maintain copy/paste functionality.

Step-by-Step

1. Search Actions for copy/paste code.
2. Create an Action base class.
   a. Move copy/paste code to base class.
   b. Modify subclasses to invoke implementation in base class.
3. Test the refactored solution.

Example

The goal of this solution is to create a set of common methods in our Action base class to support posting user interface messages, so that we can replace redundant blocks of code in subclasses with invocations to the new APIs. This should result in a significant reduction in the lines of code in our example Actions, leading, in turn, to improved readability and ease of maintenance and reducing the risk of bugs.

The example Actions introduced in the solution to Pitfall 3.1: Business-Tier Code in Actions will be modified as a starting point for our example solution. Listings 3.7 and 3.8 demonstrate.

```
// Imports, javadoc, etc.
...
public class FindInvoiceAction extends Action
{
    public ActionForward execute(ActionMapping mapping,
                                 ActionForm form,
                                 HttpServletRequest request,
                                 HttpServletResponse response)
        throws Exception
    {
        FindInvoiceForm findInvoiceForm = (FindInvoiceForm) form;
        FindInvoiceBean bean = (FindInvoiceBean)
            findInvoiceForm.getBean();
        Integer invoiceNumber = bean.getInvoiceNumber();

        InvoiceDO invoice = null;
        try {
            InvoiceDelegate delegate = InvoiceDelegate.getInstance();
            invoice = delegate.findInvoice(bean);
        }
        catch (InvoiceDelegate.NotFoundException e) {
            ActionError error =
```

Listing 3.7 FindInvoiceAction with copy/paste error-handling code.

```
                new ActionError("error.find", invoiceNumber);
            ActionErrors errors = new ActionErrors();
            errors.add(ActionErrors.GLOBAL_ERROR, error);
            saveErrors(request, errors);
            return mapping.findForward("findInvoicePage");
        }
        catch (DelegateException e) {
            e.printStackTrace();
            ActionError error = new ActionError("error.system");
            ActionErrors errors = new ActionErrors();
            errors.add(ActionErrors.GLOBAL_ERROR, error);
            saveErrors(request, errors);
            return mapping.findForward("findInvoicePage");
        }

        InvoiceForm invoiceForm = (InvoiceForm)
            request.getSession().getAttribute("invoiceForm");
        invoiceForm.populate(invoice);
        return mapping.findForward("saveInvoicePage");
    }
}
```

Listing 3.7 *(continued)*


```
// Imports, javadoc, etc.
...
public class SaveInvoiceAction extends Action
{
    public ActionForward execute(ActionMapping mapping,
                                 ActionForm form,
                                 HttpServletRequest request,
                                 HttpServletResponse response)
        throws Exception
    {
        InvoiceForm invoiceForm = (InvoiceForm)form;
        InvoiceDO invoice = (InvoiceDO) invoiceForm.getBean();

        try {
            InvoiceDelegate delegate = InvoiceDelegate.getInstance();
            invoice = delegate.applyDiscount(invoice);
            delegate.saveInvoice(invoice);
        }
        catch (InvoiceDelegate.NotFoundException e) {
            ActionError error =
                new ActionError("error.find",
                    invoice.getInvoiceNumber());
```

Listing 3.8 SaveInvoiceAction with copy/paste error-handling code. *(continues)*

```
            ActionErrors errors = new ActionErrors();
            errors.add(ActionErrors.GLOBAL_ERROR, error);
            saveErrors(request, errors);
            return mapping.findForward("saveInvoicePage");
        }
        catch (DelegateException e) {
            ActionError error = new ActionError("error.save");
            ActionErrors errors = new ActionErrors();
            errors.add(ActionErrors.GLOBAL_ERROR, error);
            saveErrors(request, errors);
            return mapping.findForward("saveInvoicePage");
        }

        invoiceForm.populate(invoice);

        ActionMessage message = new ActionMessage("message.confirm");
        ActionMessages messages = new ActionMessages();
        messages.add(ActionMessages.GLOBAL_MESSAGE, message);
        saveMessages(request, messages);
        return mapping.findForward("confirmInvoicePage");
    }
}
```

Listing 3.8 (continued)

First, let's move one of the bits of code used to post ActionErrors. We can take the following snippet and move it to a method in our base Action class.

```
ActionError error = new ActionError("error.find", invoiceNumber);
ActionErrors errors = new ActionErrors();
errors.add(ActionErrors.GLOBAL_ERROR, error);
saveErrors(request, errors);
```

Here's the new method.

```
protected void postGlobalError(String errorKey,
                               Object arg,
                               HttpServletRequest request) {
    ActionError error = new ActionError(errorKey, arg);
    ActionErrors errors = new ActionErrors();
    errors.add(ActionErrors.GLOBAL_ERROR, error);
    saveErrors(request, errors);
}
```

Note that this method is designed to support posting a single message. Additional APIs can be added later to handle posting lists of messages, if necessary.

Once we have tested our changes and made sure that they work, we can move another block of code, such as the following.

```
ActionError error = new ActionError("error.system");
ActionErrors errors = new ActionErrors();
errors.add(ActionErrors.GLOBAL_ERROR, error);
saveErrors(request, errors);
```

We'll change the base class method we created earlier so that the implementation can be shared. Here's how the new code would look in BaseAction.

```
    protected void postGlobalError(String errorKey,
                                   HttpServletRequest request) {
        postGlobalError(errorKey, null, request);
    }

    protected void postGlobalError(String errorKey,
                                   Object arg,
                                   HttpServletRequest request) {
        ActionError error = (arg == null ?
                             new ActionError(errorKey) :
                             new ActionError(errorKey, arg));
        ActionErrors errors = new ActionErrors();
        errors.add(ActionErrors.GLOBAL_ERROR, error);
        saveErrors(request, errors);
    }
```

Next we'll make FindInvoiceAction extend the BaseAction class.

```
public class FindInvoiceAction extends BaseAction
{
    ...
```

Finally we can migrate the ActionMessage code in much the same manner. Listing 3.9 demonstrates the resulting BaseAction class.

```
package com.aboutobjects.pitfalls;

import javax.servlet.http.HttpServletRequest;

import org.apache.struts.action.*;
import org.apache.struts.config.ApplicationConfig;
import org.apache.struts.util.RequestUtils;
import org.apache.struts.actions.DispatchAction;

/**
```

Listing 3.9 The BaseAction class. *(continues)*

```java
 * A Base class for our Actions.
 */
public class BaseAction extends Action
{
    protected void postGlobalError(String errorKey,
                                   HttpServletRequest request) {
        postGlobalError(errorKey, null, request);
    }

    protected void postGlobalError(String errorKey,
                                   Object arg,
                                   HttpServletRequest request) {
        ActionError error = (arg == null ?
                             new ActionError(errorKey) :
                             new ActionError(errorKey, arg));
        ActionErrors errors = new ActionErrors();
        errors.add(ActionErrors.GLOBAL_ERROR, error);
        saveErrors(request, errors);
    }

    protected void postGlobalMessage(String messageKey,
                                     HttpServletRequest request) {
        postGlobalMessage(messageKey, null, request);
    }

    protected void postGlobalMessage(String messageKey,
                                     Object arg,
                                     HttpServletRequest request) {
        ActionMessage message = (arg == null ?
                                 new ActionError(messageKey) :
                                 new ActionError(messageKey, arg));
        ActionMessages messages = new ActionMessages();
        messages.add(ActionMessages.GLOBAL_MESSAGE, message);
        saveMessages(request, messages);
    }
}
```

Listing 3.9 *(continued)*

We can now clean up our Actions to eliminate the blocks of redundant code, thereby improving the clarity and maintainability of the classes. Listing 3.10 shows the slimmer, trimmer versions of our Actions.

```java
package com.aboutobjects.pitfalls;

import java.io.IOException;
import javax.servlet.ServletException;
```

Listing 3.10 Trimmed-down version of FindInvoiceAction.

```java
import javax.servlet.http.HttpServletRequest;
import javax.servlet.http.HttpServletResponse;

import com.aboutobjects.pitfalls.delegate.DelegateException;
import com.aboutobjects.pitfalls.delegate.InvoiceDelegate;
import org.apache.struts.action.ActionForm;
import org.apache.struts.action.ActionForward;
import org.apache.struts.action.ActionMapping;

/**
 * An Action that attempts to find an InvoiceDO. If one is found,
 * the InvoiceForm in the session is initialized with its values, and
 * we forward to the Save Invoice page. Otherwise, we return to the
 * Find Invoice page and display an appropriate error message.
 */
public class FindInvoiceAction extends BaseAction
{
    public ActionForward execute(ActionMapping mapping,
                                 ActionForm form,
                                 HttpServletRequest request,
                                 HttpServletResponse response)
        throws IOException, ServletException
    {
        FindInvoiceForm findInvoiceForm = (FindInvoiceForm) form;
        FindInvoiceBean bean = (FindInvoiceBean)
            findInvoiceForm.getBean();
        Integer invoiceNumber = bean.getInvoiceNumber();

        InvoiceDO invoice = null;
        try {
            InvoiceDelegate delegate = InvoiceDelegate.getInstance();
            invoice = delegate.findInvoice(bean);
        }
        catch (InvoiceDelegate.NotFoundException e) {
            postGlobalError("error.find", invoiceNumber, request);
            return mapping.findForward("findInvoicePage");
        }
        catch (DelegateException e) {
            e.printStackTrace();
            postGlobalError("error.system", request);
            return mapping.findForward("findInvoicePage");
        }

        // Note: the following line contains a bug we'll explore later

        InvoiceForm invoiceForm = (InvoiceForm)
            request.getSession().getAttribute("invoiceForm");
        invoiceForm.populate(invoice);
```

Listing 3.10 *(continued)*

```
            return mapping.findForward("saveInvoicePage");
    }
}
```

Listing 3.10 *(continued)*

Now we can replace the error-handling code in SaveInvoiceAction, resulting in the shorter and easier-to-read version in Listing 3.11.

```
package com.aboutobjects.pitfalls;

import java.io.IOException;
import javax.servlet.ServletException;
import javax.servlet.http.HttpServletRequest;
import javax.servlet.http.HttpServletResponse;

import com.aboutobjects.pitfalls.delegate.DelegateException;
import com.aboutobjects.pitfalls.delegate.InvoiceDelegate;
import org.apache.struts.action.*;

/**
 * An Action that attempts to save an invoice. If the invoice is saved,
 * we forward to the Confirmation page. Otherwise, we return to the
 * Save Invoice page and display an appropriate error message.
 */
public class SaveInvoiceAction extends BaseAction
{
    public ActionForward execute(ActionMapping mapping,
                                 ActionForm form,
                                 HttpServletRequest request,
                                 HttpServletResponse response)
        throws Exception {
        InvoiceForm invoiceForm = (InvoiceForm)form;
        InvoiceDO invoice = (InvoiceDO) invoiceForm.getBean();

        try {
            InvoiceDelegate delegate = InvoiceDelegate.getInstance();
            delegate.saveInvoice(invoice);
        }
        catch (InvoiceDelegate.NotFoundException e) {
            Integer invoiceNumber = invoice.getInvoiceNumber();
            postGlobalError("error.find", invoiceNumber, request);
            return mapping.findForward("saveInvoicePage");
        }
```

Listing 3.11 Trimmed-down version of SaveInvoiceAction.

```
        catch (DelegateException e) {
            postGlobalError("error.save", request);
            return mapping.findForward("saveInvoicePage");
        }

        invoiceForm.populate(invoice);
        postGlobalMessage("message.confirm", request);
        return mapping.findForward("confirmInvoicePage");
    }
}
```

Listing 3.11 *(continued)*

Pitfall 3.3: Accessing ActionForms in the Session

When the Struts framework processes a request, it begins by consulting the ActionMapping configuration information coded by the developer in struts-config.xml. The framework uses the ActionMapping to resolve the URI transmitted in a request to a corresponding Action class to be used to service the request. The framework attempts to locate an instance of the class, instantiating one if none is found, and then invokes the instance's execute() method. If a form name is provided in the ActionMapping (by setting the ActionMapping's *name* attribute), the framework also attempts to locate an instance of the corresponding ActionForm, instantiating one if none is found, and passes a reference to the ActionForm instance as one of the formal parameters to the execute() method.

This convenient arrangement is often sufficient for a majority of the Actions in an application. Some Actions, though, need to work with more than one ActionForm. Because Action's execute() method has only one parameter of type ActionForm, the framework is unable to support this directly, so code must be added to Actions to locate any additional ActionForm instances.

A common example is an Action that performs a find. Here, the ActionForm that Struts passes to the execute() method would likely be used to hold query parameters submitted by the user. If the find succeeds, it returns the resulting values, perhaps as a value object, to the Action, which must now forward to a JSP to present the results to the user. The form in that JSP may be bound to a different ActionForm—one that is designed to allow the user to modify the resulting values, as opposed to the original ActionForm, which allowed the user to submit a query.

To borrow a concrete example from Pitfall 3.2, the FindInvoiceAction is passed a FindInvoiceForm in its parameter list. If it succeeds in finding an invoice, the Action then forwards to ModifyInvoice.jsp, which is bound to the InvoiceForm, not to the FindInvoiceForm. During rendering, ModifyInvoice.jsp will access the InvoiceForm to incorporate values from the invoice in the generated HTML. Because this occurs immediately after the return from FindInvoiceAction's execute() method, InvoiceForm must be populated sometime between the call to the finder method and execution of the return statement.

The question is, how does the FindInvoiceAction locate the InvoiceForm? There are four possible answers:

1. By directly calling getAttribute() on the session (and/or the request)
2. By instantiating a new InvoiceForm and calling setAttribute() on the appropriate scope

3. By implementing code that mimics the way Struts locates ActionForms

4. By directly invoking the code that Struts uses to locate ActionForms

And herein lies the pitfall: If left to their own devices, development teams are likely to use any or all of these approaches in a single application. Unfortunately, the first two methods generally cause bugs (unless you happen to be lucky), and the third is fragile, as it isn't guaranteed to be forward-compatible with future releases of Struts. Even the fourth would be messy if implemented as a copy/paste solution because it involves a fair bit of nonobvious code.

The way out of this pitfall is to provide a base Action class that the rest of your Actions can extend. The base Action class should include a method that implements the right approach to locating ActionForms, so that any Action that needs it can readily access the functionality. It then becomes a relatively simple matter to educate the members of the development team about the desired usage. This is usually an easy sell because you are handing developers a tidy, one-line solution to the problem.

Example

As noted previously, although the ActionMappings in struts-config.xml provide us with a handy facility for designating an ActionForm to be passed as a parameter when a given Action's execute() method is invoked, some execute() methods require access to more than one ActionForm.

A typical example is an execute() method that receives an ActionForm containing search criteria and then populates a different ActionForm with the resulting values before forwarding to a JSP that renders the values. It is a simple matter to get the second ActionForm from the request or the session, provided that it has been placed there previously by the framework. The problem is that when a given Action is invoked for the first time, there's no guarantee that the framework has initialized the second ActionForm yet.

Once again, we can borrow code from the solution to Pitfall 3.2: Copy/Paste Code in Actions as the basis for our example. Note that Listing 3.12 includes a line of code that gets the InvoiceAction from the session. Unfortunately, the first time its execute method is called, we have no guarantee that an InvoiceForm has been instantiated yet, so this call could result in a NullPointerException being thrown. We'll discuss the mechanics of this shortly.

```
// Imports, Javadoc, etc.
...
public class FindInvoiceAction extends BaseAction
{
    public ActionForward execute(ActionMapping mapping,
                                 ActionForm form,
                                 HttpServletRequest request,
                                 HttpServletResponse response)
        throws IOException, ServletException
    {
        FindInvoiceForm findInvoiceForm = (FindInvoiceForm) form;
        FindInvoiceBean bean = (FindInvoiceBean)
            findInvoiceForm.getBean();
        Integer invoiceNumber = bean.getInvoiceNumber();

        InvoiceDO invoice = null;
        try {
            InvoiceDelegate delegate = InvoiceDelegate.getInstance();
            invoice = delegate.findInvoice(bean);
        }
        catch (InvoiceDelegate.NotFoundException e) {
            postGlobalError("error.find", invoiceNumber, request);
            return mapping.findForward("findInvoicePage");
        }
        catch (DelegateException e) {
            e.printStackTrace();
            postGlobalError("error.system", request);
            return mapping.findForward("findInvoicePage");
        }

        // Note: the following line contains a bug
        InvoiceForm invoiceForm = (InvoiceForm)
            request.getSession().getAttribute("invoiceForm");
        invoiceForm.populate(invoice);
        return mapping.findForward("saveInvoicePage");
    }
}
```

Listing 3.12 A FindInvoiceAction that gets the InvoiceForm from the session.

A second approach that introduces a potentially more evil bug is to instantiate the InvoiceForm and place it in the session ourselves, by replacing the following line:

```
InvoiceForm invoiceForm = (InvoiceForm)
    request.getSession().getAttribute("invoiceForm");
```

with this innocuous-looking snippet.

```
InvoiceForm invoiceForm = new InvoiceForm();
request.getSession().setAttribute("invoiceForm");
```

The primary problem with this approach is that we may have just clobbered an InvoiceForm instance that had been placed in the session previously. We know that the InvoiceForm is used in other Actions—for example, in SaveInvoiceAction (see Pitfall 3.2). Developers can store and access arbitrary state in ActionForms that live in the session, so replacing the existing instance with the one we just instantiated could have unknown, harmful consequences.

Of course, we could combine the two approaches, as in the following code:

```
InvoiceForm invoiceForm = (InvoiceForm)
    request.getSession().getAttribute("invoiceForm");

if (invoiceForm == null) {
    invoiceForm = new InvoiceForm();
    request.getSession().setAttribute(Constants.INVOICE_FORM,
                                      invoiceForm);
}
```

We would, however, still be omitting a couple of steps that the framework code carries out behind the scenes when it initializes forms (for example, we are not handling ActionForms in request scope at all, nor are we calling getServlet() on the new form instance as we should), leaving us open to potential bugs and performance issues down the road.

Finally, given that Struts is an open source project, we could copy and paste the pertinent framework code right into our Action class. But then we would still be stuck with copy/paste implementations, and even worse, our Actions could have forward-compatibility problems, as future releases of Struts might change some of the underlying details, causing our implementation to break.

To understand why the call to getAttribute() we discussed in the first approach can result in a null pointer exception, we need to look at how the framework initializes ActionForms. When Struts receives a request, it locates a corresponding ActionMapping in struts-config.xml to determine which Action to invoke.

One of the optional attributes of an ActionMapping is *name*, which is used to associate the Action with an ActionForm. If the name attribute is not set, no form is passed when the Action's execute() method is invoked. If it *is* set, the specified ActionForm is passed. Struts locates an instance by first looking in the session. If an instance is found there, it is used; otherwise, Struts constructs a new instance and places it in the session.

This generally happens the first time the Action is called, although because a given form can be associated with several different Actions, the form might already have been instantiated in response to an earlier request. For this reason, the bug introduced by the first approach covered in this pitfall may be difficult to reproduce.

For example, given the following struts-config.xml, the framework will instantiate the FindInvoiceForm (based on the value of the name attribute) prior to the FindInvoiceAction's execute() method being called for the first time.

```xml
...
<form-beans>
    <form-bean name="invoiceForm"
               type="com.aboutobjects.pitfalls.InvoiceForm"/>
    <form-bean name="findInvoiceForm"
               type="com.aboutobjects.pitfalls.FindInvoiceForm"/>
</form-beans>
...
<action-mappings>
    <action path="/findInvoice"
            type="com.aboutobjects.pitfalls.FindInvoiceAction"
            validate="true"
            name="findInvoiceForm"
            input="/FindInvoice.jsp">
        <forward name="findInvoicePage" path="/FindInvoice.jsp"/>
        <forward name="saveInvoicePage" path="/SaveInvoice.jsp"/>
    </action>

    <action path="/saveInvoice"
            type="com.aboutobjects.pitfalls.SaveInvoiceAction"
            validate="true"
            input="/SaveInvoice.jsp"
            name="invoiceForm">
        <forward name="saveInvoicePage" path="/SaveInvoice.jsp"/>
        <forward name="confirmInvoicePage"
                 path="/ConfirmInvoice.jsp"/>
    </action>
    ...
<action-mappings>
...
```

Because the Form Bean is then placed in session scope, the framework will simply use that instance the next time the execute() method is invoked.

Note that the FindInvoiceForm is the form that contains the search criteria entered by the user, and it is the form that is submitted when the user clicks the Submit button on the page. The execute() method not only must access this form to get the values of the search criteria to use in performing the search, it also must do some setup for the next page if the search succeeds.

In this case, the next page will display the results of the search. The corresponding JSP therefore needs to reference values not in the FindInvoiceForm, but in the InvoiceForm, which was not passed in as an argument because only one form can be passed in at a time. Therefore, the execute() method will have to get the InvoiceForm instance itself, as illustrated in Figure 3.3.

Solving Pitfall 3.3: Add ActionForm Locator Method to Base Class

As we discovered earlier, when an Action attempts to access a form by invoking getAttribute() on the request or the session, the framework does not guarantee that the form has been initialized. Because it is common for Actions to work with more than one form, this solution will focus on moving (and improving) any such code that may already exist in the application so that it works correctly and is available in a central location.

❶ RequestProcessor passes FindInvoiceForm as parameter to execute() method.

❷ FindInvoiceAction gets InvoiceForm from session.

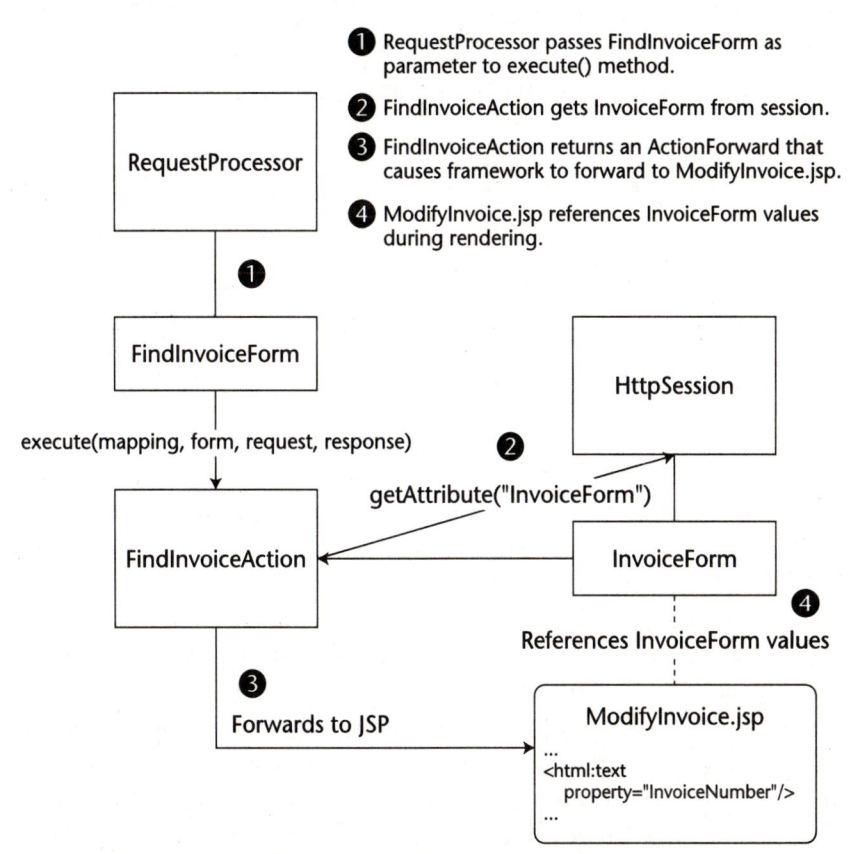

❸ FindInvoiceAction returns an ActionForward that causes framework to forward to ModifyInvoice.jsp.

❹ ModifyInvoice.jsp references InvoiceForm values during rendering.

Figure 3.3 Execute() method gets InvoiceForm instance.

The optimal solution involves writing a method to invoke the mechanism that Struts uses to locate ActionForms. We will do this by adding a new method, getForm(), to the base class for our Actions. In the solution to Pitfall 3.2: Copy/Paste Code in Actions, we created a BaseAction class that we can use as a starting point, along with the FindInvoiceAction class from that section.

This solution will serve to minimize dependencies on underlying implementation details of the Struts framework while providing a central method, readily accessible to all of our Actions, that will transparently check for the existence of a form and initialize it correctly if necessary. The caller need not be aware of these details and thus is not tied to the implementation, leaving us free to change it later if necessary.

Step-by-Step

1. Implement a getForm() method in your base Action class.
2. Locate all Actions in your application that deal with more than one form.
   a. Make sure that they extend the base Action class.
   b. Replace any code used to get forms from the session or request with calls to getForm().

Example

The first step we need to take is to add a getForm() method to our BaseAction class that will provide a centralized mechanism for looking up forms and initializing them, if necessary. At first glance it would appear that the most straightforward way to initialize a form would be to call the RequestProcessor's processActionForm() method, but closer inspection reveals that this method has been declared as protected in the current release of Struts. We could subclass RequestProcessor to get around this, but rather than sidestep the intent of the framework, let's explore an alternative: calling the createActionForm() method in RequestUtils.

Either one of these methods requires us to pass in an ActionMapping that defines the form we want to use. Our getForm() method will need callers to provide, at a minimum, a key identifying the mapping. We'll revisit this point later when we look at how to modify the code in our Actions. For now, here's an implementation of getForm() that uses RequestUtils to initialize the form, if necessary.

```
    protected ActionForm getForm(String formName,
                                 String path,
                                 HttpServletRequest request) {
        ActionForm form = (ActionForm) request.getAttribute(formName);
        if (form == null) {
            form = (ActionForm) request.getSession().getAttribute(formName);
        }
        if (form == null) {
            ApplicationConfig appConfig = (ApplicationConfig)
                request.getAttribute(Action.APPLICATION_KEY);
            ActionMapping mapping = (ActionMapping)
                appConfig.findActionConfig(path);
            form = RequestUtils.createActionForm(request,
                                                 mapping,
                                                 appConfig,
                                                 (ActionServlet) getServlet());
            String key = mapping.getAttribute();
            if (mapping.getScope().equals("request"))
                request.setAttribute(key, form);
            else
                request.getSession().setAttribute(key, form);
        }
        return form;
    }
}
```

Now we can modify the code in our Actions to invoke this method whenever they need to access a form other than the one passed in as a parameter. First, though, we will need to find the appropriate ActionMapping to reference in struts-config.xml. Here's a mapping we could use to access the InvoiceForm.

```
<action path="/saveInvoice"
        type="com.aboutobjects.pitfalls.SaveInvoiceAction"
        validate="true"
        input="/SaveInvoice.jsp"
        name="invoiceForm">
    <forward name="saveInvoicePage" path="/SaveInvoice.jsp"/>
    <forward name="confirmInvoicePage" path="/ConfirmInvoice.jsp"/>
</action>
```

Now we can modify the code in the FindInvoiceAction to call getForm(), using the value of the *path* attribute to identify the mapping. Here is the new version of FindInvoiceAction, shown in Listing 3.13.

```
package com.aboutobjects.pitfalls;

import javax.servlet.http.HttpServletRequest;
import javax.servlet.http.HttpServletResponse;
```

Listing 3.13 FindInvoiceAction after moving code to the getForm() method. *(continues)*

```java
import com.aboutobjects.pitfalls.delegate.DelegateException;
import com.aboutobjects.pitfalls.delegate.InvoiceDelegate;
import org.apache.struts.action.ActionForm;
import org.apache.struts.action.ActionForward;
import org.apache.struts.action.ActionMapping;

/**
 * An Action that attempts to find an InvoiceDO. If one is found,
 * the InvoiceForm in the session is initialized with its values, and
 * we forward to the Save Invoice page. Otherwise, we return to the
 * Find Invoice page and display an appropriate error message.
 */
public class FindInvoiceAction extends BaseAction
{
    public ActionForward execute(ActionMapping mapping,
                                 ActionForm form,
                                 HttpServletRequest request,
                                 HttpServletResponse response)
        throws Exception
    {
        FindInvoiceForm findInvoiceForm = (FindInvoiceForm) form;
        FindInvoiceBean bean = (FindInvoiceBean)
            findInvoiceForm.getBean();
        Integer invoiceNumber = bean.getInvoiceNumber();

        InvoiceDO invoice = null;
        try {
            InvoiceDelegate delegate = InvoiceDelegate.getInstance();
            invoice = delegate.findInvoice(bean);
        }
        catch (InvoiceDelegate.NotFoundException e) {
            postGlobalError("error.find", invoiceNumber, request);
            return mapping.findForward("findInvoicePage");
        }
        catch (DelegateException e) {
            e.printStackTrace();
            postGlobalError("error.system", request);
            return mapping.findForward("findInvoicePage");
        }

        InvoiceForm invoiceForm = (InvoiceForm)
            getForm("invoiceForm", "/saveInvoice", request);
        invoiceForm.populate(invoice);
        return mapping.findForward("saveInvoicePage");
    }
}
```

Listing 3.13 *(continued)*

Note that by applying the combined solutions from the previous sections, we have reduced the code size by more than half, as can be seen by comparing Listing 3.13 with the original version of Listing 3.1. The result is a more readable class, less code to maintain, and fewer places that require modification when a given change needs to be introduced.

Pitfall 3.4: Overloaded ActionMappings

It's not unusual to find developers writing Actions that both navigate to a page and handle forms submitted from that page. Apart from adding one extra level of confusion to the mix, there's nothing inherently wrong with coding Actions this way. However, unless extra care is taken when defining the ActionMappings that correspond to such Actions, the application may begin to exhibit some odd and befuddling quirks. For example, you may end up with a page that displays validation error messages when users first navigate to it, before they have had a chance to fill in a field—much less submit the form.

The general form of this pitfall is to write an execute() method that performs two or more entirely different functions, depending on the value of a request parameter, and to use a single ActionMapping in struts-config.xml to configure it.

```
String invoiceNum = request.getParameter("invoiceNum");
if (invoiceNum != null) {
    // Do something
    ...
    return mapping.findForward("modifyInvoicePage");
}
else {
    // Do something completely different
    ...
    return mapping.findForward("modifyInvoicePage");
}
```

Example

The execute() method in the ModifyInvoiceAction that follows can be used either to navigate to the Modify Invoice page or to handle submission of the Modify Invoice page's form. The method looks for a magic parameter, invoiceNum, in the request. If the parameter is there, the method assumes that this is a request to navigate to the page, and it uses the value invoiceNum to find the invoice to display. If invoiceNum is not in the request, then the method assumes that the user has submitted a form from the Modify Invoice page, and it attempts to save the values passed in via the ActionForm in the parameter list, as you can see in Listing 3.14.

```java
public class ModifyInvoiceAction extends BaseAction
{
    public ActionForward execute(ActionMapping mapping,
                                 ActionForm form,
                                 HttpServletRequest request,
                                 HttpServletResponse response)
        throws Exception {

        String invoiceNum = request.getParameter("invoiceNum");
        if (invoiceNum != null) {
            // If magic request parameter "invoiceNum" is set
            // then we're navigating to the Modify Invoice page, so
            // use the value of invoiceNum to find the invoice
            Integer invoiceNumber = new Integer(invoiceNum);
            try {
                InvoiceDelegate delegate =
                    InvoiceDelegate.getInstance();
                FindInvoiceBean bean =
                    new FindInvoiceBean(invoiceNumber);
                InvoiceDO invoice = delegate.findInvoice(bean);
                InvoiceForm invoiceForm = (InvoiceForm)
                    getForm("invoiceForm", "/saveInvoice", request);
                invoiceForm.populate(invoice);
            }
            catch (InvoiceDelegate.NotFoundException e) {
                postGlobalError("error.find", invoiceNumber, request);
            }
            catch (DelegateException e) {
                e.printStackTrace();
                postGlobalError("error.system", request);
            }
            // We're going to the Modify Invoice Page
            return mapping.findForward("modifyInvoicePage");
        }
        else {
            // The user is submitting a modify request from the
            // Modify Invoice page, so attempt to save the
            // submitted form
            InvoiceForm invoiceForm = (InvoiceForm)form;
            InvoiceDO invoice = (InvoiceDO) invoiceForm.getBean();
            try {
                InvoiceDelegate delegate =
                    InvoiceDelegate.getInstance();
                delegate.saveInvoice(invoice);
            }
            catch (InvoiceDelegate.NotFoundException e) {
                Integer invoiceNumber = invoice.getInvoiceNumber();
                postGlobalError("error.find", invoiceNumber, request);
                return mapping.findForward("modifyInvoicePage");
```

Listing 3.14 ModifyInvoiceAction.java. *(continues)*

```
            }
            catch (DelegateException e) {
                postGlobalError("error.save", request);
                return mapping.findForward("modifyInvoicePage");
            }
            invoiceForm.populate(invoice);
            postGlobalMessage("message.confirm", request);
            // We're going to the Confirmation Page
            return mapping.findForward("confirmInvoicePage");
        }
    }
}
```

Listing 3.14 *(continued)*

Here's one of the more comical scenarios that can ensue when employing this pitfall. Let's assume that while one developer, Developer A, is working on the ModifyInvoiceAction Action, another developer, Developer B, is adding validation code in the InvoiceForm. In order to avoid holding up other developers, Developer B goes into struts-config.xml and turns validation off in the appropriate ActionMappings until the new validations have been fully tested (using JUnit, of course).

```
<action path="/modifyInvoice"
        type="com.aboutobjects.pitfalls.ModifyInvoiceAction"
        validate="false"
        input="/ValidationErrors.jsp"
        name="invoiceForm">
    <forward name="modifyInvoicePage" path="/ModifyInvoice.jsp"/>
    <forward name="confirmInvoicePage" path="/ConfirmInvoice.jsp"/>
</action>
```

Note in particular that the value of the input attribute is set to point to ValidationErrors.jsp. This is the JSP that is to be rendered when validation fails.

Getting back to our scenario, Developer A now tests the ModifyInvoiceAction, and it works perfectly. Sometime later, when the validation code is working properly in the test harness, Developer B goes back into struts-config.xml and sets the validate attribute in the ActionMapping back to true. The result? The Modify Invoice Page is now unreachable.

What happened? The problem here is that the modifyInvoice ActionMapping specifies that the InvoiceForm should be passed to the Action (name="invoiceForm") and that the form should be validated (validate="true"). As we learned in the previous pitfall, Struts automatically initializes a given ActionForm the first time a submitted URI selects an ActionMapping that binds it.

In our case, the path "/modifyInvoice" is first encountered when we try to navigate to the Modify Invoice page, so Struts initializes the InvoiceForm at this point. Because it is a brand new instance, all of its fields are initially null. Assuming that at least one of the fields on the InvoiceForm is being validated as a required field in the new validation rules that Developer B just added, we are guaranteed that a new instance of InvoiceForm will fail validation because null is not an allowable value for a required field.

Doh! Developer B just set validate to true in struts-config.xml, so the brand new instance of InvoiceForm is going to be validated whenever we attempt to navigate to the page we need to get to in order to change its values! And remember, as we mentioned earlier, the input attribute of the ActionMapping identifies the JSP to forward to if there are validation errors. In this case, it is ValidationErrors.jsp, so when our futile attempts to navigate to the Modify Invoice page result in a validation failure, we are taken directly to the Validation Errors page. Sweet! There is now an unreachable page in our application.

One way to avoid this pitfall completely is to code separate Actions for navigation and form submission, though that may be a bit drastic. A simpler and less restrictive way is to create separate ActionMappings in struts-config.xml for navigation and form submission—and to make sure that the name attribute is never set in ActionMappings used for navigation, so that navigating doesn't have the side effect of processing an ActionForm.

Solving Pitfall 3.4: Create Separate ActionMappings for Navigation and Form Submission

This pitfall can be resolved by applying the Create Separate ActionMappings for Uncohesive Methods solution, which simply requires adding an ActionMapping to struts-config.xml and enables us to avert potential runtime errors.

Step-by-Step

1. Locate overloaded ActionMappings.
2. Create additional ActionMappings in struts-config as necessary.

Example

All we need to do to fix the problem outlined in this pitfall is to provide an additional ActionMapping in struts-config.xml. Assuming that we have already defined an ActionMapping such as the following, which handles submission of the InvoiceForm from the Modify Invoice page, we can simply add another ActionMapping to handle navigation to the Modify Invoice page. Here's the existing ActionMapping for modifying an invoice:

```
<action path="/modifyInvoice"
        type="com.aboutobjects.pitfalls.ModifyInvoiceAction"
        validate="true"
        input="/ValidationErrors.jsp"
        name="invoiceForm">
    <forward name="modifyInvoicePage" path="/ModifyInvoice.jsp"/>
    <forward name="confirmInvoicePage" path="/ConfirmInvoice.jsp"/>
</action>
```

We'll add a new ActionMapping to navigate to the ModifyInvoice page:

```
<action path="/goToModifyInvoice"
        type="com.aboutobjects.pitfalls.ModifyInvoiceAction"
        input="/ModifyInvoice.jsp"">
    <forward name="modifyInvoicePage" path="/ModifyInvoice.jsp"/>
</action>
```

Note that the navigation mapping no longer requires the name attribute to be provided because we don't need to and should not submit a form when navigating.

Of course, our simple Modify Invoice scenario could have been just as well carried out by the separate find and save actions that we have used in our previous examples, which had the virtues of being simpler and relatively fool-proof. The important thing is that we now have the flexibility to pick the design that best fits the needs of a given set of Web pages.

CHAPTER 4

Struts TagLibs and JSPs

TagLibs are the extension mechanism for JSPs. Struts takes advantage of this mechanism to provide a comprehensive set of TagLibs that ease the development of view components. Used correctly, they can help promote a cleaner separation of model, view, and controller components and simplify JSPs by eliminating the need for most scriptlet code. Pitfalls in using these TagLibs usually arise from a lack of specific knowledge of how the TagLibs that Struts provides are intended to be used, and from a lack of understanding of TagLibs in general.

TagLibs are architecturally part of the view of the application and are best used as such. Due to TagLibs' inherent flexibility however, developers somtimes introduce model or controller code into their JSPs. When TagLibs are used to blur the lines between the model, view, and controller components, it's a good sign that some pitfall-infected code is creeping into your JSP. This chapter examines these and other pitfalls developers may encounter in coding JSPs using the Struts TagLibs.

Pitfall 4.1: Hard-Coded Strings in JSPs describes the habit of many developers to hard-code string values directly into their JSPs. The pitfall shows its teeth when *name* shows up more than once, resulting in a dual maintenance point.

Pitfall 4.2: Hard-Coded Keys in JSPs is related to Pitfall 4.1 because developers will often turn from hard-coded strings to this pitfall and hard-code the names of the properties into their JSPs. This usually turns into a maintenance hassle over time.

Pitfall 4.3: Not Using Struts Tags for Error Messaging describes the habit of developers to manage error messages themselves, resulting in developers doing manually what is already provided (that is, tested and well designed) in Struts.

Pitfall 4.4: Calculating Derived Values in JSPs examines the consequences of using scriptlets to perform calculations in JSPs.

Pitfall 4.5: Performing Business Logic in JSPs involves an even more serious form of blurring the lines between the models, views, and controllers in a Struts application. If business logic is in a JSP, then each point in the user interface that needs that processing will have to have a copy of the code—definitely not recommended.

Pitfall 4.6: Hard-Coded Options in HTML Select Lists describes the problems developers often encounter with HTML select lists in Struts. Many developers find the Struts html:options tag confusing when they initially encounter it, and they simply find it expedient to code the values that they need directly in their JSP using the html:option tag instead. This leads to a lot more code than is required, thereby potentially increasing maintenance costs.

Pitfall 4.7: Not Checking for Duplicate Form Submissions addresses a common scenario involving the lack of synchronization between the interface presented in a browser and the state of the model on the server. This has the potential to corrupt the underlying data store by creating duplicate records, overwriting current data with stale values, and more.

Pitfall 4.1: Hard-Coded Strings in JSPs

Struts provides a tag for rendering string values by first looking them up in a resource bundle. Many developers, though, hard-code the strings directly into their JSPs. When the JSPs are first being written it may not be apparent that anything else could or should happen—if the string "Name" appears on only one form in a Web application, then why would we want to have to look up that string to get it onto the Web page? The pitfall shows its teeth when "Name" shows up more than once. If that string is hard-coded in both places and if it ever needs to be changed (for example, to "First Name") there is a dual maintenance point. Whenever a dual maintenance point arises you can be fairly confident that a pitfall is lurking somewhere, making your life more difficult than it needs to be.

When the same instructional text, field label, or other string value appears to vary depending on which page the user is looking at, you are experiencing this pitfall. You will also notice that it is often painful and time-consuming to make simple changes and that far too many defect tickets are written against trivial JSP coding errors during system test.

This pitfall will be much more obvious if your development team faces language localization requirements. If your JSPs are trapped in this pitfall, each one will have to be translated individually. Usually the local language version of the user interface has already been coded by the time support for additional languages is addressed. If you have to translate your pages, don't brute-force the translation—apply the solution first.

Generally, this pitfall affects those newer to Struts who are usually distracted by other, more pressing issues during the earlier stages of development. The typical developer new to Struts is usually just trying to keep his or her head above water while riding the learning curve for Struts' major architectural aspects, much less trying to learn many of the seemingly unimportant tags in the extensive TagLib. Here's a simple example of a hard-coded string that might appear in a JSP.

```
...
<h1>Modify Invoice</h1>
...
```

At first pass, this might appear to be the right solution; the heading is Modify Invoice, and that is what it will remain for the foreseeable future. Why would you want to look it up? Well, let's go back to the example of translating the application into multiple languages and suppose that Modify Invoice appears on several pages. If localization is a requirement for your application, each page that the string appears on will have to be translated. Modifying all the pages will be an expensive proposition.

Example

Listing 4.1 provides an example of a JSP caught in this pitfall. Notice all the hard-coded strings.

The first hard-coded string is somewhat innocuous because it is probably unique to the current JSP. Unique strings can sometimes be the exception to the rule on hard-coding strings in JSPs (for apps that *don't* require localization) because they appear only once.

The next hard-coded string in the example is instructional text that may be used in several similar pages in the application. If the requirements for the text to be displayed change, every JSP the string appeared in will have to be updated. If the same text appears in more than a few places, it would be easy to miss an instance or mangle it, potentially resulting in bug reports being written against the affected page during system test. That, of course, means that you'll have to rummage through those same pages to make the same edits again.

Finally, we see a couple of hard-coded field labels. These same labels may occur on many other pages, sometimes in more than one place on a given page. Finding all occurrences of a given label and changing them all by hand can be quite tedious and has the potential to introduce errors.

Some content may be truly unique to a given page, and in that case there is little to be gained by abstracting it away (unless there are language localization requirements). Applications with a small page count are also less vulnerable to the downsides of this pitfall, particularly if there is little overlap between the content of the various pages.

```
...
<h1>Modify Invoice</h1> <%-- HARDCODED --%>
<p>
Modify one or more of the values below and press Submit<%-- HARDCODED --%>
<p>
<html:form action="/saveInvoice" method="post">
    <table>
        <tr>
            <td>Invoice Number: <td> <%-- HARDCODED --%>
            <td><html:text property="invoiceNumber"/></td>
        </tr>
        <tr>
            <td>Invoice Date: <td> <%-- HARDCODED --%>
            <td><html:text property="billingDate"/></td>
        </tr>
...
```

Listing 4.1 Hard-coded strings in a JSP.

To avoid this pitfall altogether, spend some time early in the project thinking through how strings will be presented in your JSP pages and setting guidelines for using resource bundles.

Solving Pitfall 4.1: Move Common Strings to Resource Bundles

In solving this pitfall, our goal is to allow for sharing of common string values across multiple JSPs. This solution is essential if your application has language localization requirements, but it is helpful in any case because it provides a centralized location for the storage of UI strings so that they can be shared by multiple JSPs, rather than be copied into each of the JSPs.

Step-by-Step

1. Create a .properties file.
    a. Place the .properties file somewhere in the path at runtime. It is typical to place the .properties file alongside the struts-config.xml file in the WAR file.
2. Begin with a single JSP.
    a. Start with the simplest JSP.
3. Search for hard-coded strings.
    a. Any string that will appear in the final HTML on the user's browser is a candidate to be a hard-coded string.
4. Create an entry in the .properties file for each unique string.
5. Replace the hard-coded strings with bean:message tags.
6. Deploy and test the changes.
7. Repeat for each JSP.

Example

In this example, we will walk through the steps laid out earlier to solve this pitfall. The first step is to create a messages.properties file to hold the strings. The next step is to choose a simple JSP to start with. We will begin with Listing 4.1. The next step is to identify all the hard-coded strings and put them into the properties file that we created. Here is a listing of the properties that are in the file.

```
...
example.title=Jakarta Pitfalls Example
invoice.modify.heading=Modify Invoice
label.invoice.number=Invoice Number:
label.billing.date=Billing Date:
instruction.modify=Modify one or more of the values below and press
Submit
...
```

The next step for this JSP is to replace the hard-coded values in the JSP with bean:message tags. Listing 4.2 is a partial listing of the code for the JSP with the strings replaced with bean:message tags.

Notice that the newly improved JSP does not have any display strings hard-coded in it. If localization ever becomes an issue for this page, then it will be easy to translate because all the user visible strings are in one file. In this listing the display strings are no longer hard-coded, but the names of the keys in the properties file are. Pitfall 4.2 addresses this issue.

```
...
<head>
    <title><bean:message key="example.title"/></title>
</head>

<body bgcolor="white">
<h1><bean:message key="modify.heading"/></h1>
<p>
<bean:message key="instruction.modify"/>
<p>
<html:form  action="/saveInvoice" method="post">
    <table>
        <tr>
            <td><bean:message key="label.invoice.number"/><td>
            <td><html:text property="invoiceNumber"/></td>
        </tr>
        <tr>
            <td><bean:message key="label.billing.date"/><td>
            <td><html:text property="billingDate"/></td>
        </tr>
    ...
```

Listing 4.2 JSP with bean:message tags.

Pitfall 4.2: Hard-Coded Keys in JSPs

This pitfall is related to Pitfall 4.1 because what usually happens (as we saw in the solution to Pitfall 4.1) is that a developer will turn from hard-coded strings to this pitfall and hard-code the names of the properties into his or her JSPs. This usually turns into a maintenance hassle over time. Suppose for example that the initial naming scheme for properties is outgrown, and a new naming scheme is introduced. The new naming scheme will require the old properties to be renamed. Searching through each JSP looking for each instance of the old property name becomes very tedious very quickly.

As an application grows in size and complexity, the burden required to maintain the hard-coded strings grows as well. Another issue is that the hard-coded values don't scale up to large teams well. Even though this pitfall seems rather harmless, it can lead to countless hours of tedious work to rename a single property.

Example

Here is the solved code from Listing 4.2. It is stuck in this pitfall because the names of the properties are hard-coded in the JSP.

```
...
<head>
    <title><bean:message key="example.title"/></title>
</head>

<body bgcolor="white">
<h1><bean:message key="modify.heading"/></h1>
<p>
<bean:message key="instruction.modify"/>
<p>
<html:form  action="/saveInvoice" method="post">
    <table>
        <tr>
            <td><bean:message key="label.invoice.number"/><td>
            <td><html:text property="invoiceNumber"/></td>
        </tr>
        <tr>
            <td><bean:message key="label.billing.date"/><td>
            <td><html:text property="billingDate"/></td>
        </tr>
...
```

Over time, we might decide that we want the properties used for labels in our forms to be named in a consistent three-part naming scheme where the first part of the name is an action of the string, the second part identifies a part of the model, and the third part of the name identifies the kind of string. Under this scheme the properties names would look like this:

```
...
modify.invoice.heading=Modify Invoice
label.invoice.number=Invoice Number:
label.billing.date=Billing Date:
modify.invoice.instruction =Modify one or more of the values below and
press Submit
...
```

If each of these names were spread out over several JSPs, we'd have to go to each JSP and update each occurrence of the property names. If you find yourself doing similar things, you are stuck in this pitfall.

Solving Pitfall 4.2: Replace Hard-Coded Keys with Constants

To solve this pitfall, the constant Strings should be captured in a Java constants class. One really nice thing about this solution is that it allows developers to take advantage of the syntax-checking facilities of IDEs in order to avoid runtime errors caused by invalid keys. The IDE can validate that Constants.MY_PROPERTY_NAME is a real attribute on the Constants class, but the IDE cannot validate my.property.name. Applying this solution also makes maintaining property definitions easier. If a key is changed in the properties file, only the constants class must be updated. Instead of performing a global search and replace on the key name in all of the JSPs, one simple value change is all that is needed.

Something to consider as you are applying the solution to this pitfall is not to go overboard on putting all your constants into one Java class. On a medium-sized project, you can end up with hundreds of properties; if each of those properties ends up in one Constants class, the class will then itself become a pitfall. Group the constants into related properties, and put the groups into a class together.

I've been on projects where all the message constants are jumbled into one Constants file that also contains constants for request/session attributes and every other imaginable use for a constant. I think it's much more manageable to have a MessageConstants.java file that contains only message key constants.

Step-by-Step

1. Create a Constants class.
   a. Depending on which approach is taken to the replacement of constant keys in the JSP, you might also need to create accessors for each property constant.
2. Begin with a single, simple JSP.
   a. Keep in mind that you will be repeating these steps, so it is best to start simple and work your way up.
   b. Another equally valid approach is to go through your home page, then each page that is accessible from there and so on until you have covered all the pages.
3. Search for hard-coded keys.
4. Create a new constant in the Java class for each unique key.
   a. Keep in mind that if there are a lot of constants, say more than 30 or 40 as a rule of thumb, the constants should be grouped and split into separate classes.
5. Replace each hard-coded key with a reference to the appropriate constant.
   a. Or use an expression referring to the property.
6. Test the changes.
7. Continue with the next JSP, until all keys have been replaced with the constant.

Example

In this example, we will apply the solution to the same JSP that we looked at earlier in the pitfall (Listing 4.2). Here is the code for the JSP that is stuck in the pitfall for reference.

```
...
<head>
    <title><bean:message key="example.title"/></title>
</head>

<body bgcolor="white">
<h1><bean:message key="modify.heading"/></h1>
<p>
<bean:message key="instruction.modify"/>
```

```
<p>
<html:form  action="/saveInvoice" method="post">
    <table>
        <tr>
            <td><bean:message key="label.invoice.number"/><td>
            <td><html:text property="invoiceNumber"/></td>
        </tr>
        <tr>
            <td><bean:message key="label.billing.date"/><td>
            <td><html:text property="billingDate"/></td>
        </tr>
...
```

The first step is to create a Constants class that will contain the strings. We will skip grouping the constants for brevity, but keep that in mind on larger projects. You have several choices for how to group the properties. For example, the properties can be grouped in functional areas; in an online store, for example, the areas would include a shopping cart section, a catalog section, an account management section, and probably others. Another equally valid way is to group the constants along functional lines, like shopping, purchasing, and shipping. Just about any way you organize the constants is fine as long as the method is well documented so that others can follow it. Just remember that the idea is to keep from building a single class with 400 static variables in it.

Now that we have chosen the JSP to work with first, the next step is to find the list of hard-coded property names. Here is the list of properties that are referred to in the JSP.

```
example.title
modify.heading
instruction.modify
label.invoice.number
label.billing.date
```

The next step is to put the constants into the Java class that we created. Here is the code for that class.

```
...
public abstract class Constants {
    /** The key to the string displayed in the browser's title bar */
    public final static String BROWSER_TITLE_KEY =
        "example.title";
    /** The key to the heading for the Modify Invoice page */
    public final static String MODIFY_INVOICE_HEADING_KEY =
        "modify.heading";
    /** The key to instructional text for forms users can modify */
```

```
    public final static String MODIFY_INSTRUCTION_KEY =
        "instruction.modify";
    /** The key to the label for the <b>invoice number</b> field */
    public final static String INVOICE_NUMBER_LABEL_KEY =
        "label.invoice.number";
    /** The key to the label for the <b>billing date</b> field */
    public final static String BILLING_DATE_LABEL_KEY =
        "label.billing.date";
}
```

The next step is to replace the hard-coded key names in the JSPs with the constants we just created. There are two ways to do this. The first involves scriptlets; the second involves the JSP expression language. If you are able to use the expression language, then you should do so because it provides a cleaner separation of Java code from the JSP. If you are unable to use the expression language, then use scriptlet code in your JSP.

Using scriptlets involves first adding an *import* statement to the JSP. That import should look like this:

```
<%@ page import="com.aboutobjects.pitfalls.Constants" %>
```

Next, the hard-coded strings are replaced with references to the constants defined in Constants.java:

```
<head>
    <title><bean:message
key="<%=Constants.BROWSER_TITLE_KEY%>"/></title>
</head>

<body bgcolor="white">

<h1><bean:message key="<%=Constants.MODIFY_INVOICE_HEADING_KEY%>"/></h1>
<p>
<bean:message key="<%=Constants.MODIFY_INSTRUCTION_KEY%>"/>
<p>
<html:form  action="/saveInvoice" method="post">
    <table>
        <tr>
            <td><bean:message
                    key="<%=Constants.INVOICE_NUMBER_LABEL_KEY%>"/><td>
            <td><html:text property="invoiceNumber"/></td>
        </tr>
        <tr>
            <td><bean:message
                    key="<%=Constants.BILLING_DATE_LABEL_KEY%>"/><td>
            <td><html:text property="billingDate"/></td>
        </tr>
...
```

The final step is to deploy and test the newly modified JSP. It is always a good idea to test each individual JSP before moving on to the next. The final step is to start over and do it all again for the next JSP.

If you are able to use the JSP expression language, the approach is very similar. Instead of using a scriptlet, you write a JSP expression to access the constant value. The scriptlet engine works against JavaBeans, so we must add a bean façade over the Constants class that we already created. Here is the additional code that must be added to the Constants class.

```
public abstract class Constants {
    public Constants() {
    }
    public String getBrowserTitleKey() {
        return BROWSER_TITLE_KEY;
    }
    public String getModifyInvoiceHeadingKey() {
        return MODIFY_INVOICE_HEADING_KEY;
    }
    // Continue on with this approach for each key added to the
    // constants file
    ...
}
```

Now we'll modify the JSP to use the expression language:

```
<jsp:useBean id="constants"
             class="com.aboutobjects.pitfalls.Constants"/>
<head>
    <title><bean:message key="${constants.browserTitleKey}"/></title>
</head>

<body bgcolor="white">

<h1><bean:message key="${constants.modifyInvoiceHeadingKey}"/></h1>
```

You can now continue through the JSP, replacing scriptlet code with corresponding expressions. It should be pointed out that the choice between scriptlets and expression language for this particular usage is not terribly meaningful. Keep in mind, though, that scriptlets represent a maintenance issue for non-Java programmers. Web developers know the Web-based languages (XHTML, JavaScript, etc.) but do not usually know Java. Having Java embedded in the JSP sometimes forces the Web developer to wait for a Java developer to consult before he or she can make a change. If it is possible to use the expression language, you are better off doing that.

Pitfall 4.3: Not Using Struts Tags for Error Messaging

Struts provides a fairly comprehensive set of facilities for managing and rendering error (and other) messages. Developers, however, may have already acquired the habit of managing these messages themselves through working in other JSP environments, or they simply may not have had sufficient time to understand how to use the Struts messaging facilities. This results in the developers doing manually what is already provided (that is, tested and well designed) in Struts. It is generally better to use an existing piece of well-tested software than to build your own solution.

The symptoms of this pitfall typically are inconsistent error messaging, extra copy/paste code to format values to be displayed as part of the message, and difficulty maintaining scattered, hard-coded messages.

This pitfall typically arises because the Struts error-messaging mechanism is a bit difficult to grasp at first and the documentation is sparse. Developers often find themselves wrestling with more pressing design issues, so error messaging may get short shrift early in the life of the project.

This pitfall usually shows up in two places. First, the JSP has a logic:present tag that looks for a marker saying that an error occurred. Second, the Action class notices error conditions and sets the marker so that the JSP will find and display it. Here is some typical code you'd find in an application trapped in this pitfall.

```
<logic:present name="errorMessage">
    <bean:write name="errorMessage"/>
</logic:present>
try {
    ...
}
catch (SomeException e) {
    request.setAttribute("errorMessage", "Some error message");
    ...
}
```

Keep in mind that this is just one of several forms that this pitfall may take. In general, any time you find yourself managing error messages in your application and you are not using the Struts error tags, you are probably stuck in this pitfall.

Example

Here is another example of an Action class and a JSP that are stuck in the pitfall. The try/catch block from the FindInvoiceAction is putting the error messages directly in the request:

```
try {
    InvoiceDelegate delegate = InvoiceDelegate.getInstance();
    invoice = delegate.findInvoice(bean);
}
catch (InvoiceDelegate.NotFoundException e) {
    request.setAttribute("errorMessage",
        "Unable to find invoice number " + invoiceNumber);
    return mapping.findForward("findInvoicePage");
}
```

And the ModifyInvoice.jsp is looking for the request value and placing it into the output if it is found:

```
<logic:present name="errorMessage">
    <bean:write name="errorMessage"/>
</logic:present>
```

This works perfectly well (as long as you don't have any localization requirements), but it is difficult to maintain as messages have to be copy/pasted in numerous places, along with any formatting code. Of course, you could pull the strings out into a properties file and use the java.text.MessageFormat class to allow for parameterization and formatting of values, but then you'd have to embark on the path of re-implementing existing Struts functionality, which would obviously be counterproductive.

To avoid this pitfall use Struts ActionError and ActionMessage classes to generate user interface messages, and reference them with html:errors and html:messages tags in your JSPs.

Solving Pitfall 4.3: Replace Custom Messaging with Struts Messaging

The Struts messaging functionality allows us to maintain our message strings in properties files, and it automatically supports parameterized messages, so we can supply values that will be plugged into the strings when necessary. Instead of coding this ourselves in Action classes and JSPs, we should use the functionality that comes with Struts. Using the error mechanism also neatly handles keeping the strings in one place for easy maintenance and localization (if we need localization). At the same time, this solution will allow us to simplify the code in our Actions.

Step-by-Step

1. Start with the simplest Action containing custom messaging code.
2. Move the error strings to the appropriate properties file.
   a. Add placeholders for dynamic values as necessary.
3. Add a constant to your constants class for the new property key.
   a. Don't forget to add the simple accessor method so that the property can be used in a JSP expression statement.
4. Replace messaging implementation with code to generate ActionError or ActionMessage instances, and place them in the appropriate scope.
5. Identify associated JSPs.
6. Modify rendering code in the JSPs to display the Struts messages.
7. Test the new implementation.
8. Search for additional Actions that contain custom messaging code and repeat the steps as necessary.

Example

The first step is to identify the simplest Action class to start with. For this example, we will solve the example presented in the pitfall. Here's the code snippet from the Action:

```
try {
    InvoiceDelegate delegate = InvoiceDelegate.getInstance();
    invoice = delegate.findInvoice(bean);
}
catch (InvoiceDelegate.NotFoundException e) {
    request.setAttribute("errorMessage",
        "Unable to find invoice number " + invoiceNumber);
    return mapping.findForward("findInvoicePage");
}
```

The next step is to move the message string to ApplicationResources.properties:

```
error.find=Unable to find invoice with invoice number {0,number,#}.
```

Note that we have added an expression (not to be confused with JSP expression language) at the end of the line to act as a placeholder for the invoice number.

> **FORMATTING MESSAGES**
>
> Struts uses the class java.text.MessageFormat to perform substitution on bracketed expressions in message strings. The ActionMessage class and its subclass ActionError allow you to provide an array of arguments that will be used by MessageFormat to replace the bracketed expressions. There are also convenience methods that take one to four explicit arguments.
>
> In the preceding example, we used a couple of optional features of MessageFormat to control how one of the values was formatted. Note that the only value MessageFormat requires inside the curly braces is a number specifying by position the parameter to be applied. The additional values in the example represent the type of formatting to apply (for example, *number* in this case), as well as a formatting pattern to use. We specified #, which will prevent MessageFormat from inserting commas as thousands separators. (For more details, see the javadoc for java.text.MessageFormat.)

The next step is to add a line to our Constants class to refer to the key. If you're using expression language in your JSP, you will also need to add an accessor method.

```
/** The key to the <i>not found</i> error message */
public final static String FIND_ERROR = "error.find";
...
public String getFindError() {
    return FIND_ERROR;
}
```

The next step is to rewrite the catch block to generate an ActionError instead of putting the error string into the response.

```
catch (InvoiceDelegate.NotFoundException e) {
    ActionError error =
        new ActionError(Constants.FIND_ERROR, invoiceNumber);
    ActionErrors errors = new ActionErrors();
    errors.add(ActionErrors.GLOBAL_ERROR, error);
    saveErrors(request, errors);
    return mapping.findForward("findInvoicePage");
}
```

You may recall that in a previous solution we created a convenience method on our Action base class to perform most of this work, so we can actually rewrite the previous code as follows:

```
catch (InvoiceDelegate.NotFoundException e) {
    postGlobalError(Constants.FIND_ERROR, invoiceNumber, request);
```

```
        return mapping.findForward("findInvoicePage");
}
```

Next we need to find the associated JSPs and replace any custom error presentation code, as in the following snippet:

```
<logic:present name="myMessage">
    <bean:write name="myMessage"/>
</logic:present>
```

with a Struts errors tag:

```
<html:errors/>
```

Note that if we were posting an ActionMessage rather than (or in addition to) an ActionError, we would need to add the following code to our JSP:

```
<html:messages id="messageId" message="true"/>
    <logic:present name="messageId">
        <h4><font color="red"><bean:write name="messageId"/></font></h4>
    </logic:present>
</html:messages>
```

The final step is to deploy and test the new implementation. When it works, you can continue on to fix any additional Actions and JSPs that are stuck in this pitfall.

Pitfall 4.4: Calculating Derived Values in JSPs

This pitfall examines the consequences of using scriptlets to perform calculations in JSPs. Developers are often tempted to take shortcuts, and one of the easiest to take is inserting a bit of scriptlet code in a JSP to calculate a value derived from other fields displayed in the same JSP.

The MVC model states that there are specific layers to which certain types of activities should be confined. One of the key benefits of using Struts is achieving a cleaner separation between these layers. Implementing calculations in JSP scriptlet code begins to erode this separation, though, coupling the view to the model, which leads to more difficult maintenance and harder-to-find bugs.

The main symptom of this pitfall is increased complexity of JSP code. This extra complexity makes the JSPs more difficult to maintain. Also, because there's no compile-time checking of the scriptlet code, the JSP code will be more vulnerable to runtime errors. Anyone who has had to track down an error in a JSP page knows how difficult it can be—especially compared to how straightforward tracking down exceptions in the regular Java code that makes up the Model and Controller classes usually is.

Usually this pitfall is seen as a scriplet that performs a calculation in a JSP. Here is a typical piece of scriptlet code that adds the employees' bonuses to their base salaries.

```
<%
    ...
    BigDecimal compensation = salary.add(bonus);
    ...
%>
```

Example

In this example, we will see some of the responsibilities of the earlier InvoiceDO (from Chapters 2 and 3) implemented in scriptlet code in a JSP. Suppose our InvoiceDO had a Balance field that represented the balance carried forward from the previous billing cycle. We could then present a Balance field on the Modify Invoice page as well as an Amount Due field. The amount due is derived by subtracting the prior balance from the invoice amount.

One way to accomplish this is to calculate the difference directly in the JSP. First we need to add some imports.

```
<%@ page import="com.aboutobjects.pitfalls.Constants,
            java.math.BigDecimal,
            com.aboutobjects.pitfalls.InvoiceForm,
            com.aboutobjects.pitfalls.Formatter" %>
```

Next we need a scriptlet to perform the calculation. Note that we need to use Formatter to unformat and format the values.

```
<%
Formatter formatter = Formatter.getFormatter(BigDecimal.class);
InvoiceForm form = (InvoiceForm) session.getAttribute("invoiceForm");
BigDecimal amount = (BigDecimal) formatter.unformat(form.getAmount());
BigDecimal balance = (BigDecimal) formatter.unformat(form.getBalance());
String amountDue;
if (amount == null)
    amountDue = "";
else if (balance == null)
    amountDue = formatter.format(amount);
else {
    BigDecimal difference = amount.add(balance.negate());
    amountDue = formatter.format(difference);
}
%>
```

Now we can add code to display the resulting value.

```
<tr>
    <td>Amount Due: </td>
    <td><%= amountDue%></td>
</tr>
```

If one or more additional pages need to display the same value, we will have to resort to copying and pasting this code to the new pages. A page containing numerous derived values could get quite complicated.

Pitfall 4.5: Performing Business Logic in JSPs is similar to this pitfall. Any time you have scriptlet code in your JSP, you should make sure that the code could not possibly belong somewhere else, and that it is confined to rendering logic. In addition to blurring the lines between the model, view, and controller, scriptlet code tends to increase maintenance costs and almost always leads to copying and pasting code from one JSP to another.

Solving Pitfall 4.4: Move Calculations to Value Object

The goal of this solution is to calculate the derived values in only one place, rather than copying a scriptlet implementation into several JSPs. The benefit to solving this pitfall is that the derived value calculation can be shared not only between Web pages, but also with the business tier. It should also allow us to used typed values in performing the calculations, eliminating the need to perform extra type conversions.

The code to calculate the derived values can be in the value object or in the Session Bean, whichever is more convenient. The value object generally makes more sense if the values in question pertain only to the user interface, but if the derived value is used in further business logic or processing, the Session Bean probably makes more sense.

Step-by-Step

1. Begin with the simplest JSP that contains one or more calculations.
2. Add a getter method in the corresponding value object that performs the calculation and returns the derived value.
   a. As noted earlier, the right place to put the code could also be the Session Bean, depending on your implementation.
3. Add a property, including a getter and a setter, for a string version of the value in the corresponding ActionForm.
4. Modify the rendering code in the JSP to display the new form property.
   a. If you are using the dynamic mapping infrastructure from Chapter 2, add the property's name to the outbound keysToSkip array.
5. Test the new implementation.
6. Continue with the next JSP.

Example

The first step is to choose the JSP to start with; remember to keep it simple the first time you apply this solution to your existing code. We will start with the JSP that was described in the pitfall example. Here is the original scriptlet code.

```
<%
Formatter formatter = Formatter.getFormatter(BigDecimal.class);
InvoiceForm form = (InvoiceForm) session.getAttribute("invoiceForm");
BigDecimal amount = (BigDecimal) formatter.unformat(form.getAmount());
BigDecimal balance = (BigDecimal) formatter.unformat(form.getBalance());
String amountDue;
if (amount == null)
    amountDue = "";
else if (balance == null)
    amountDue = formatter.format(amount);
```

```
    else {
        BigDecimal difference = amount.add(balance.negate());
        amountDue = formatter.format(difference);
    }
%>
```

The next step is to add a getter method to InvoiceDO that performs the same calculation being done in the scriplet. Note that, in our current scenario, the code for our getter method will be quite a bit simpler because we're taking advantage of the typed values in InvoiceDO as well as the dynamic formatting infrastructure:

```
public BigDecimal getAmountDue() {
    if (amount == null)   return null;
    if (balance == null) return amount;
    return amount.add(balance.negate());
}
```

Now we need to add a property to the InvoiceForm to hold the formatted string version of the amountDue value. Here is the new code for InvoiceForm.

```
private String amountDue;
...
public String getAmountDue() { return amountDue; }
public void setAmountDue(String amountDue) {
    this.amountDue = amountDue;
}
```

Now we can modify our JSP to display the new property:

```
<tr>
    <td>Amount Due: </td>
    <td><bean:write name="invoiceForm" property="amountDue"/></td>
</tr>
```

Finally, before we start testing, we need to make sure that the mapping infrastructure doesn't try to transfer the amountDue value to the InvoiceDO because this is a derived value and therefore cannot be set. We need to add the corresponding key to the keysToSkip array in InvoiceForm, as follows:

```
protected ArrayList keysToSkip(int mode) {
    ArrayList keysToSkip = super.keysToSkip(mode);
    if (mode == TO_OBJECT) {
        ...
        keysToSkip.add("amountDue");
    }
    return keysToSkip;
}
```

Pitfall 4.5: Performing Business Logic in JSPs

This pitfall doesn't just blur the lines between the models, views, and controllers in a Struts application—it obliterates them. Coding business logic in the presentation tier is problematic because the implementation cannot be shared with business-tier objects that may require access to the same functionality. If the presentation tier and the business tier each have to have their own separate implementations of the same piece of logic, it becomes difficult to ensure consistent behavior. Placing the code in JSPs rather than Java classes only makes matters worse, making it impossible to share the logic even among presentation-tier classes. (Admittedly, you could use JSP include statements to source in a file containing scriptlet code in order to share business logic between JSPs, but other presentation-tier objects, such as Actions and ActionForms would still be unable to access the functionality.)

This pitfall is similar to Pitfall 4.4: Calculating Derived Values in JSPs, although the consequences are potentially even more serious, as it affects the critical business behavior of the application.

A couple of paths lead developers into this pitfall. One is simply lack of experience with applying the Model-View-Controller design pattern to developing Web applications. The other is the understandable tendency to take shortcuts under deadline pressure. Unfortunately, this shortcut will almost certainly cost the developer more time than it saves in the end.

The general form of this pitfall is a chunk of scriptlet code that implements business logic. In the following example, a bit of the business logic that properly belongs in the InvoiceDO has been implemented in a scriptlet in one of the JSPs.

```
<%
    InvoiceDO invoice = (InvoiceDO)
        request.getSession().getAttribute("invoice");
    GregorianCalendar dueDateCal = new GregorianCalendar();
    GregorianCalendar invoiceCal = new GregorianCalendar();
    invoiceCal.setTime(invoice.getBillingDate());
    dueDateCal.add(Calendar.DATE, -30);
    boolean thirtyDaysPastDue = invoiceCal.before(dueDateCal);
%>
```

Another block of code in the JSP renders the resulting value.

```
<% if (thirtyDaysPastDue) { %>
    <bean:message key="invoice.past.due"
              arg0="<%= invoice.getInvoiceNumber().toString()%>"/>
<% } %>
```

How will this calculation of the past-due date be handled in other JSPs that need to present the same information? Unfortunately, the answer in this case is that the implementation will have to be duplicated in each JSP that requires the derived value.

Example

Below is a slightly more elaborate example involving a past-due invoice calculation. Calculated past-due dates may need to be presented in several different places in the user interface, but with the code presented here, we will have to copy and paste the scriptlet implementation in each JSP that displays these values.

```
<%
    InvoiceDO invoice = (InvoiceDO)
        request.getSession().getAttribute("invoice");
GregorianCalendar dueDateCal = new GregorianCalendar();
GregorianCalendar invoiceCal = new GregorianCalendar();
invoiceCal.setTime(invoice.getBillingDate());
int interval;
switch (invoice.getPaymentTerm().intValue()) {
    case InvoiceDO.PAYMENT_TERM_30: interval = -30; break;
    case InvoiceDO.PAYMENT_TERM_60: interval = -60; break;
    default:                        interval = 0;
}
dueDateCal.add(Calendar.DATE, interval - 30);
boolean thirtyDaysPastDue = invoiceCal.before(dueDateCal);
%>
```

Note that the first step in the scriptlet is to extract an InvoiceDO from the session. This in itself could be considered a pitfall, in that placing value objects directly in the session unnecessarily exposes them to being accidentally modified elsewhere. The more objects we have floating around in the session, the more difficult our application's code is to understand, as the reader of a given JSP generally has no clue about how the values got there and how or when they may be modified.

Of course, in real life, the logic could be quite a bit more complex, so the scriptlet could get considerably more convoluted. A great question to ask yourself as you check if any of your scriptlets have caused your JSPs to be trapped in this pitfall is, should this code be shared? If the answer is yes, then you are probably stuck in this pitfall and you should look at the solution. Your application is almost certainly going to need to apply the same logic elsewhere.

The next problem is that the container compiles this code, so you're at its mercy regarding compiler warnings and error messages, and container compiler error messages are notoriously hard to follow. If you're not pre-compiling your JSPs, compilation errors won't occur until you load the page in the Web container.

In addition, we still need code to implement the user interface logic associated with the above scriptlet. Let's suppose we simply wish to display a message regarding the lateness of the invoice. Here is the message as it is defined in the properties file:

```
invoice.past.due=Invoice {0} is {1} or more days past due
```

Here's the code we would need to render the message:

```
<% if (thirtyDaysPastDue) { %>
    <bean:message key="invoice.past.due"
                  arg0="<%= invoice.getInvoiceNumber().toString()%>"
                  arg1="thirty"/>
<% } %>
```

Note that the argN parameters of the bean:message tag require arguments of type String, so that we can no longer use the formatting capabilities of java.util.MessageFormat to format the supplied value. In other words, a specification like this:

```
invoice.past.due=Invoice {0,number,#} is {1} or more days past due
```

would fail at runtime because the specification {0, number, #} requires an argument of type Number.

Therefore, any formatting would also have to be done in scriptlet code inside the JSP. Again, such formatting code could not be easily shared and thus would likely be copy/pasted around, with all its inherent evils. To avoid this pitfall, you can use helper classes to contain business logic so that the logic can be easily shared across the layers of your application.

Solving Pitfall 4.5: Move Business Logic to a Helper Class

Business logic can easily wind up being duplicated throughout the layers of your application. Obviously, that makes it difficult to maintain the code, and it usually frustrates attempts to reuse the implementations.

By creating a helper class to contain our business logic, we will be able to access the behavior easily anywhere in our application that it may be needed. This of course applies equally to business logic coded in Actions and ActionForms, though for the sake of this example we will focus on business logic coded in JSPs.

Step-by-Step

1. Start with the JSP with the simplest business logic scriptlet.
   a. Make sure to identify any copies of the scriptlet so that they can be deleted in favor of an expression to invoke the new implementation in the helper class.
2. Move the scriptlet code to a helper class.
3. Modify the implementation as necessary so that it can be shared as needed.
4. Modify rendering code in the JSP to take advantage of the new implementation.
5. Add code to the related Action to invoke the business logic.
6. Test the new implementation.
   a. After you have tested the new implementation, you can go back to the other JSPs that had the scriptlet copied into them and apply the same steps. It is a good idea not to move on to the next scriptlet until you have removed all the copies of the current scriptlet.
7. Continue with the next JSP that has business logic captured in scriptlets.

Example

In this example, we will apply the steps of this solution to the example we looked at in the pitfall and see how we can get the JSP and Action out of this pitfall. Making this choice completes the first step of the solution. Remember that you should start your solution with the simplest scriptlet to get the hang of applying this solution. Here is the scriptlet for reference.

```
<%
    InvoiceDO invoice = (InvoiceDO)
        request.getSession().getAttribute("invoice");
    GregorianCalendar dueDateCal = new GregorianCalendar();
    GregorianCalendar invoiceCal = new GregorianCalendar();
    invoiceCal.setTime(invoice.getBillingDate());
    int interval;
    switch (invoice.getPaymentTerm().intValue()) {
        case InvoiceDO.PAYMENT_TERM_30: interval = -30; break;
        case InvoiceDO.PAYMENT_TERM_60: interval = -60; break;
        default:                        interval = 0;
    }
    dueDateCal.add(Calendar.DATE, interval - 30);
    boolean thirtyDaysPastDue = invoiceCal.before(dueDateCal);
%>
```

The next step in our solution is to move the preceding implementation to a helper class. Let's call this class BusinessRules. The initial implementation is found in Listing 4.3.

```java
package com.aboutobjects.pitfalls.rule;

import com.aboutobjects.pitfalls.InvoiceDO;
import java.util.Calendar;
import java.util.GregorianCalendar;

/**
 * The business rules for our application.
 */
public class BusinessRules {

    /**
     * Determines whether the provided invoice is past due by the
     * given number of days.
     * @param invoice The invoice to be checked
     * @param days The number of days before the invoice is considered
     *             past due
     * @return <code>true</code> if the invoice is past due;
     *         <code>false</code> otherwise
     */
    public static boolean isPastDue(InvoiceDO invoice, int days) {
        GregorianCalendar dueDateCal = new GregorianCalendar();
        GregorianCalendar invoiceCal = new GregorianCalendar();
        invoiceCal.setTime(invoice.getBillingDate());
        int interval;
        switch (invoice.getPaymentTerm().intValue()) {
            case InvoiceDO.PAYMENT_TERM_30: interval = -30; break;
            case InvoiceDO.PAYMENT_TERM_60: interval = -60; break;
            default:                        interval = 0;
        }
        dueDateCal.add(Calendar.DATE, interval - days);
        return invoiceCal.before(dueDateCal);
    }

    /**
     * Determines whether the provided invoice is thirty or more days
     * past due.
     * @param invoice The invoice to be checked.
     * @return <code>true</code> if the invoice is thirty or more days
     *         past due; <code>false</code> otherwise
     */
    public static boolean isThirtyDaysPastDue(InvoiceDO invoice) {
        return isPastDue(invoice, 30);
    }
}
```

Listing 4.3 BusinessRules.java.

Notice that we have made the basic implementation a bit more general by allowing the caller to pass the number of days past due. We have also added a convenience method isThirtyDaysPastDue() to invoke the generic method with a well-known value. This code can now easily be made available to business-tier classes as well as to all levels of the presentation tier.

Accordingly, we can now invoke these methods from our Actions. In this case, we simply need to add the following code to our FindInvoiceAction:

```
if (BusinessRules.isThirtyDaysPastDue(invoice)) {
    postGlobalMessage(Constants.INVOICE_PAST_DUE, invoiceNumber,
                    "thirty", request);
}
```

The next step is to update the JSP so that it takes advantage of the new implementation. First, we will need to modify the string specification in our properties file to prevent java.util.MessageFormat from inserting comma separators in the invoice number during formatting:

```
invoice.past.due=Invoice {0,number,#} is {1} or more days past due
```

Now we can clean up the rendering logic in the JSP by replacing this code:

```
<% if (thirtyDaysPastDue) { %>
    <bean:message key="<%= Constants.INVOICE_PAST_DUE%>"
                    arg0="<%= invoice.getInvoiceNumber().toString()%>"
                    arg1="thirty"/>
<% } %>
```

with this obviously much more generic code:

```
<html:messages id="messageId" message="true"/>
    <logic:present name="messageId">
        bean:write name="messageId"/>
    </logic:present>
</html:messages>
```

This makes our JSP more adaptable to future changes. Since the invocation of the business logic now takes place in the Action, we can now delete the business logic scriptlet from our JSP as well.

The next step is to deploy and test the new code to make sure that everything works as it should. Once the new implementation is working correctly we can search for any other JSPs that had copies of the scriptlet and clean them up as well. The final step is to repeat this whole process for each JSP that is trapped in this pitfall.

Pitfall 4.6: Hard-Coded Options in HTML Select Lists

This pitfall deals with problems developers often encounter with HTML select lists in Struts. One of the trickier issues developers face when coding their JSPs is how to populate the value lists displayed in the drop-down menus rendered by the HTML select element. Struts provides an html:options tag that allows developers to specify a bean containing a collection that provides the labels to display in the UI, and another collection for their associated values, if different. Unfortunately, many developers find the Struts html:options tag confusing when they initially encounter it, and they simply find it expedient to code the values that they need directly in their JSP using the html:option tag instead. This leads to a lot more code than is required, thereby increasing maintenance costs. The cause of this problem is twofold: First, populating HTML select lists is one of the less straightforward mappings developers need to work out, and second, the associated Struts tags are correspondingly less intuitive. In addition, documentation on this feature of Struts has historically been sparse.

Example

Here's an example of a JSP that is stuck in this pitfall. The code uses hard-coded values to populate the labels and values of an html:select tag.

```
<html:form  action="/saveInvoice" method="post">
    ...
    <html:select property="paymentTerm">
        <html:option value="0">None</html:option>
        <html:option value="1">Net 30 Days</html:option>
        <html:option value="2">Net 60 Days</html:option>
    </html:select>
    ...
</html:form>
```

And here is the HTML it generates:

```
<form name="invoiceForm"
      method="post"
      action="/pitfalls/saveInvoice.do">
    ...
    <select name="paymentTerm">
        <option value="0">None</option>
        <option value="1" selected="selected">Net 30 Days</option>
        <option value="2">Net 60 Days</option>
    </select>
</form>
```

The html:select tag binds the value of its property element, in this case paymentTerm, to the value of the underlying bean. In our example, the bean will be the ActionForm bound to the path /saveInvoice (the html:form's action) in struts-config.xml. The tag will automatically preselect a matching value (if one is found) from the options list during rendering, and the user-selected value will automatically be bound to the ActionForm's paymentTerm property when the form is submitted.

The problem with this approach is that we will be forced to copy/paste this code to other JSPs that need to render the same select list. Any changes would then have to be applied by hand, opening the door to inconsistency and bugs. For example, suppose a developer accidentally switched two of the value's settings. The user interface would display the user's selection correctly, but the underlying bean value would be incorrect. This type of bug is often hard to diagnose. Clearly, it would be best if we could maintain a single instance of the list and share it among various JSPs.

Another potential problem is that some applications may require the flexibility of having the values lists determined dynamically. For example they might be fetched from a database table, which would allow new values to be added at runtime. Obviously if the values are hard-coded in a JSP, the application would lack this kind of flexibility.

You can avoid this pitfall by using a helper class to provide the label/value mappings for select lists, along with the Struts html:options tag to populate html select lists. See the solution for details on how to do this.

Solving Pitfall 4.6: Move Options Values to a Helper Class

Moving the label/value mappings from JSP options lists to one or more helper classes will allow us to share the implementation across multiple JSPs and conceivably other code that may be able to use them. It also provides a central location for viewing the mappings, which makes it easier to verify that they are correct and to modify them when necessary.

Step-by-Step

1. Start with any JSP containing an options list with hard-coded values.
2. Add constants to the associated value object for each of the allowable bean values.
3. Create a method in a helper class that returns a Collection corresponding to the label/value pairs in the options list.
    a. You might have to create a new helper class if there is no logical place to put the method.

4. Add a method to your base ActionForm class to provide access to an instance of the helper class.
5. Replace the hard-coded options with an html:options tag.
6. Test the implementation.
7. Repeat for additional options lists until all have been refactored.

Example

The first step of the solution is to choose the JSP to start with. We will start with the example from the pitfall. Here is the options list for reference.

```
...
<html:select property="paymentTerm">
      <html:option value="0">None</html:option>
      <html:option value="1">Net 30 Days</html:option>
      <html:option value="2">Net 60 Days</html:option>
</html:select>
...
```

First, we'll define constants in InvoiceDO or in Constants to represent the allowable bean values. (Note: it's generally best to place constant definitions in the class with which they are most closely associated whenever possible and to avoid dumping everything into the Constants class.)

```
public final static int PAYMENT_TERM_NONE = 0;
public final static int PAYMENT_TERM_30 = 1;
public final static int PAYMENT_TERM_60 = 2;
```

Next, we'll create a helper class to provide the label/value mappings. Struts offers us some assistance in the form of the LabelValueBean class, which provides predefined label and value properties that we can use to contain the values, as seen in Listing 4.4.

```
package com.aboutobjects.pitfalls;

import java.util.ArrayList;
import java.util.List;
import java.io.Serializable;
import org.apache.struts.util.LabelValueBean;

/**
 * The label/value mappings used in options lists.
 */
```

Listing 4.4 Options.java.

```java
public class Options {
    private static Options uniqueInstance = new Options();

    // Don't allow direct instantiation.
    private Options() { }

    public static Options getInstance() { return uniqueInstance; }

    public List getPaymentTerms() {
        ArrayList paymentTerms = new ArrayList();
        String none = Integer.toString(InvoiceDO.PAYMENT_TERM_NONE);
        String net30 = Integer.toString(InvoiceDO.PAYMENT_TERM_30);
        String net60 = Integer.toString(InvoiceDO.PAYMENT_TERM_60);
        paymentTerms.add(new LabelValueBean("None", none));
        paymentTerms.add(new LabelValueBean("Net 30 Days", net30));
        paymentTerms.add(new LabelValueBean("Net 60 Days", net60));
        return paymentTerms;
    }
    ...
}
```

Listing 4.4 *(continued)*

Now we can make the Options instance visible to the JSPs by adding an accessor method to the ActionForm base class:

```java
/**
 * Returns the unique instance of the Options class.
 * @return the Options instance
 */
public Options getOptions() { return Options.getInstance(); }
```

The next step is to replace the hard-coded options list in the JSP with a bit of slightly tricky Struts tag code, as seen here:

```
<html:select property="paymentTerm">
    <bean:define id="values"
                 name="invoiceForm"
                 property="options.paymentTerms"
                 type="java.util.ArrayList"/>
    <html:options collection="values"
                  property="value"
                  labelProperty="label"/>
</html:select>
```

The bean:define tag puts the List returned by getPaymentTerms() in scope so that the html:options tag can access it, using the arbitrary identifier values. The html:options tag will then iterate the collection, rendering an html option tag for each entry.

The next step is to deploy and test the cleaned-up code. After testing to make sure that this fix has been completed successfully, you can proceed to other hard-coded option lists in your other JSPs.

Pitfall 4.7: Not Checking for Duplicate Form Submissions

A side effect of the stateless nature of the HTTP protocol is that the interface presented in the browser can easily get out of sync with the state of the model on the server. There is a common pitfall involving this lack of synchronization that must be dealt with in nearly every application. This occurs when a user submits values using a form on a given page and then, at some later point, backtracks to the cached page, edits the now stale values, and resubmits the form. This has the potential to corrupt the underlying data store by creating duplicate records, overwriting current data with stale values, and so on. In the best case, it creates a bad transaction that is rejected by the data store.

This pitfall potentially affects nearly every JSP containing a form tag. In most projects, the problems show up during system test. Fortunately for developers, system testers are generally wise enough to include scenarios in their test scripts that expose this type of bug. Developers, on the other hand, rarely test for these conditions.

Example

The code that follows represents a typical naive form implementation that is trapped in this pitfall. If we don't do anything special to prevent it, the user can use the HTML generated by this JSP to submit the same form multiple times.

```
<html:form  action="/saveInvoice" method="post">
  <table>
    <tr>
      <td><bean:message
            key="<%=Constants.INVOICE_NUMBER_LABEL_KEY%>"/><td>
      <td><html:text property="invoiceNumber"/></td>
    </tr>
    <tr>
      <td><bean:message
            key="<%=Constants.BILLING_DATE_LABEL_KEY%>"/><td>
      <td><html:text property="billingDate"/></td>
    </tr>
    <tr>
      <td><bean:message
            key="<%=Constants.AMOUNT_KEY%>"/><td>
      <td><html:text property="amount"/></td>
    </tr>
```

```
            <td colspan=3 align="right"><html:submit/></td>
        </tr>
    </table>
</html:form>
```

One of the common mechanisms to control this pitfall, and the one that will be explored in the accompanying solution, is to have forms submit tokens that the application can check to ensure that the forms are not submitted more than once.

Solving Pitfall 4.7: Add Tokens to Generated JSP

To solve this pitfall, we will make use of one of the more obscure features of Struts. The token management facility is provided by the Action and FormTag classes, comprising a small group of Action methods that provide for token generation and checking, and largely undocumented code in the FormTag to render the generated tokens automatically. Taken together, these two features make it quite easy to check for duplicate submissions.

Our goal here is to ensure that forms are submitted only when they contain fresh data. In essence, we're trying to exert some control over the flow of the application. To do that, we can call on Struts to place tokens in our forms as necessary, so that we can check the submitted token against a copy cached on the server.

Step-by-Step

1. Choose a form.
2. Identify the Action that navigates to the form.
    a. Add code to generate a token.
3. Identify the Action that handles submission of the form.
    a. Add code to check the generated token and to generate a new one if the Action is successful.
4. Test the implementation.
5. Continue with other Actions until all form-submission scenarios have been covered.

Example

The first step in the solution is to choose a form. We will begin this example by choosing the FindInvoice form. The next step is to identify the

Action that navigates to the form and add code to generate the token. The Action that navigates to the form is the FindInvoiceAction. This is the code for that action with the token generation added.

```
public class FindInvoiceAction extends BaseAction
{
    public ActionForward execute(ActionMapping mapping,
                                 ActionForm form,
                                 HttpServletRequest request,
                                 HttpServletResponse response)
        throws IOException, ServletException
    {
        ...
        saveToken(request); // This is all we need to add

        return mapping.findForward("saveInvoicePage");
    }
}
```

The FormTag class takes care of inserting the token for you if a value for it has been set, as we did above with saveToken in the FindInvoiceAction.

The next step is to identify the action that handles submission of the form and add code to that form that will make sure that the tokens match and then generate a new token if the form submission was successful. Listing 4.5 is the code for the SaveInvoiceAction that has been modified to check the token.

```
public class SaveInvoiceAction extends BaseAction
{
    public ActionForward execute(ActionMapping mapping,
                                 ActionForm form,
                                 HttpServletRequest request,
                                 HttpServletResponse response)
        throws Exception {

        // Check the token. If it doesn't match the token currently in
        // the session, it's stale.
        if (!isTokenValid(request)) {
            postGlobalError(Constants.DUPLICATE_FORM_ERROR, request);
            return mapping.findForward("saveInvoicePage");
        }

        ...

        // if we got this far, everything worked okay, so generate
```

Listing 4.5 Checking the token in SaveInvoiceAction. *(continues)*

```
            // a new token.
            saveToken(request);

            return mapping.findForward("confirmInvoicePage");
    }
}
```

Listing 4.5 *(continued)*

The final step is to deploy and test the code to make sure it functions properly. Once you have a working implementation, you can add token generation and checking wherever else it is needed. Extra care should be taken in testing the solution to ensure that forms cannot be resubmitted under any odd combinations of circumstances.

CHAPTER 5

Ant

Ant is a great tool that has replaced make as the build tool of choice for Java developers. Almost every major Java development effort involves the use of Ant. The tool deserves its notoriety. It is straightforward, simple to understand, and cross-platform, and it can be extended when necessary with a simple Java class.

So what can possibly go wrong? Even though Ant is easy to pick up, developers still build poorly with it, particularly due to bad planning. For example, the build file can grow over time to include everything that comes up. The build file should be planned for the same reason that applications are planned: Planning leads to a better implementation that is easier to understand and maintain. Build files that are not planned are much harder to maintain and understand than those that are. An unplanned build file becomes something like a kitchen sink; everything gets thrown into it and in the end all that is discernable is that the content is messy. A typical example of failure to plan becoming an issue in an Ant build file is captured later in one of the pitfalls: not distinguishing between deployment and development builds. A build process that does not distinguish between the two types of builds will be much more complex than it needs to be.

Most of the pitfalls covered in this chapter relate to the lack of planning that so often happens. While it is not entirely necessary to design the content of your Ant files, it is important at least to spend enough time thinking through the process to get the big stuff done consistently. For example, plan up front that the libraries and .jar files that your application depends on will be upgraded during development, and make your build file able to accommodate these changes. Again, there is no need to pull out your favorite UML tool and start trying to figure out how to represent a build process. But you do need to do at least some "back of the napkin" planning so that you get the important pieces of your build correct. You don't need a 40-page document to describe the process, but you do need what will fit on the back of a napkin.

A thought-through build process will work much better than one that is just patched over time. After all, the build file is part of the source code for your application, and just like source code, the build file will become large and incomprehensible over time if it's not well planned.

Pitfall 5.1: Copy-and-Paste Reuse describes what happens when developers copy and paste various pieces of the build file to accomplish the build. Copying code means copying bugs, and as the bugs get fixed in one part of the build, the copies will go unfixed. Also, as parts of the build grow and mature, the copies will not.

Pitfall 5.2: No Distinction between Different Types of Builds describes how there is often a lack of distinction between different types of builds. Often on big projects, the final production deployment environment is not completely formed when development first gets started. The build will undoubtedly become geared for the development environment and will often be hard to modify or enhance for production deployment.

Pitfall 5.3: Building Subprojects addresses how developers often write Ant build file hierarchies that mimic the way they used to write make files. Many developers are making the switch from make to Ant, so we end up with lots of build files spread throughout the directory structure of many projects.

Pitfall 5.4: No Logging from Custom Tasks details the common mistake of not putting proper logging statements into tasks. With the declarative nature of an Ant build, it is very important to have good logging to help users discover why the task is not performing as expected.

Pitfall 5.1: Copy-and-Paste Reuse

This pitfall describes what happens when developers copy and paste various pieces of the build file to accomplish the build.

Just as in any other area of development, copying and pasting is easy, quick, and bad for long-term productivity. Copying code is copying bugs, and—even worse—as the bugs get fixed in one part of the build, the copies will go unfixed. Also, as parts of the build grow and mature, the copies will not. This is a classic mistake that developers make in just about every area of programming. There are lots of different reasons why copy and paste happen—laziness, looming deadlines, ignorance, to name a few—but what looks good for the short term turns out to be very painful to deal with in the long term. And, for whatever reason, we developers insist on having to learn this lesson over and over.

The most common cause for this pitfall is not knowing how to parameterize aspects of the build or not even realizing that parameterization is possible. The general root here is inexperience.

The first symptom that usually points to this pitfall is having one aspect of the build work fine and another (very similar) aspect not work; for example, one EJB .jar has the proper deployment descriptor and manifest copied into it and another EJB .jar does not have these things copied properly. Another way to spot this pitfall is to notice that the build file is very hard to change without breaking something. Several parts of the build file (all the copies) end up dependent on assumptions. If the assumptions are wrong or if they change, all the copies will stop working.

This pitfall generally takes the form of very similar tasks copied and pasted, then renamed throughout the build file. The copies are then slightly modified to meet the subtly different requirement. Tasks that typically are copied include building various EJB .jar files and deploying them to different servers.

Example

Listing 5.1 shows a piece of a build file that compiles and *jars* up the Entity and Session Beans into two separate .jar files (this is not meant to prescribe how you should organize your EJBs), one called entity.jar and the other called session.jar.

```xml
<target name="compile.entity" description="Compile the Entities">
    <mkdir dir="${build.destdir}/entity"/>

    <javac srcdir="${src.dir}"
           compiler="modern"
           destdir="${build.destdir}/entity"
           deprecation="off"
       debug="off"
       verbose="off"
           includes="${ejb.src.dir}/entity/**/*.java">
      <classpath refid="classpath"/>
      <classpath refid="_jboss.classpath"/>
    </javac>

    <mkdir dir="${build.destdir}/entity/META-INF"/>
    <copy todir="${build.destdir}/entity/META-INF">
      <fileset dir="${ejb.src.dir}/entity/META-INF"
               includes="**/*"
               excludes="**/.DS_Store"/>
    </copy>
    <jar destfile="${build.destdir}/entity.jar"
         manifest="config/entity.mf"
         basedir="${build.destdir}/entity"/>
  </target>

  <target name="compile.session" description="Compile the Sessions">
    <mkdir dir="${build.destdir}/session"/>

    <javac srcdir="${src.dir}"
           compiler="modern"
           destdir="${build.destdir}/session"
           deprecation="off"
       debug="off"
       verbose="off"
           includes="${ejb.src.dir}/session/**/*.java">
      <classpath refid="classpath"/>
      <classpath refid="_jboss.classpath"/>
    </javac>

    <mkdir dir="${build.destdir}/session/META-INF"/>
    <copy todir="${build.destdir}/session/META-INF">
      <fileset dir="${ejb.src.dir}/session/META-INF"
               includes="**/*"
               excludes="**/.DS_Store"/>
    </copy>
    <jar destfile="${build.destdir}/session.jar"
         manifest="config/session.mf"
         basedir="${build.destdir}/session"/>
  </target>
```

Listing 5.1 Copied-and-pasted targets.

These two targets are exactly the same except for the string *entity* being replaced with *session*. These two targets could easily be combined into one target that takes the name of the EJB .jar as a parameter; then our two real targets would just collapse into *antcalls* to this new target.

Another common issue that causes copy and paste in build files is deploying to the development, test, and production servers. These deployment targets often end up looking the same except for parameters related to hostname, port, and so on. Unfortunately, this pitfall is usually part of the problem that causes other pitfalls, namely Pitfall 5.3: Building Subprojects and Pitfall 5.2: No Distinction between Different Types of Builds. If you discover that your build files are stuck in either of those pitfalls, come back to this solution for more information on how to clean up your build files.

For small applications that have a small team where there will be little or no maintenance in the future, it is often not worth the effort to keep the build file maintainable. Watch out, though, because small projects tend to become large projects. Small projects that "will not be maintained" often live for years and years.

Every time you are tempted to copy and paste a piece of the XML in a build file, create a new internal or private parameterized target instead and use antcall to invoke the target. This seems like second nature to developers; breaking a problem into small reusable pieces and stringing them together into a program are what we do. For whatever reason, though, developers often do not think in these terms when writing the build file.

Solving Pitfall 5.1: Introduce Antcall

Introducing antcall is most useful as a means to organize your build file. Over time, a build file tends to become less organized, new requirements come up, and changes to the deployment structure occur. These changes can lead to various problems with maintainability in the build file. As the build file grows and changes over time, it can become impossible to understand. Apply this solution to clean up the build file so that it is easier to understand and maintain. Over the life of a project, this solution should probably be applied several times to keep the build file simpler and easier to understand.

Step-by-Step

1. Review the targets in the build file for similar structure.
    a. If you know of targets that have been copied and pasted, start with them.

b. Another great place to find similar targets is the targets associated with various deployment units—that is, each EJB .jar file, each .war file, and so on.

2. Start with one similar group, and create another target that is a copy of one of the existing targets.

   a. This may seem like a step backward, but see it through.

3. Rename the target, and remove the description attribute if there was one.

   a. This is going to be a private target, so adopt a naming convention for your private targets. A decent naming convention is to put an underscore in front of the name. The particulars are not so important as having a convention. Put a comment at the top of the build file that specifies the convention.

4. Replace the body of one of the other similar targets with an antcall block.

   a. Don't choose the one that you used to copy this new private target; it's too similar and won't show what needs to be parameterized.

   b. Start with a simple invocation: <antcall target="_newtarget"/>.

   c. Compare the body of this target with the body of the target that will be called.

   d. Parameterize the called target where appropriate.

5. Comment out the old body for this target.

   a. Wait to delete the XML until everything is working.

6. Invoke and test the reworked target.

7. Once the reworked target works, repeat these steps until each of the similar targets is cleaned up.

Example

Listings 5.2 and 5.3 show a piece of a build file that compiles two EJB .jar files. One .jar has all the entity code in it; the other has all the session code in it. (This is not meant to be a recommendation on how to package your EJBs.) The first step is to do what we have already done: identify similar targets. Both of these targets are basically the same except for the directory names.

```xml
<target name="compile.entity" description="Compile the Entities"
        depends="build.po">
   <mkdir dir="${build.destdir}/entity"/>
   <javac srcdir="${src.dir}"
          compiler="modern"
          destdir="${build.destdir}/entity"
          deprecation="${javac.deprecation}"
       debug="${javac.debug}"
       verbose="off"
          includes="subject/invoice/entity/**/*.java">
     <classpath refid="classpath"/>
     <classpath path="${j2eeri.classpath}"/>
     <classpath location="build/po.jar"/>
   </javac>

   <mkdir dir="${build.destdir}/entity/META-INF"/>
   <copy todir="${build.destdir}/entity/META-INF">
     <fileset dir="${src.dir}/subject/invoice/entity/META-INF"
              includes="**/*"/>
   </copy>
   <jar destfile="${build.destdir}/entity.jar"
        manifest="config/entity.mf"
        basedir="${build.destdir}/entity"/>
</target>
```

Listing 5.2 Build file with entity code.

```xml
<target name="compile.session" description="Compile the Sessions"
        depends="compile.entity">
   <mkdir dir="${build.destdir}/session"/>
   <javac srcdir="${src.dir}"
          compiler="modern"
          destdir="${build.destdir}/session"
          deprecation="${javac.deprecation}"
       debug="${javac.debug}"
       verbose="off"
          includes="subject/invoice/session/**/*.java">
     <classpath refid="classpath"/>
     <classpath path="${j2eeri.classpath}"/>
     <classpath location="build/po.jar"/>
     <classpath location="build/entity.jar"/>
   </javac>

   <mkdir dir="${build.destdir}/session/META-INF"/>
   <copy todir="${build.destdir}/session/META-INF">
     <fileset dir="${src.dir}/subject/invoice/session/META-INF"
```

Listing 5.3 Build file with session code. *(continues)*

```
                    includes="**/*"/>
    </copy>
    <jar destfile="${build.destdir}/session.jar"
         manifest="config/session.mf"
         basedir="${build.destdir}/session"/>
</target>
```

Listing 5.3 *(continued)*

Now that we have identified the two similar tasks, we need to copy one, rename it, remove the description, and make the other one (the one we did not copy) call the renamed target. The target compile.session is copied so the first target to resolve is compile.entity, as shown in Listing 5.4.

```
<target name="compile.entity" description="Compile the Entities"
        depends="build.po">
  <antcall target="_compile.ejb">
    <param name="ejbpkg" value="entity"/>
  </antcall>
</target>

<target name="_compile.ejb">
  <mkdir dir="${build.destdir}/${ejbpkg}"/>
  <javac srcdir="${src.dir}"
         compiler="modern"
         destdir="${build.destdir}/${ejbpkg}"
         deprecation="${javac.deprecation}"
         debug="${javac.debug}"
         verbose="off"
         includes="subject/invoice/${ejbpkg}/**/*.java">
    <classpath refid="classpath"/>
    <classpath path="${j2eeri.classpath}"/>
    <classpath location="build/po.jar"/>
  </javac>

  <mkdir dir="${build.destdir}/${ejbpkg}/META-INF"/>
  <copy todir="${build.destdir}/${ejbpkg}/META-INF">
    <fileset dir="${src.dir}/subject/invoice/${ejbpkg}/META-INF"
             includes="**/*"/>
  </copy>
  <jar destfile="${build.destdir}/${ejbpkg}.jar"
       manifest="config/${ejbpkg}.mf"
       basedir="${build.destdir}/${ejbpkg}"/>
</target>
```

Listing 5.4 Solved compile.entity target.

The next step is to comment out the old entity target and test the resultant artifacts. If the test passes, it is time to move on to the session target. It will look a lot like the entity target, but there is a slight issue in this modification. The entity.jar file created by the entity target must be in the *classpath* for the session to build. It seems to be bad form to include the entity .jar file in the classpath in the general target because the entity build can hardly depend on itself to complete. We will have to modify our resolved private target to accommodate this issue. Another property needs to be introduced to hold the extra classpath items. The line in the private target _compile.ejb that has the po.jar file in it should change to use the new property. The final form of the entity and session targets is shown here.

```
<target name="compile.entity" description="Compile the Entities"
        depends="build.po">
  <antcall target="_internal.compile.ejb">
    <param name="ejbpkg" value="entity"/>
    <param name="classpath.extras" value="build/po.jar"/>
  </antcall>
</target>

<target name="compile.session" description="Compile the Sessions"
        depends="compile.entity">
  <antcall target="_internal.compile.ejb">
    <param name="ejbpkg" value="session"/>
    <param name="classpath.extras"
           value="build/po.jar;build/entity.jar"/>
  </antcall>
</target>
```

The next step is to test the whole build process again and make sure that both the entity and session targets are leaving behind the artifacts they are supposed to leave behind.

Another way this solution can be used to clean up and organize a build file is to further factor out common activity into private targets. In the _compile.ejb target, a couple of steps can be taken out and reused by other targets. Specifically, the creation of the directory where the .class files will be placed and the compile could be combined into another private target that could be reused to compile the rest of the objects (the Web classes, for example). Here is the target reworked with the parameterized compile step.

```
<target name="_compile.ejb">
  <antcall target="_internal.compile">
    <param name="build.destdir" value="${build.destdir}/${ejbpkg}"/>
    <param name="included.files"
           value="subject/invoice/${ejbpkg}/**/*.java"/>
```

```xml
        </antcall>
        <mkdir dir="${build.destdir}/${ejbpkg}/META-INF"/>
        <copy todir="${build.destdir}/${ejbpkg}/META-INF">
          <fileset dir="${src.dir}/subject/invoice/${ejbpkg}/META-INF"
                   includes="**/*"/>
        </copy>
        <jar destfile="${build.destdir}/${ejbpkg}.jar"
             manifest="config/${ejbpkg}.mf"
             basedir="${build.destdir}/${ejbpkg}"/>
    </target>
    <target name="_internal.compile">
        <mkdir dir="${build.destdir}"/>
        <javac srcdir="${src.dir}"
               compiler="modern"
               destdir="${build.destdir}"
               deprecation="${javac.deprecation}"
               debug="${javac.debug}"
               verbose="off"
               includes="${included.files}">
           <classpath refid="classpath"/>
           <classpath path="${classpath.extras}"/>
        </javac>
    </target>
```

Now that we have this target in place, it can be used in several places to do the compile, and we won't have to remember to make the directory. The only downside to this approach is that you don't want to go overboard and start defining a private target for each task used in your build. You have to consider whether creating a private target is worth the trouble. If you want at least two steps or a lot of configuration to be the same (like the *javac* task in this example), then you should consider applying this solution to these areas as well.

Pitfall 5.2: No Distinction between Different Types of Builds

This pitfall describes how there is often a lack of distinction between different types of builds. For example, the build for testing is one type of build. Another distinction that could be made is that the build for development might include all the test classes, but the build for deployment might not. The build for a development server deployment will almost always be different from the build for deployment on a test or production server.

Often on big projects, the final production deployment environment has not completely gelled when development first gets started. Questions about what kind of hardware will be required and other considerations are not completely answered, so the environment is not completely known. This can lead to an attitude of: "Oh, I'll deal with that later" when writing the build file. This is a dangerous approach because the build will be geared specifically for the development environment and will often be hard to modify or enhance for production deployment.

Because deployment of the application into the test or production environment is so far down the road, developers often ignore the implications on the build file. When the day to deploy onto a test machine finally comes, there are numerous problems with hard-coded host names, ports, passwords and other configuration information.

The first symptom of this pitfall usually appears when it is time to deploy to the test environment for the first time. The most common thing probably will be a failure to deploy properly inside the environment, but from time to time even the host is hard-coded and the application cannot get into the environment.

Most of the time this pitfall comes up because of ignorance or lack of experience. Sometimes, when development first gets started, it happens because the build file writer did not want to hassle with setting up the build file from the beginning to handle multiple types of deployment. Note that developers often fall into Pitfall 5.1: Copy-and-Paste Reuse in trying to achieve the quick fix to this pitfall; of course, there are inherent issues in that, all documented in that pitfall.

The most common form of this build file is a flat set of targets that do not distinguish between development and test, with all the deployment-related values hard-coded to the development environment. Another form of this pitfall is not distinguishing the files that get built. Often one set of files is put into a development build, and another set is put into a production build. Test classes are the most common example, but things like properties files and other resources can vary depending on the environment as well.

Example

In this example, a deployment is done to a J2EE reference implementation application server.

```xml
<property name="j2eeri.home" value="~/DevTools/j2sdkee1.3.1"/>

<target name="deploy.j2eeri" depends="build.ear">
  <echo message="Deploying ear to the RI ...."/>
  <java classname="com.sun.enterprise.tools.deployment.main.Main"
        fork="yes">
    <classpath path="${j2eeri.classpath}"/>
    <sysproperty key="com.sun.enterprise.home"
                 value="${j2eeri.home}"/>
    <sysproperty key="org.omg.CORBA.ORBInitialPort" value="1050"/>
    <sysproperty key="java.security.policy"
                 value="${j2eeri.home}/lib/security/java.policy"/>
    <arg line="-deploy build/application.ear localhost"/>
  </java>
</target>
```

Notice that the port for the server is hard-coded to 1050 to prevent the application from deploying into an environment that does not have 1050 (the default) as the port for the server. Also the j2eeri.home property is set to the home directory of the user who is currently logged in. Not all developers like to clutter their home directory with an instance of an application server.

Another example of not distinguishing is often found in compiling the classes. The following is a section of a build file that compiles everything in the package, including the test classes. That is exactly what we want to happen during development; the tests need to be easy to run so that they will be run often. When the code moves to another environment (testing or production, for example), it is often the case that the tests should not be included. Here is the example target.

```xml
<target name="compile" description="Compile the classes">
    <mkdir dir="${build.destdir}"/>
    <javac srcdir="${src.dir}"
           compiler="modern"
           destdir="${build.destdir "
           deprecation="off"
           debug="off"
           verbose="off">
      <classpath refid="classpath"/>
    </javac>
</target>
```

The test classes could easily be excluded with an *excludes* attribute for the javac task (assuming a common naming standard like *Test.java). That would keep the tests out of the build entirely, and the tests should be included in the development build. The inclusion/exclusion of test classes should be parameterized so that the build targets for development will include the test classes but the production targets will not. This target could be copied and renamed compile.dev, and the copy could be renamed compile.prod. That puts us right into Pitfall 5.1: Copy-and-Paste Reuse.

The best way to avoid getting stuck in this pitfall is to think through what the build needs to do before writing the build file. This seems obvious, but it is often overlooked. The build process is sometimes just an afterthought for the development team—and it shows. Spend the time up front to determine the different environments that the application must run in and how they vary. Make sure to parameterize based on the things that vary.

Solving Pitfall 5.2: Introduce Properties File

One of the most effective solutions to Pitfall 5.2 is to introduce a properties file. The properties file contains the values for the various distinctions between the different kinds of builds that are performed. The build file then uses the properties to parameterize the build process. This allows the build to use the correct environment values for the type of build being done.

This solution will help you better organize your build file so that the build can be performed in many different environments. Several different aspects of the build would benefit from being more parameterized. Deployment is often different in the development environment than it is in a test or production environment. With a parameterized build file, values can be set to allow the same build file to deploy to either environment.

This solution is also helpful with medium-sized to large development groups where variability occurs in the location of the tools used for the build (that is, all developers do not install the app server into the same directory). Using this solution, you can add flexibility to your process that will accommodate the developer's preferences.

Step-by-Step

1. Create an empty file called build.properties.
    a. This will become the location of all the default values for the properties.
2. Create an empty file called build.properties.local.
    a. This is where developers will override the defaults for their particular environment.

3. Identify aspects of the build that depend on the environment.
   a. Look for things like absolute paths, host names, port numbers, and so on.
4. Place a property for each of the aspects that are likely to change into the build.properties file.
   a. This file is formatted according to the specification for java.util.Properties.
   b. Be consistent in the naming of the properties—that is, if you are adding several properties related to EJBs, use a prefix like "ejb." so that the properties are more easily recognized.
5. Place two properties import lines near the top of the build file, one for each properties file.
   a. Use the "file" attribute of the properties task.
   b. Make sure to put the import for the build.properties.local first so that the properties there will override anything set in the build.properties file.
6. Replace all the hard-coded values in the build file with the property names introduced into the build.properties file.
   a. Be sure to keep track of each target that is changed so that you know what to test in the next step.
7. Invoke each changed target, and review the artifacts.

Example

In this example, we will apply a solution to a build file that is hard-coded to the development environment and cannot deploy to the test environment without changes. Here is a deploy target that will deploy an ear file to the J2EE reference implementation.

```
<target name="deploy.j2eeri" depends="build.ear">
  <echo message="Deploying ear to the RI ...."/>
  <java classname="com.sun.enterprise.tools.deployment.main.Main"
        fork="yes">
    <classpath path="${j2eeri.classpath}"/>
    <sysproperty key="com.sun.enterprise.home"
                 value="/Users/bdudney/DevTools/j2sdkee1.3.1"/>
    <sysproperty key="org.omg.CORBA.ORBInitialPort" value="1050"/>
    <sysproperty key="java.security.policy"
       value="/Users/bdudney/DevTools/j2sdkee1.3.1/lib/security/java.policy"/>
```

```
        <arg line="-deploy build/invoice.ear localhost"/>
    </java>
</target>
```

This is particularly bad because the location of the app server is hard-coded to use my home directory. This will not work on any other user's machine on the team. Also, if there were a need to vary the port, this target would fail. The first step is to create the two properties files that contain properties for the hard-coded values here, namely the J2EE Reference Implementation installation directory and the port on which it is configured to listen. Other values that need to be parameterized are the host name the server is running on and the port where the *httpd* server is listening. Here is the build.properties file with each of the values specified.

```
# j2ee reference implementation properties
j2eeri.host.name=localhost
j2eeri.host.port=8000
j2eeri.orb.port=1050
j2eeri.home=/DevTools/j2sdkee1.3.1
```

Because I installed the application server in my home directory I would put the following line in my build.properties.local file.

```
# local overides of the j2ee reference implementation properties
j2eeri.home=/Users/bdudney/DevTools/j2sdkee1.3.1
```

The next step in the solution is to add the property import lines to the main build file. The code for that is shown here.

```
<!-- load the local version of the properties first -->
<property file="build.properties.local"/>
<!-- load the default version of the properties second -->
<property file="build.properties"/>
```

The next step is to replace the hard-coded values with properties.

```
<target name="deploy.j2eeri" depends="build.ear">
  <echo message="Deploying ear to the RI ...."/>
  <java classname="com.sun.enterprise.tools.deployment.main.Main"
        fork="yes">
    <classpath path="${j2eeri.classpath}"/>
    <sysproperty key="com.sun.enterprise.home"
                 value="${j2eeri.home}"/>
    <sysproperty key="org.omg.CORBA.ORBInitialPort"
                 value="${j2eeri.orb.port}"/>
    <sysproperty key="java.security.policy"
                 value="${j2eeri.home}/lib/security/java.policy"/>
```

```
        <arg line="-deploy build/invoice.ear ${j2eeri.host.name}"/>
    </java>
</target>
```

Now when the build goes into another environment and is deployed onto different ports, the SCM person can create his or her own copy of the build.properties.local file that reflects the correct values for that environment and thus deploys the application properly.

The final step is to build and deploy the application and test the artifacts that are created. This is another place where a good set of unit tests would come in handy. If the invoice.ear file were fully covered by a set of Cactus tests, the deployment would be easy to test by invoking the Cactus tests. If they succeed, then everything should be fine.

Pitfall 5.3: Building Subprojects

This pitfall describes how developers often write Ant build file hierarchies that mimic the way they used to write make files. This follows an idiom that was used to manage multiple subdirectories with the old build management tool called make.

As expected, this pitfall usually shows up in build files written by developers experienced in writing make files. With make, they had to put a make file into each directory and then invoke that make file from the one in the parent directory. With Ant's sophisticated file sets, there is no longer any reason to do that. But, given the breadth of experience with make and the growing popularity of Ant, many developers are making the switch, so we end up with lots of build files spread throughout the directory structure of many projects.

Symptoms of this pitfall are usually related to maintenance of the build and are something like what happens in Pitfall 5.1: Copy-and-Paste Resuse. Instead of copying targets, though, entire files are copied. As with all copy and paste operations, the functionality and bugs are copied together, so bug fixes in one copy must be applied across every single copy or there will be regression-like bugs.

The general form of this pitfall is a master build file in the root directory of the project and a separate build file in each of the subprojects. Generally, there is not a build.xml file in each subdirectory, but more than one build file increases maintenance overhead and makes the build harder to understand.

Example

In this example, there are two subprojects: the entity and session EJBs for a project. The entities are kept in one source tree, and the sessions are kept in another. The source tree looks like this.

```
project_root/src/entity/build.xml
                       META-INF/ejb-jar.xml
                                jboss.xml
                                jbosscmb-jdbc.xml
                       CustomerBean.java
                       Customer.java
                       CustomerHome.java
              session/build.xml
                      META-INF/ejb-jar.xml
                               jboss.xml
                      ProcessCustomerBean.java
                      ProcessCustomer.java
                      ProcessCustomerHome.java
```

Notice that each directory has its own build file. These build files should be exactly the same because the build can be done in the same way for both subprojects. Here is a portion of the build file that would invoke these two build files.

```xml
<target name="build.entity">
  <ant dir="src/entity"
       target="build.entity"/>
</target>

<target name="build.session">
  <ant dir="src/session"
       target="build.session"/>
</target>
```

The two subbuild files would invoke several steps, but both would go through the same process. Part of the entity file is here.

```xml
<target name="compile.entity"
        description="Compile the files, build the jar">
    <!-- make sure the destination directory is present -->
    <mkdir dir="${build.destdir}/entity"/>
    <!-- compile all the .java files -->
    <javac srcdir="${src.dir}"
           compiler="modern"
           destdir="${build.destdir}/entity"
           deprecation="off"
           debug="off"
           verbose="off"
           includes="**/*.java">
      <classpath refid="classpath"/>
      <classpath refid="_jboss.classpath"/>
    </javac>
    <!-- make sure the META-INF directory is present -->
    <mkdir dir="${build.destdir}/entity/META-INF"/>
    <!-- copy the deployment descriptors,
         .DS_Store is a Mac OSX file that does not need to be copied -->
    <copy todir="${build.destdir}/entity/META-INF">
      <fileset dir="META-INF"
               includes="**/*"
               excludes="**/.DS_Store"/>
    </copy>
    <!-- jar up the artifacts -->
    <jar destfile="${build.destdir}/entity.jar"
         manifest="config/entity.mf"
         basedir="${build.destdir}/entity"/>
</target>
```

The session file would look exactly like this one except the word *entity* would be replaced with the word *session*. The build will suffer from the same problems, lack of maintainability chief among the issues.

Note that with subprojects that are very different in nature, it is sometimes OK to put another build file down in the subproject. A common reason to have subprojects that are very different is a different implementation technology for the subproject. A good example is a group of C++ code that is used as the implementation of a group of JNI calls. C++ has different conventions regarding source code placement (that is, no packages), so it might warrant a new build file. Another good reason to use subprojects is for truly different building needs in various subsets of an application. For example, an application that has a plug-in architecture might have a very different type of build process for the plug-ins than for the application itself. These are good places to introduce subprojects.

To avoid this pitfall, there must be a plan for the build file. What are the subprojects, and what will need to be done to build them? If the build process for each subproject is similar, put the similar targets into the master build file as parameterized targets that you can invoke with the various subdirectories as arguments. For each aspect of the build process that is different, create a new build file in the subproject and invoke it from the master.

This pitfall probably underscores the need to plan the build more than any other pitfall covered so far. For each type of subproject (EJB, Web, Web service, etc.), there needs to be a common set of tasks and a common directory layout so that the tasks can function in a similar manner. Sometimes developers copy and paste build XML to keep out of this pitfall, which leads to Pitfall 5.1: Copy-and-Paste Reuse. The result is just as difficult to maintain.

Solving Pitfall 5.3: Centralize the Build

This solution describes steps to consolidate the building of your application in one place instead of having the build spread out over several files. When projects are built with a distributed build system (a separate build file for each subproject), often each of the build files ends up looking more or less the same. One group of targets compiles the source code, and another packages the products into a .jar file. This practice leads to the same problems with maintainability that copying and pasting parts of the build have. Namely, if there is a bug in one of the subproject build files, that same bug is likely to be replicated across each subproject build file. Also, if a change needs to be made to meet a new requirement, then that same change probably needs to be made across all the subprojects. Applying this solution will help you to get your build consolidated into one build file that is much easier to maintain and thus get you out of this pitfall.

Step-by-Step

1. Identify common structures or targets in the subprojects.
   a. Drawing a graph of the targets in the build files is a great way to see the structure and similarities.
   b. This will become the basis for restructuring the top-level build file.
2. Create a target in the top-level build file that is a copy of one of the existing similar targets from the subproject build files.
   a. Make sure to start with the common target with the fewest dependencies.
3. Rename the new target, and remove the description if there was one.
   a. This will become a private target. The name should reflect the old name but should follow a naming convention to denote that this is a "private" target. Using a leading underscore is a typical convention, but use whatever works, as long as it's consistent.
   b. Make sure that you put a comment at the top of your build file specifying the convention you adopt.
4. Parameterize the private target so that it can be used to accomplish the tasks on each subproject.
   a. This is the most complex step by far. There can be considerable work in refactoring the directory structure on the subprojects if they were not created similarly.
5. Add two new public targets to the top-level build file that invoke the new private target with antcall.
   a. It is important to adopt a naming convention for these targets. Because they are doing the same thing for different subprojects, some part of the name should be the same. A decent starting convention is to put the name of the subproject followed by the old name of the target. The particulars are not that important as long as you are consistent.
   b. Make sure to get the dependencies from the subproject's target. This requirement means that it is important to start at the top of the dependency chain.
6. Specify the parameters so that the tasks will execute against the proper subproject.

7. Invoke the new public targets, and test the results.
8. Repeat these steps for each target.

Example

In this example, the build files from the Petstore sample application from Sun will be solved according to the mechanism laid out there. The Petstore sample has quite a few build files spread out through the source code. Many of the build files are more or less identical, so it is a prime example of how consolidation can help with maintainability. We will focus on the build files in apps/petstore/src and apps/supplier/src.

The first step is to figure out the similarities between the subproject build files. Figure 5.1 is a graphical representation of the targets in the Petstore build.

Figure 5.2 is the same graphing technique applied to the build file for the supplier build file.

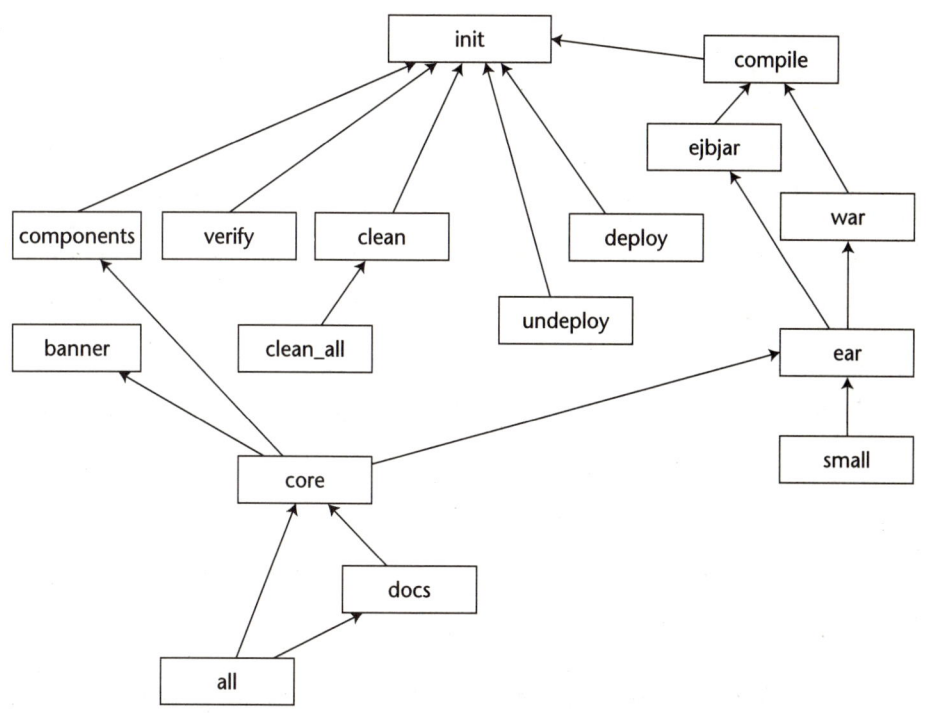

Figure 5.1 Graphical depiction of targets for the Petstore application.

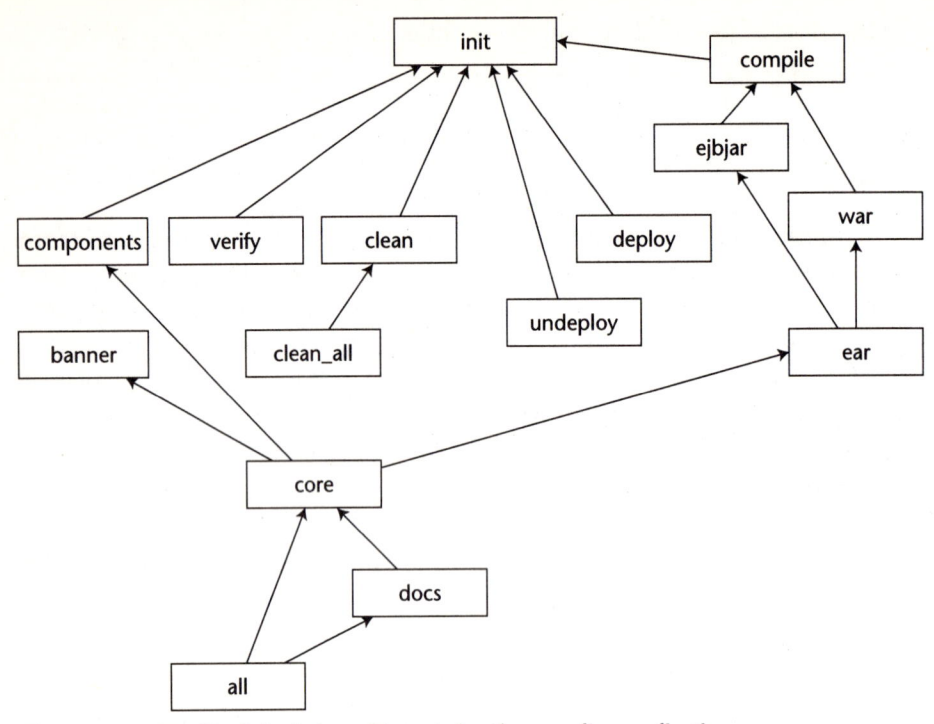

Figure 5.2 Graphical depiction of targets for the supplier application.

Notice that the two files have basically the same structure and have the same target names. The next step in the process is to copy one of the subproject targets into the root build file and make it private (remove the description and name it according to your naming convention). Even though we should start with the *init* target for the example (because it has no dependencies), we will start with the deploy target so that we can get to the interesting stuff right away. In your build scripts it is important to start with the simple targets first so that they can build on each other. Listing 5.5 shows the code for the two deploy targets for comparison.

```xml
<!--
    The deploy target for the petstore application
-->
<target name="deploy" depends="init">
  <java classname="com.sun.enterprise.tools.deployment.main.Main"
        fork="yes">
    <classpath path="${j2ee.classpath}"/>
    <sysproperty key="com.sun.enterprise.home" value="${j2ee.home}"/>
    <sysproperty key="org.omg.CORBA.ORBInitialPort" value="1050"/>
    <sysproperty key="java.security.policy"
```

Listing 5.5 Deploy targets from the Petstore and supplier build files.

```xml
                    value="${j2ee.home}/lib/security/java.policy"/>
            <!--
                This line was reformatted from the original so it would fit
            -->
            <arg value="-deploy ${petstore.build}/${petstore.ear}"/>
            <arg value="${j2ee.server.name}"/>
        </java>
    </target>

    <!--
        The deploy target for the supplier application
    -->
    <target name="deploy" depends="init">
        <java classname="com.sun.enterprise.tools.deployment.main.Main"
              fork="yes">
            <classpath path="${j2ee.classpath}"/>
            <sysproperty key="com.sun.enterprise.home" value="${j2ee.home}"/>
            <sysproperty key="org.omg.CORBA.ORBInitialPort" value="1050"/>
            <sysproperty key="java.security.policy"
                    value="${j2ee.home}/lib/security/java.policy"/>
            <!--
                This line was reformatted from the original so it would fit
            -->
            <arg value="-deploy ${supplier.ear}"/>
            <arg value="${j2ee.server.name}"/>
        </java>
    </target>
```

Listing 5.5 *(continued)*

Notice how very similar these two targets are. The only difference is the build location and ear file that is being deployed. The major problem with this is, of course, that if something needs to be changed in one it must be changed in all (that is, if the ORBInitialPort needed to be changed for some reason). Another issue that is apparent only if you look very closely is the way the ear file is referred to by a property. In the Petstore file it is referred to via ${petstore.build}/${petstore.ear}. In the supplier file it is referred to simply as ${supplier.ear}. The values are named similarly but are defined differently. This is another one of the issues that arise when build files are not consolidated: Properties and targets become inconsistent. Maintenance is harder because there is so much more to know in order to understand the whole build.

The next step in this solution is to copy one of the targets, make it private, rename it, and parameterize it so that it can be called with antcall. Antcall is part of the consolidated build; where the Introduce Antcall solution is about reducing copy-and-paste problems in a single build file, this solution is about reducing copy and paste between the build files that are spread out throughout the subprojects. The copied and parameterized code is listed here.

```xml
<target name="_deploy.application">
  <java classname="com.sun.enterprise.tools.deployment.main.Main"
        fork="yes">
    <classpath path="${j2ee.classpath}"/>
    <sysproperty key="com.sun.enterprise.home" value="${j2ee.home}"/>
    <sysproperty key="org.omg.CORBA.ORBInitialPort" value="1050"/>
    <sysproperty key="java.security.policy"
                 value="${j2ee.home}/lib/security/java.policy"/>
    <arg value="-deploy ${application.build}/${application.ear}"/>
    <arg value="${j2ee.server.name}"/>
  </java>
</target>
```

All that we had to change for this target is the build location (to application.build) and the *ear* file to deploy (to application.ear). The next step in the solution is to add targets that will invoke the private target with the specific values required for the subprojects. The private target is invoked with an antcall like this.

```xml
<target name="deploy.petstore" depends="build.petstore">
    <!-- deploy the petstore application -->
    <antcall name="_deploy.application">
      <param name="application.build" value="${build.dir}/petstore"/>
      <param name="application.ear" value="petstore.ear"/>
    </antcall>
</target>
<target name="deploy.supplier" depends="build.supplier">
    <!-- deploy the supplier application -->
    <antcall name="_deploy.application">
      <param name="application.build" value="${build.dir}/supplier"/>
      <param name="application.ear" value="supplier.ear"/>
    </antcall>
</target>
<target name="deploy" depends="deploy.petstore, deploy.supplier"/>
```

Notice that we retained the "deploy" target so that users of the build will not even have to know that the internals were changed. Another thing to notice is that all the properties that are specified in the project are inherited so you do not have to supply the j2ee.server.name property to invoke the private target. The final step is to invoke the target and review the results.

Pitfall 5.4: No Logging from Custom Tasks

This pitfall describes a common mistake of new task developers in not putting proper logging statements into their tasks. With the declarative nature of an Ant build, it is very important to have good logging to help users discover why the task is not performing as expected.

As with other reusable software, the developer is responsible for building something that is usable (if he or she wants it used). The writer has to ensure that the task can actually be used by other developers who are not as experienced or who don't want to know all the details about the internals of Ant. Often, though, developers forget about making the task mistake-friendly. Users putting a task into their build files should not be left to guess why the task is not doing what the documentation led them to believe it would do. The task needs to put into a log exactly what it is doing and why. Of course, this kind of information should show up only if the *debug* or *verbose* arguments are used.

Developers should be concerned about the task not only for other users but also for themselves. In all likelihood, the task will not remain the main development task for long; the actual application needs to be built. In six months will the task still be understandable? That question needs to be asked more often, about all kinds of software.

This pitfall almost always shows up as developers who use a custom tag complaining about how hard the task is to use. It can also be seen by an increase in complexity or difficulty in maintaining the build file.

The most common cause for this pitfall is inexperience. Developers usually fall into this pitfall only once and then they learn from it by having to use the task again three or six months later. Developers who have to go back and use their own poorly written code often benefit from the experience.

This pitfall generally takes the form of a task that is really hard to get to know. Each attempt to incorporate the task into a build leads to a lot of frustration in trying to figure out how to make the attribute values correct. Remember that a poorly written task can often lead to a poorly structured build file as the build file is modified to try to make the task work.

Example

This example is a simple reimplementation of the copy task that ships with Ant. Most of the functionality is not here, but Listing 5.6 illustrates the poor practice of not logging from custom tasks.

```java
public class CopyTask extends Task {
    protected File file = null;       // the source file
    protected File destFile = null; // the destination file
    /**
     * Copy task constructor.
     */
    public CopyTask() {
    }

    /**
     * Sets a single source file to copy.
     */
    public void setFile(File file) {
        this.file = file;
    }

    /**
     * Sets the destination file.
     */
    public void setTofile(File destFile) {
        this.destFile = destFile;
    }

    /**
     * Performs the copy operation.
     */
    public void execute() throws BuildException {
        try {
            if (file != null && destFile != null) {
                BufferedReader in =
                    new BufferedReader(new FileReader(file));
                BufferedWriter out =
                    new BufferedWriter(new FileWriter(destFile));
                String line = in.readLine();
                String newline = null;
                while (line != null) {
                    newline = line;
                    out.write(newline);
                    line = in.readLine();
                }
            }
        } catch(IOException ioe) {
            throw new BuildException(ioe.getMessage());
        }
    }
}
```

Listing 5.6 CopyTask.java.

There is no way to tell why the copy failed from this implementation. If one of the files passed in is a directory, the task would fail, and it would be very difficult to tell why. This task would be very hard to use as it is written.

Remember that there is always cause to put logging into a task. At the very least, log each attribute value in the execute method so that users can see what actually got passed into the task. For very simple tasks, there is less reason to log than for more complex tasks.

The best way to stay out of this pitfall is to spend some up-front time, before the task is written, thinking through what is likely to go wrong and how the task can log indicators of the problem. Any task takes parameters, and unless the task is very simple (like echo, for example), some things can and will go wrong with what is passed in. For example, the real copy task that comes with Ant logs if it cannot find the source file or destination directory, but it does not stop at a simple "I can't find it" message. The actual path that copy thinks should be copied is printed out. All tags should have useful logs like this to help users find out what is wrong.

Solving Pitfall 5.4: Add Logging

Usually the solution is straightforward and simple to apply. As a rule, if the task takes more than two property values or the processing done is more than a few lines of Java code, it is important to log from that task. Adding logging is also straightforward so there is no reason not to do it. Something to keep in mind as you are applying this solution to your custom tasks is to log at the appropriate level. Logging informational messages at the error level is almost as irritating as not logging errors at all.

Because Ant is a declarative means of describing the build and not a programming language, it can be very difficult to debug the declaration, especially if the runtime representation of the target does not provide assistance. There can be no breakpoints set in the execution of an Ant file (unless you want to run Ant in a debugger), so the only debugging technique is to log messages. If a task does not provide debugging messages, developers using a tag will often give up trying and perform the build in another way with tasks that they can make work. It would be a shame to have the task go unused just because it does not provide sufficient logging messages.

Step-by-Step

1. Look for places where the task could fail.
   a. The first place to look is in any catch block. There should, at the very least, be a debug log for every exception caught.

260 Chapter 5

      b. Another good spot to look for possible errors is ignored return values.

2. Log a message for each point of failure, informing the user what happened and why the task fails because of it.

      a. As an aside, potential failures are a great thing to keep in the documentation as well as good logging about them.

3. Recompile, and test the task.

Example

In this example, we will solve the earlier example of a simplified copy task shown in Listing 5.6. This task is greatly simplified from the task that ships with Ant; it will not deal with file sets or directories, and its main purpose is to provide an illustration of the solution. Listing 5.7 details the code for the execute method.

```java
public class CopyTask extends Task {
    protected File file = null;     // the source file
    protected File destFile = null; // the destination file

. . . constructor and get/set methods elided . . .

    /**
     * Performs the copy operation.
     */
    public void execute() throws BuildException {
        try {
            if (file != null && destFile != null) {
                BufferedReader in =
                    new BufferedReader(new FileReader(file));
                BufferedWriter out =
                    new BufferedWriter(new FileWriter(destFile));
                String line = in.readLine();
                String newline = null;
                while (line != null) {
                    newline = line;
                    out.write(newline);
                    line = in.readLine();
                }
            }
        } catch(IOException ioe) {
            throw new BuildException(ioe.getMessage());
        }
    }
}
```

Listing 5.7 CopyTask execute method.

The first step in this solution is to look for potential failure points in the execution of the task. The obvious one here is in catching the IOException. Because it is being rethrown as a BuildException, the user will get some indication, but it would be better to be more explicit. Now that a failure spot has been identified, the next step is to log a message that the user can understand. The catch block should change to look like this.

```
    . . .
        } catch(IOException ioe) {
            String msg = "Failed to copy " + file + " to " + destFile
                + " due to " + ioe.getMessage();
            log(msg, Project.MSG_ERROR);
            throw new BuildException(ioe.getMessage());
        }
    . . .
```

Also notice that the task silently fails if either file or destFile is null. This is especially irritating to users of a task (at least this user). There should be an else clause that throws a BuildException so that the copy can be cleaned up. To fix this aspect of the pitfall, the code should look like this.

```
    . . .
        } else {
            log("You must specify both source and destination files",
                MSG_ERROR);
            throw new BuildException("source or destination not set",
                                     location);
        }
    . . .
```

Another thing to think about is to put in debug logging so that when Ant is run in verbose mode the developer can see exactly what is happening inside the task. The final resolved code is listed here.

```
    public void execute() throws BuildException {
        try {
            if (file != null && destFile != null) {
                log("file = " + file, Project.MSG_DEBUG);
                log("destFile = " + destFile, Project.MSG_DEBUG);
                BufferedReader in =
                    new BufferedReader(new FileReader(file));
                BufferedWriter out =
                    new BufferedWriter(new FileWriter(destFile));
                String line = in.readLine();
                String newline = null;
                while (line != null) {
                    newline = line;
                    out.write(newline);
                    line = in.readLine();
```

```
            }
        } else {
            log("You must specify both source and destination files",
                MSG_ERROR);
            throw new BuildException("source or destination not set",
                                    location);
        }
    } catch (IOException ioe) {
        String msg = "Failed to copy " + file + " to " + destFile
            + " due to " + ioe.getMessage();
        log(msg, Project.MSG_ERROR);
        throw new BuildException(msg, ioe, location);
    }
}
```

Each failure scenario is logged, and debugging information is provided as well. After the solution is applied, this task will be much easier to use.

APPENDIX A

Pitfall Catalog

Pitfall 1.1: No Assert — p. 4

This pitfall describes the tendency of developers new to unit testing to forget about asserts completely. New developers often assume that invoking the method is a sufficient test. They assume that if no exceptions are thrown when the method is called, then everything must be OK. Many bugs escape this kind of testing.

Pitfall 1.2: Unreasonable Assert — p. 20

This pitfall describes the tendency of inexperienced developers to assert everything that can be imagined. Often developers new to unit testing will take one of two tracks: They will have read about asserts before and thus recognize the concept when they see it in JUnit, or they will not have heard of asserts before and skip over them. The first kind of developer typically gets trapped in this pitfall. Tests end up bloated with a lot of asserts that just make sure that the JVM is working.

Pitfall 1.3: Console-Based Testing — p. 24

This pitfall describes the practice of using System.out.println in the test code and then visually inspecting the output to validate that the test subject is doing what it should. Developers new to unit testing typically don't know how to write good test code and will not have enough experience to write good assertions. Often in these cases, the developer knows something more needs to be done but does not know quite what to do, so he or she decides that the results should be printed to the console.

Pitfall 1.4 Unfocused Test Method — p. 34

This pitfall describes test methods that are unfocused in nature and tend to become unwieldy as they grow to test more and more of the API. It usually comes from experienced developers who have gotten lazy about building the setUp code for the test, so they cram all the testing they can into one large, complex test method. Even though this sometimes results in a well-tested subject, the tests become unwieldy and are less likely to be maintained over time.

Pitfall 1.5: Failure to Isolate Each Test — p. 45

This pitfall usually takes the form of some external script that must be run before the tests will succeed. Examples of external scripts include things like initialization data (or scripts that clean out the database) in an SQL script that must be run against the database. Another typical form is for the test methods to have order dependencies. In either form, the tests will become unreliable if they remain stuck in this pitfall because, over time, the order of the methods will change and they will start to fail, or people will forget to run the database script often enough that they get fed up with the tests. Tests that are not reliable will cease to be used because they show too many false bugs and catch too few actual bugs.

Pitfall 1.6: Failure to Isolate Subject — p. 58

Test subjects that rely on other classes to function properly are harder to test because the underlying classes might have bugs. Bugs in an underlying class might cause the test to fail even though the bug is not in the subject of the test. In a perfect world, there would be no test failures that are caused by code other than the test subject. In that kind of scenario, the test would pass or fail based solely on the bugs (or lack of) in the test subject. While the ideal scenario is hard to achieve, it is worth pursuing. Developers often don't even think about trying and thus end up stuck in this pitfall.

Pitfall 2.1: Copy/Paste Formatting   p. 70

Ensuring that the values displayed in the user interface are consistently and correctly formatted can be painstaking work. Because Struts doesn't provide generic facilities to automate this task, the temptation is to code the required behavior directly in value object getter methods, which quickly leads to copying and pasting a particular formatting behavior to all the getter methods that need it. This copy/paste formatting code is used to convert Java types (for example, BigDecimal, Date, etc.) into formatted strings suitable for display in the user interface, as well as to populate ActionForms with the values derived via this technique. If you find yourself copying and pasting formatting code in numerous classes or maintaining redundant formatting code, you are stuck in this pitfall.

Pitfall 2.2: Copy/Paste Conversion   p. 96

This pitfall is related to Pitfall 2.1: Copy/Paste Formatting because it represents the inverse of the problem of formatting values for presentation in the user interface. One of the challenges facing Struts developers is converting the form values transmitted in HTTP requests from Strings to the wide variety of object types into which they have to ultimately be bound, while removing any formatting characters added during rendering (for example, thousands separators and currency symbols in currency amounts). If you find yourself scratching your head at the rapid growth of the code size for the user interface, and spending way too much time and energy messing around with type conversion code, you're probably experiencing the Copy/Paste Conversion pitfall.

Pitfall 2.3: Copy/Paste Validation   p. 119

Struts provides a simple hook, the empty validate() method in the ActionForm class, as a starting point for validation of HTML form values submitted in the request. Your subclasses can override this method to provide the necessary validation logic. While it may be tempting simply to hand-code whatever logic is needed on a case-by-case basis, there are a number of problems with this approach. The most obvious of these is the proliferation of copy/paste code across the ActionForms that perform validation. If the validate() methods in your ActionForms are getting huge, you are experiencing this pitfall.

Pitfall 3.1: Business-Tier Code in Actions   p. 149

Actions are controller objects that typically contain application logic, coordinating the other components of the system to respond to user requests. Because Actions are the entry point for the request cycle, developers often find it handy simply to hard-code whatever logic is needed. This can result in business-tier code being sprinkled liberally through a number of Action classes. Coupling the presentation tier with the business tier this way can make your application inflexible and difficult to maintain. If there is JNDI lookup code in your Actions, you have fallen prey to this pitfall.

Pitfall 3.2: Copy/Paste Code in Actions   p. 172

This pitfall describes the tendency for redundant code to proliferate throughout a project's Action classes. While this pitfall may seem relatively minor in terms of its potential negative consequences, resolving it can lead to dramatic improvements in the readability and maintainability of Actions. The issue here is that the code contained in most Actions tends to be quite similar. If a great deal of this kind of code is copied, it can become a burden to maintain, and it can obscure the more significant bits of code in a given method. If you find yourself copying and pasting blocks of code from one Action to another, you are experiencing this pitfall.

Pitfall 3.3: Accessing ActionForms in the Session   p. 182

Struts can be configured to pass an ActionForm automatically as a parameter when it invokes an Action's execute() method. If an Action needs to work with more than one ActionForm, there's no way to extend this behavior, so the Action has to be coded to locate the other ActionForms that it needs. Unfortunately, some of the techniques that developers use can lead to runtime errors. In addition, developers often resort to copy-and-paste reuse for this type of functionality. If you have strange intermittent bugs in your user interface, you may be experiencing this pitfall.

Pitfall 3.4: Overloaded ActionMappings   p. 192

It's not unusual to find developers writing Actions that both navigate to a page and handle forms submitted from that page. Apart from adding one extra level of confusion to the mix, there's nothing inherently wrong with coding Actions this way. Unless extra care is taken when defining the ActionMappings that correspond to such Actions, the application may begin to exhibit some odd and befuddling quirks. If you tend to write execute() methods that perform two or more entirely different functions depending on the value of a request parameter and then use a single ActionMapping in struts-config.xml to configure it, you are vulnerable to this pitfall.

Pitfall 4.1: Hard-Coded Strings in JSPs   p. 199

Struts provides a tag for rendering string values by first looking them up in a resources bundle. Many developers, though, hard-code the strings directly into their JSPs. When the JSPs are first being written it is sometimes not apparent that anything else could or should happen. If the string *Name* appears on only one form in a Web application, then why would we want to have to look that string up to get it onto the Web page? The pitfall shows its teeth when Name shows up more than once. If that string is hard-coded in both places and if it ever needs to be changed (for example, to *First Name*), there is a dual maintenance point. Whenever a dual maintenance point arises, you can be fairly confident that a pitfall is lurking somewhere and making your life more difficult than it needs to be.

Pitfall 4.2: Hard-Coded Keys in JSPs   p. 203

This pitfall is related to Pitfall 4.1: Hard-Coded Strings in JSPs because what usually happens is that a developer will turn from hard-coded strings to this pitfall and hard-code the names of the properties into their JSPs. This usually turns into a maintenance hassle over time. What typically happens is that the initial naming scheme for properties is outgrown and a new naming scheme is introduced. The new naming scheme will require the old properties to be renamed. It becomes tedious very quickly to search through each JSP looking for each instance of the old property name. If your property names are in your JSPs, then you are stuck in this pitfall.

Pitfall 4.3: Not Using Struts Tags for Error Messaging p. 209

Struts provides a fairly comprehensive set of facilities for managing and rendering error (and other) messages. Developers may have already acquired the habit of managing these messages themselves by working in other JSP environments, or they simply may not have had sufficient time to fully understand how to use the Struts messaging facilities. This results in the developers doing manually what is already provided (that is, tested and well designed) in Struts. It is always better to use an existing piece of well-tested software than to build your own solution. If you are managing your own errors in Struts, then you are almost certainly caught in this pitfall.

Pitfall 4.4: Calculating Derived Values in JSPs p. 214

This pitfall examines the consequences of using scriptlets to perform calculations in JSPs. Developers are often tempted to take shortcuts, and one of the easiest to take is inserting a bit of scriptlet code in a JSP to calculate a value derived from other fields displayed in the same JSP. If you are performing a calculation in your JSP, chances are you are stuck in this pitfall.

Pitfall 4.5: Performing Business Logic in JSPs p. 218

This pitfall involves an even more serious form of blurring the lines between the models, views, and controllers in a Struts application. Remember that the model contains the data and business logic of the application, the view displays the data to the user, and the controller glues user interface events from the views to the business logic in the models. If business logic is in a JSP, then each point in the user interface that needs that processing will have to have a copy of the code. As has been said countless times, copying code is always bad.

This pitfall is similar to Pitfall 4.4: Calculating Derived Values in JSPs, although the consequences are potentially even more serious. If one of the JSPs does not get a copy of the code, then the business logic will not be executed at all. If you have any scriptlet code in your JSPs that performs any business logic, you are caught in this pitfall.

Pitfall 4.6: Hard-Coded Options in HTML Select Lists   p. 224

This pitfall deals with the problems developers often encounter with HTML select lists in Struts. One of the trickier issues developers face when coding their JSPs is how to populate the value lists displayed in the drop-down menus rendered by the HTML select element. Struts provides an html:options tag that allows developers to specify a bean containing a collection that provides both the labels to display in the UI and their associated values. Unfortunately, many developers find the Struts html:options tag confusing when they initially encounter it and find it expedient to code the values that they need directly in their JSP using the html:option tag instead. This leads to a lot more code than is required, thereby increasing maintenance costs. If you have built an HTML select list manually, you are stuck in this pitfall.

Pitfall 4.7: Not Checking for Duplicate Form Submissions   p. 229

A side effect of the stateless nature of the HTTP protocol is that the interface presented in the browser can easily get out of sync with the state of the model on the server. This pitfall addresses a common scenario involving the lack of synchronization that arises in nearly every application. It is common for a user to submit values using a form on a given page and then, at some later point, backtrack to the cached page, edit the now stale values, and submit the form again. This has the potential to corrupt the underlying data store by creating duplicate records, overwriting current data with stale values, and so on. In the best case, it creates a bad transaction that is rejected by the data store. Unless you have explicitly made sure that your forms will not submit more than once, you are stuck in this pitfall.

Pitfall 5.1: Copy-and-Paste Reuse   p. 235

This pitfall describes what happens when developers copy and paste various pieces of the build file to accomplish the build.

Just as in any other area of development, copy-and-paste reuse is easy, quick, and bad for long-term productivity. Copying code is copying bugs, and—even worse—as the bugs get fixed in one part of the build, the copies will go unfixed. Also, as parts of the build grow and mature, the copies will not. This is a classic mistake that developers make in just about every area of programming. There are lots of different reasons why copy and paste happens, including laziness, looming deadlines, and ignorance. but what looks good for the short term turns out to be very painful to deal with in the long term. If you have any copied build file xml, you are caught in this pitfall.

Pitfall 5.2: No Distinction between Different Types of Builds p. 243

This pitfall describes how there is often a lack of distinction between different types of builds. For example, the build for testing is one type of build. Another distinction that could be made is that the build for development might include all the test classes, but the build for deployment might not. The build for a development server deployment will almost always be different from the build for deployment on a test or production server. Often on big projects, the final production deployment environment has not completely gelled when development first gets started. Questions about what kind of hardware will be required and other considerations are not completely answered, so the environment is not completely known. This can lead to an attitude of "I'll deal with that later" when writing the build file. This is a dangerous approach because the build will become geared specifically for the development environment and will often be hard to modify or enhance for production deployment. Unless you have explicitly planned your final deployment environment, you are probably trapped in this pitfall.

Pitfall 5.3: Building Subprojects p. 249

This pitfall describes how developers often write Ant build file hierarchies that mimic the way they used to write make files. This follows an idiom that was used to manage multiple subdirectories with the old build management tool called make.

As expected, this pitfall usually shows up in build files written by developers experienced in writing make files. With make, they had to put a make file into each directory and then invoke that make file from the one in the parent directory. With Ant's sophisticated file sets, there is no longer any reason to do that. But, given the breadth of experience with make and the growing popularity of Ant, many developers are making the switch, so we end up with lots of build files spread throughout the directory structure of many projects.

Pitfall 5.4: No Logging from Custom Tasks p. 257

This pitfall describes a common mistake of new task developers in not putting proper logging statements into their tasks. With the declarative nature of an Ant build, it is very important to have good logging to help users discover why the task is not performing as expected. If your custom tasks do not contain logging, you are definitely in this pitfall.

APPENDIX B

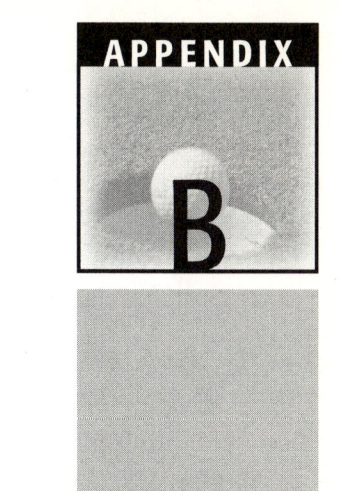

References

Ant

**Java Development with Ant by Erik Hatcher
and Steve Loughran (Manning, 2002)**

This is a terrific book on Ant. There is extensive documentation about the way that Ant works and how to extend it as well as a good treatment of the fundamental data types found in Ant (that is, file sets, etc.).

**Java Tools for eXtreme Programming by Richard Hightower
and Nicholas Lesiecki (Wiley, 2001)**

This is a wonderful resource for Ant as well as unit testing. This book does not go into the detail that Hatcher and Loughran go into, but there is a wealth of practical information on how to build and deploy your J2SE and J2EE applications with Ant.

http://jakarta.apache.org/ant

This is the root of the Ant project. You will find all kinds of information here about Ant as well as downloads of the latest versions.

Struts

***Refactoring: Improving the Design of Existing Code* by Martin Fowler et al. (Addison Wesley, 1999)**

The definitive work on refactoring, Fowler's book is a comprehensive treatment of the topic that offers profound insights into how to reorganize code for clarity, flexibility, and reusability.

***Core J2EE Patterns: Best Practices and Design Strategies* by Deepak Alur, John Crupi, and Dan Malks (Prentice Hall PTR, 2001)**

This is an authoritative book on design patterns for J2EE applications that contains many useful suggestions for refactoring. Developers often refer to the the patterns delineated in this book by name, so this book is an important reference.

***Bitter Java* by Bruce A. Tate (Manning, 2002)**

Tate focuses quite effectively on some of the generic anti-patterns of server-side Java applications, and he offers practical alternatives to help avoid them.

***Effective Java* by Joshua Bloch (Addison Wesley, 2001)**

This is one of the best books available on the fundamental techniques of Java programming.

***Programming Jakarta Struts* by Chuck Cavaness (O'Reilly, 2002)**

One of a recent spate of books focused on Struts, Cavaness's book offers a comprehensive and thorough guide to the essentials of Struts programming.

***Struts in Action* by Ted Husted et al. (Manning, 2002)**

This is another excellent, comprehensive introduction to the essentials of Struts programming. The lead author is one of the original Struts committers.

http://www.husted.com/struts

Ted Husted's Web site containing much useful information about Struts, as well as links to other helpful resources.

http://jakarta.apache.org/struts

This is the official Struts Web site, from which you can download current and previous releases and browse the API JavaDoc. The site contains numerous helpful links, as well as some fundamental documentation on Struts.

Unit Testing

http://junit.sourceforge.net/doc/testinfected/testing.htm

This is a "getting started" document that goes into why people who do unit testing get hooked and continue to do unit testing.

http://www.xprogramming.com

This is a site on XP that has general information about test first design and other information and motivation about unit testing.

http://www.extremeprogramming.org

This is another great resource for XP.

***Java Tools for eXtreme Programming* by Richard Hightower and Nicholas Lesiecki (Wiley, 2001)**

An excellent resource with really good examples and information on how to use JUnit and its J2EE counterpart called Cactus.

http://www.junit.org

This is the location to find everything there is to know about JUnit. There is a ton of documentation, plus pointers to variations and extensions to JUnit.

APPENDIX C

What's on the Web Site

This appendix provides you with information on the contents of the Web site that accompanies this book. Here is what you will find:

- System Requirements
    - JDK   1.3.1 or higher
    - JBoss (www.jboss.org) or
    - Sun's J2EE Reference Implementation (java.sun.com)
    - Jakarta Struts 1.1 (jakart.apache.org/struts)
- What's on the Web site
    - Source code for the examples in the book.

System Requirements

Make sure that your computer meets the minimum system requirements listed in this section. If your computer doesn't match up to most of these requirements, you may have a problem using the Web site.

Appendix C

For Windows 9x, Windows 2000, Windows NT4 (with SP 4 or later), Windows Me, or Windows XP:
- PC with a Pentium processor running at 600 Mhz or faster
- At least 128 MB of total RAM installed on your computer; for best performance, we recommend at least 256 MB
- Ethernet network interface card (NIC) or modem with a speed of at least 28,800 bps
- A CD-ROM drive
- JDK 1.3.1 or higher (tested with Sun's JDK)

For Linux:
- PC with a Pentium processor running at 600 Mhz or faster
- At least 64 MB of total RAM installed on your computer; for best performance, we recommend at least 128 MB
- Ethernet network interface card (NIC) or modem with a speed of at least 28,800 bps
- A CD-ROM drive
- JDK 1.3.1 or higher

For Macintosh:
- Mac OS X computer with a G3 or faster processor running OS 10.1 or later
- At least 64 MB of total RAM installed on your computer; for best performance, we recommend at least 128 MB
- JDK 1.3.1 or higher

Author-Created Materials

All author-created materials from the book, including code listings and samples, are on the Web site.

If you still have trouble with the CD, please call the Wiley Customer Care phone number: (800) 762-2974. Outside the United States, call 1 (317) 572-3994. You can also contact Wiley Customer Service by e-mail at techsupdum@wiley.com. Wiley will provide technical support only for installation and other general quality control items; for technical support on the applications themselves, consult the program's vendor or author.

Index

A

access ActionForms in session pitfall
  about, 182–183, 266
  add ActionForm locator method to base class, 187–191
  example, 183–187
  solution, 187–191
Action call sequence, 160
ActionErrors, 176
ActionForm locator method, add to base class, 187–191
ActionForms. *See* Struts ActionForms
ActionMapping, 182, 196
Actions. *See* Struts Actions
addValidationRule(), 131
Alur, Deepak, 158, 274
Ant
  about, 233–234
  build subprojects pitfall, 249–256, 270
  copy-and-paste reuse pitfall, 235–242
  no distinction between different types of builds pitfall, 243–248, 270
  no logging from custom tasks pitfall, 257–262, 271
  references, 273
  Web site, 273
antcall, 237–242
API intent, 5
append method, 5
Apple JVM, 49
asserts
  no assert pitfall, 4–19, 263
  System.out Becomes assert solution, 28
  unreasonable assert pitfall, 20–28, 21–22, 263

B

base class
  add ActionForm locator method, 187–191
  Formatter, 76
  move common code to, 173–181
BaseAction class, 177–178
bean population code, consolidate and generalize, 101–118
bean population, framework facilities, 96

Index

bean:define tag, 228
bean:message tags, 202
beanutils, 78, 96
BeanUtils package, 68
Big Process code, 8
BigDecimal, 70
Bitter Java (Tate), 274
Bloch, Joshua, 274
build subprojects pitfall, Ant
  about, 249, 270
  centralize build, 251–256
  example, 249–251
  solution, 251–256
build types pitfall, 243–248
BuildException, 261
business logic
  in JSPs pitfall, 218–223, 268
  move to helper class, 220–223
BusinessRules.java, 222
business-tier code in Actions pitfall
  about, 149–151, 266
  example, 151–157
  solution, 157–171

C

cache, 25
CachedCustomerListingTest, 26–27
Cactus
  console-based testing pitfall, 24–25
  difference from JUnit, 2–3
  mock object application servers, 45
  no assert pitfall, 4–6
  simplify test method pitfall
    solution, 39–44
  unit testing and, 20
  Web site, 3
calculation of derived values in JSPs pitfall
  about, 214, 268
  example, 214–215

move calculations to value object, 215–217
  solution, 215–217
call sequence before and after
  solution, 89–90
CartItem class, 19
Cavaness, Chuck, 274
classpath, 241
common code, move to base class, 173–181
compile.entity target, 240
console-based testing pitfall
  about, 24, 264
  example, 25–28
  solution, Cactus, 31–33
  solution, JUnit test, 29–31
consolidate and generalize bean
  population code, 101–118
Consolidate and Generalize
  Formatting Code, 74–75
consolidate and generalize
  validation code, 123–126
constants, replace hard-coded keys
  with, 204–208
Constants.java, 207–208
controller components, 147
copied-and-pasted targets, 236–237
copy-and-paste reuse pitfall, Ant
  about, 269–270
  example, 235–237
  solution, 237–242
copy/paste code in Actions pitfall
  about, 172, 266
  example, 172–173
  move common code to base class, 173–181
  solution, 173–181
copy/paste conversion pitfall
  about, 96–98, 265
  example, 98–101
  solution, 101–118

Index

copy/paste format pitfall
  about, 70–71, 265
  Consolidate and Generalize Formatting Code, 74–75
  example, 72–74
  solution, 74–95
copy/paste validation pitfall
  about, 119–120, 265–266
  example, 121–123
  solution, 123–145
CopyTask execute method, 260
CopyTask.java, 258
Core J2EE Patterns (Alur, Crupi, Malks), 158, 274
Crupi, John, 158, 274
CurrencyFormatter.java, 77, 103–104
custom messages, replace with Struts messages pitfall, 210–213
custom tasks, no logging from custom tasks pitfall, 257–262, 271
Customer bean API, 36, 47
Customer Entity Bean, 35–36
Customer Entity EJB, 46–47
CustomerCache, 25
CustomerCactusTest, 47–49
CustomerLoaderTestDecorator, 56–57

D

DateFormatter.java, 82–83, 110–111
debug argument, 257
decouple, Struts, 68
derived values, calculation, 214–217, 268
Design by Contract (DBC), 5
design with tests in mind, 59
duplicate form submissions pitfall, 229–232, 269

E

ear file, 256
Effective Java (Bloch), 274
empty validate() method, 119–120
entity, 237
Entity Beans, 150
entity code, 239
entity.jar, 235
equals methods, 6
error messages, Struts Tags, 209–213
execute() method, 129, 150, 187
Extreme Programming (XP), 1

F

failure to isolate each test pitfall
  about, 45, 264
  example, 46–50
  solution with setUp and tearDown methods, 50–54
  solution with test decorators, 55–57
failure to isolate subject pitall
  about, 58, 264–265
  example, 59–61
  solution with Mock Objects Pattern, 62–65
field labels, 200
FilterTestRedirector, 2
find Action, 152–154
FindInvoiceAction, 163–164, 168–170, 174–175, 178–180, 182–186, 189–190
FindInvoiceForm, 186
Form Bean, 186
format
  messages, 212
  Struts framework and, 70
Formatter base class, 76
FormattingException.java, 85
FormattingExceptions, 127, 128

Index

FormTag class, 231
Fowler, Martin, 274
framework bean population
   facilities, 96

G

generalize bean population code, 101–118
generated JSP, tokens to, 230–232
get...AsString() methods, 71, 74
getCount method, 18
getForm() method, 188
getFormatter(), 94

H

hard-coded keys in JSPs pitfall
   about, 203, 267
   example, 203–204
   replace with constants, 204–208
   solution, 204–208
hard-coded options in HTML select
   lists pitfall
   about, 224, 269
   example, 224–225
   move options values to helper
      class, 225–228
   solution, 225–228
hard-coded strings in JSPs pitfall
   about, 199, 267
   example, 200–201
   solution, 201–202
hard-coded validation, 121
hashCode methods, 6
Hatcher, Erik, 273
helper class
   move business logic to, 220–223
   move options values to, 225–228
Hightower, Richard, 273, 275
HTML select lists, hard-coded
   options in, 224–228
Husted, Ted, 274

I

import statements, 207
"in container" tests, 2
incremental test improvement, 9
inexperienced developers, 46
init target, 254
IntegerFormatter.java, 83–84, 110
intent of API, 5, 13
introduce properties file, builds
   pitfall, Ant, 245–248
Invoice bean, 39
Invoice class, 59–61
Invoice value class with formats
   logic, 72–73
InvoiceCactusTest, 40
InvoiceDelegate class, 163
InvoiceDelegate.java, 164–167
InvoiceDO class, 73, 98–100, 214
InvoiceDO.java, 86–88
InvoiceForm.java, 82, 121–123, 144–145
InvoiceTest, 60, 62–63

J

.jar files, 58, 235
Java Development with Ant (Hatcher
   and Loughran), 273
Java Tools for eXtreme Programming
   (Hightower and Lesiecki),
   273, 275
java.util.MessageFormat, 220
JSPs
   calculate derived values in JSPs
      pitfall, 214–217
   hard-coded keys in JSPs pitfall,
      203–208
   hard-coded strings in JSPs pitfall,
      199–202
   perform business logic in JSPs
      pitfall, 218–223
JSPTestRedirector, 2

Index

J

JUnit
  console-based test pitfall, 29–31
  difference from Cactus, 2–3
  no assert pitfall, 9–15
  unreasonable assert pitfall, 21–22
  Web site, 3, 275
JVM, 2

K

keys, hard-coded, in JSPs pitfall, 203–208
keysToSkip(), 104

L

LabelValueBean class, 226
left string properties, 6
Lesiecki, Nicholas, 273, 275
LineItem class, 65
log, no log from custom tasks pitfall, Ant, 257–262
logic
  business, 218–223, 268
  format, 72–73
Loughran, Steve, 273
lower-level components, tests, 9

M

Malks, Dan, 158, 274
messages
  custom messages, replace with Struts messaging pitfall, 210–213
  error messages, Struts Tags, 209–213
Mock Object
  application servers, Cactus, 45
  Mock Objects Pattern, 2, 62–65
  tests, 2
Model-View-Controller design, 218
ModifyInvoiceAction, 192–194

ModifyInvoice.jsp, 182, 199
MyForm populate() method, 124–126
MyForm.java, 79–81, 90–94, 105–109, 135–144

N

name attributes, 185
navigation maps, 196
nested ActionForms, 112–118
new Action, 154
no assert pitfall
  about, 4, 263
  example, 6–9
  solution with Cactus, 15–19
  solution with JUnit, 9–15
no check for duplicate form submissions pitfall
  about, 229, 269
  add tokens to generated JSP, 230–232
  example, 229–230
  solution, 230–232
no distinction between different types of builds pitfall, Ant
  about, 243, 270
  example, 244–245
  introduce properties file, 245–248
  solution, 245–248
no logging from custom tasks pitfall, Ant
  about, 257, 271
  add logging, 259–262
  example, 257–259
  solution, 259–262
no use of Struts Tags for error messages pitfall
  about, 209, 268
  example, 210

284 Index

no use of Struts Tags for error
    messages pitfall *(continued)*
  replace custom messaging with
    Struts messaging, 210–213
  solution, 210–213
null pass to constructor, 15
NullPointerException, 46, 183

O

options values, move to helper class,
    225–228
options.java, 226–227
overloaded ActionMappings pitfall
  about, 192, 267
  example, 192–195
  solution, 195–196

P

perform business logic in JSPs pitfall
  about, 218–219, 268
  example, 219–220
  move business logic to helper class,
    220–223
  solution, 220–223
populate(), 78, 109
populate() method, 129
Populate servlet, 31–33
populateProperty(), 128, 134
population code, consolidate and
    generalize, 101–118
Programming Jakarta Struts
    (Cavaness), 274
properties file, introduce, 245–248
PropertyUtils, 78

R

Range.java, 133
redirectors, 2–3
refactor, 86–87
Refactoring (Fowler), 274

replace custom messaging with
    Struts messaging pitfall, 210–213
replace hard-coded keys with
    constants pitfall, 204–208
RequestProcessor, 188
right string properties, 6

S

save Action, 155–157
SaveInvoiceAction, 170–171,
    175–176, 180–181, 231
scatter, 68, 70, 78
ServiceLocator class, 159, 161
ServiceLocator.java, 161–163
ServletTestRedirector, 2
session, 251
Session Bean, 150–151, 216
session code, 239–240
session.jar, 235
setFormatter(), 127
setUp methods, 50–54
ShoppingCartCactusTest, 16–17
simplify test method pitfall, 38–44
solutions
  access ActionForms in session
    pitfall, 187–191
  build subprojects pitfall, Ant,
    251–256
  business-tier code in Actions
    pitfall, 157–171
  calculation of derived values
    in JSPs pitfall, 215–217
  call sequence before and after
    solution, 89–90
  console-based testing pitfall, 29–33
  copy-and-paste reuse pitfall, Ant,
    237–242
  copy/paste code in Actions pitfall,
    173–181

Index 285

copy/paste conversion pitfall, 101–118
copy/paste formatting pitfall, 74–95
copy/paste validation pitfall, 123–145
failure to isolate each test pitfall, 50–57
failure to isolate subject pitall, 62–65
hard-coded keys in JSPs pitfall, 204–208
hard-coded options in HTML select lists pitfall, 225–228
hard-coded strings in JSPs pitfall, 201–202
Mock Objects Pattern, 62–65
no assert pitfall, 9–19
no distinction between different types of builds pitfall, Ant, 245–248
no logging from custom tasks pitfall, Ant, 259–262
not checking for duplicate form submissions pitfall, 230–232
not using Struts Tags for error messaging pitfall, 210–213
overloaded ActionMappings pitfall, 195–196
performing business logic in JSPs pitfall, 220–223
with setUp and tearDown methods, 50–54
System.out Becomes assert solution, 28
test decorators, 55–57
unreasonable assert pitfall, 23
StringBuffer, 5
StringPair, 10–12
StringPair Class, 6
StringPairTest, 7–8, 21–22

strings, hard-coded, 199–202
Struts
framework, 68
references, 274
Web site, 274–275
Struts ActionForms
about, 67–69, 182
accessing ActionForms in session pitfall, 182–191
ActionForm locator method, adding to base class, 187–191
copy/paste conversion pitfall, 96–118, 265
copy/paste formatting pitfall, 70–95, 265
copy/paste validation pitfall, 119–145, 265–266
Struts Actions
about, 147–148
accessing ActionForms in session pitfall, 182–191
business-tier code in Actions pitfall, 149–171, 266
copy/paste code in Actions pitfall, 172–181, 266
overloaded ActionMappings pitfall, 192–196
Struts in Action (Husted), 274
Struts TagLibs and JSPs
about, 197–198
calculating derived values in JSPs pitfall, 214–217
hard-coded keys in JSPs pitfall, 203–208
hard-coded options in HTML select lists pitfall, 224–228
hard-coded strings in JSPs pitfall, 199–202
not checking for duplicate form submissions pitfall, 229–232

286 Index

Struts TagLibs and JSPs *(continued)*
  not using Struts Tags for error
    messaging pitfall, 209–213, 268
  performing business logic in JSPs
    pitfall, 218–223
subprojects, building pitfall, 249–256
Sun's Windows JVM, 49
system requirements for Web site,
  277–278
System.out Becomes assert
  solution, 28
System.out.println, 24

T
TagLib, 68
targets, copied-and-pasted, 236–237
Tate, Bruce A., 274
tearDown methods, 50–54
testBean method, 41–42
testCreateCustomer, 47
TestDecorators, 44
testEqualsHashCodeConsistency, 13
testEqualsReturn, 13
testLineItemRelationship
  method, 43
testLookupCustomer, 47
tests
  CachedCustomerListingTest, 26–27
  console-based testing pitfall, 29–33
  CustomerCactusTest, 47–49
  CustomerLoaderTestDecorator,
    56–57
  designed with testing in mind, 59
  existing code, 19
  failure to isolate each test pitfall,
    45–57, 264
  FilterTestRedirector, 2
  "in container" testing, 2
  incremental test improvement, 9
  InvoiceCactusTest, 40

InvoiceTest, 60, 62–63
JSPTestRedirector, 2
lower-level components, 9
Mock Object, 2
ServletTestRedirector, 2
setUp and tearDown methods,
  50–54
ShoppingCartCactusTest, 16–17
simplify test method pitfall, 38–44,
  39–44
StringPairTest, 7–8, 21–22
test decorators, 55–57
testing existing code, 19
unfocused test method pitfall,
  34–38, 264
unit, 1–2, 20, 275
unreasonable assert pitfall, JUnit
  test, 21–22
written before code, 6
testSetAddress, 47
testSetValues method, 8
testTotal method, 64
tokens to generated JSP, 230–232

U
unfocused test method pitfall
  about, 34, 264
  example, 35–38
  solution, 38–44
unformat()implementation, 102–103
unit tests
  about, 20
  pitfalls, 1–2
  references, 275
  Web sites, 275
unreasonable assert pitfall
  about, 20, 263
  example, 20–23
  JUnit test, 21–22
  solution, 23
updateQuantity method, 18

V

validate() method, 130
validateRequired(), 134–144
validation, hard-coded, 121
validationMap, 130
ValidatorForm, 120
value object, move calculations to, 215–217
values, derived, 214–217, 268
verbose argument, 257, 260

W

Web sites
　Ant, 273
　Cactus, 3
　JUnit, 3, 275
　Struts, 274–275
　for this book, 277–278
　unit tests, 275
wrapper classes for Java, 94